Clare: Her Light and Her Song

Clare: Her Light and Her Song

Karen Karper Fredette

Originally published by Franciscan Herald Press

Copyright © 1984, 1990, 2012 by Karen Karper Fredette

ISBN: 978-1-5040-3689-4

Distributed in 2016 by Open Road Distribution
180 Maiden Lane
New York, NY 10038
www.openroadmedia.com

Clare: Her Light and Her Song

Bright and barefoot on the earth,
the night her mantle light,
Clare appraises all as loss
and sings:
    "All wonders of the world
    are only way for me—
    my light is Christ!"

Warrior woman, strong she fought
for dearest depth of poverty
found within dark flowering
of now and nothing.
    "All wonders of the world
    are only way for me—
    my wealth is Christ!"

Power flowing from a Cross,
resurrection light in Francis' limbs,
stirs and steals her song,
bridal-dancer of the Crucified:
    "All wonders of the world
    are only way for me—
    my Song is Christ!"

TO ALL MY POOR CLARE SISTERS
ESPECIALLY
TO THOSE NEAREST AND DEAREST
WITH WHOM I DAILY SHARE
THE DISCOVERY AND DEEPENING OF CLARE'S
DREAM,
THIS WORK IS GRATEFULLY DEDICATED.

HOW THIS WORK HAPPENED

After Vatican Council II issued its call to all communities to rediscover the charism of their founder/foundress, I realized that my conception of St. Clare's charism was decidedly thin. In fact, she herself was a very hazy figure in my mind, more of a name than a living person whose dream I was supposed to be incarnating in the twentieth century.

So in the mid-sixties I began asking the question and seeking the answers which have led me on a course of exciting discoveries about this marvelous woman named Clare. Gradually material gathered from diverse sources began to flesh out the life, the times, and the personality of Clare di Favarone, daughter of one of the noblest houses of Assisi. I encountered a woman who was one of the most well known figures in the Church and Europe in her own century and who was described at her death as "the new captain of womankind."

At that time (1253) over one hundred monasteries of women following her way of life were flourishing in Europe. Clare was the first woman to write her own Rule and obtain Papal approbation for it. She guarded the original inspiration of St. Francis with more energy and tenacity than did most of the Friars during the tumultous years directly following Francis' death in 1226.

This was a woman I wanted to know—as intimately and clearly as the seven-hundred year gap between her life and mine would permit. Although there are not too many documents deriving directly from Clare or writings about her by contemporaries, there are sufficient to piece together a chronological development of her life, lived at the heart of the brilliant thirteenth century.

I also had the inestimable advantage of learning and writing about Clare from the inside out; that is, from within a cloister where her Rule and spirit were the guiding norm of daily life. This work is only a pioneering venture, a beginning of what can and, hopefully, will be written about Clare in the years to come.

I have attempted to write not only Clare's life-story but something of her dream, her song. I have tried to capture in some small measure a hint of the Light she became, a reflection of that Light which came into the world to illumine the hearts of all who would receive Him.

My gratitude for assistance with this project of many years extends to innumerable persons, especially to those many who prayed with me and for me for the successful completion of this work. First of all, I wish to thank my own community of Sancta Clara. My sisters have not only shown me many facets of Clare's light but have also supported me, believed in me, and encouraged me. They have learned "to possess their souls in patience" as they listened to portions of this manuscript in early drafts and have made valuable contributions and offered constructive criticisms.

Beyond the cloister walls, I must acknowledge my deep gratitude to Sister Madge Karecki S.S.J.-T.O.S.F. who read the manuscript chapter by chapter and shared her scholarship and insights with me generously.

I wish also to thank my many Franciscan brothers who have assisted me by making the fruits of their research available. Among these are Fathers Conrad Harkins O.F.M., Bernardine Beck O.F.M., Caesar van Hulst O.F.M., Regis Armstrong O.F.M.Cap., and Brother Charles McCarron O.F.M.Cap. I want to mention the assistance given to me by many Poor Clare sisters in other communities, especially Sisters Dolores Steinberg O.S.C. and M. Michael O.S.C.

Valuable information about Assisi and its environs has been given to me by many friends who have visited the city of Francis and Clare and who related to me their visual and felt impressions of this homeland of all Franciscans.

Last of all, I feel I should thank my own family whose loving support, interest, and encouragement have heartened me to continue the work. The prayers of my loving parents, brothers, and sister, their spouses, my nieces and nephews, aunts and uncles, cousins of first, second and third degree, including Tommy who asked for special mention, have helped me to understand and write about Clare who also enjoyed the grace of an extended family.

To all these and so many more, I pray that Clare will grant a share in her love and joy in the Lord.

August 11, 1983

Preface

Though St. Clare is rightly called the most faithful follower of St. Francis, relatively few people know of the stature of her personality or the wisdom of her spiritual teaching. It has only been within the last thirty years that her writings have become available to the English speaking world. Biographies of Clare have, for the most part, been more the product of the individual author's musings than of painstaking research.

Clare di Favarone of the Offreduccio family emerged from what sociologists call a closed social system as a source of true liberation for men and women of her day. Her spirit would not be constricted by the rigid boundaries of life in the Middle Ages. She became attracted to a style of gospel living articulated by Francis of Assisi, son of the wealthy clothier, Pietro Bernardone, despite the differences in their social and economic status. Together they form the two great lights of the Franciscan family shedding their light upon their brothers and sisters for the past seven centuries.

Clare was captivated by the Poor Christ much as Francis was during his lifetime. Though she had to live the last twenty-seven years of her life without the support of her "soul-friend," her fidelity to walking in the footprints of Jesus was undiminished. Poverty was the context of her life and her spiritual teaching.

Clare so treasured poverty that she procured the "Privilege of Poverty" from Innocent III and had it renewed by Gregory IX. This document freed forever the Poor Ladies of any constraint to accept property or other material security that would insure for them regular income. This was unheard of in the history of the Church.

As is evident from her example and her writings Clare taught that poverty made her and her sisters wholly dependent on God. Material poverty was the framework and foundation for her prayer and contemplation. She wrote these words of praise for poverty to her friend Agnes of Prague:

> What a great laudable exchange:
> to leave the things of time for those of eternity,
> to choose the things of heaven for the goods of
>   earth,
> to receive the hundred-fold in place of one,
> and to possess a blessed and eternal life.[1]

This letter written in the early 1230's is as challenging to us of the twentieth century as it was to the medieval Agnes, all of us journeying to the kingdom of God.

Sister M. Karen's biographical study of Clare of Assisi brings the light of this medieval woman into prominence for us and thus serves us well. For in looking to the light of Clare and listening to her message we find direction and aid as we too endeavor to follow in the footprints of Jesus.

As Sister looks at Clare in the context of her times and reflects on the meaning of her life and writings against the backdrop of medieval life what emerges is a clarion call to all of us to examine our lives in the light which Clare reflects, Jesus the Lord.

Clare: Her Light and Her Song is a welcome addition to the world of Franciscan literature written in a way that excites the mind and refreshes the heart.

Madge Karecki S.S.J.-T.O.S.F.
July 1983

---

1. Regis Armstrong and Ignatius Brady, *Francis and Clare* (New York: Paulist Press, 1982) p. 193.

Contents

Prologue: Something New Under the Sun

Time-stained and riddled by insects, the roughly hewn crossbeams cast intricate shadows in the constantly shifting light. One's eyes are drawn to them as they overhang the room in their brooding utility. The ancient wood, gouged by a workman's adze centuries ago, dominates this long, low room. At the far end sunlight pours through a window and splashes on the floor, bright in this bluntly austere place.

A cross etched on the wall marks the place where a woman died. Seven centuries later we can gaze at the beams which join wall to wall, rooftree to rafter, knowing that we are seeing the backdrop to her reveries and prayers of forty-one years. Under these beams she slept and dreamed, here she suffered years of continual illness, here she worked, wept, and prayed. These rafters echoed her laughter and hushed her dying breath.

How is it that this empty corner of a barn-like room is so full of light? What lingers here that fills one with a wideness of spirit reminiscent of mountain heights? Why does the very bareness sing?

On a summer morning in 1253 Clare di Favarone died here in chosen poverty. The quenching of her mortal light mingled so subtly with the rising dawn that earth's day was brightened by her breach of the immortal realms. Lying here, Clare may have breathed a tender farewell to these beams which roofed her home, seeing them again as she had the first time more than forty years earlier. Then as now, she had been poised on the

1

verge of transition, of a journey toward an unknown but compelling destiny.

Spring in the year 1212! The building is empty, so very empty. The brightness of its stone walls dazzles Clare as she approaches, coming up the steep path shaded by olive trees. A bright, light-washed future beckons her. Her whole being stirs as she treads in Francis' dusty footprints toward the abandoned chapel of San Damiano. She is eighteen, her sister Agnes at her side, fifteen. Scattered clouds do not dim the bright May sunlight. The Umbrian countryside lies somnolent under its rays as if it also enjoys the noonday siesta of its citizens.

Francis had carefully chosen this time of day to conduct Clare and Agnes from the community of recluses of Sant' Angelo de Panzo down the slope of Monte Subasio and around the outskirts of Assisi. He and Brother Philip lead them up the cart lane which passes through the city's Porta Nuova from the plain. Few persons are stirring at this hour and they pass along it unnoticed except by the breeze which gently tugs at their rough lazzo garments.

When the steep path brings them within sight of the facade of San Damiano, Clare feels the urge to run and embrace the rugged walls that glint in the sun. This! This is to be the place where her searching spirit can expand unfettered. Perhaps Francis hears the catch in her breath and softly chants:

> When Israel came forth from Egypt
> the house of Jacob from an alien land,
> the mountains skipped like rams,
> the hills like the lambs of the flock![1]

And exuberantly they run until they stand in breathless joy in the cool shade of the portico.

Does Clare realize how monumental this moment is when her bare feet first step into the sanctuary of San Damiano? Forty years later, bequeathing to her sisters her most precious memories, she will write: "And thus by the will of God and of our most blessed Father Francis we came to dwell at the church of San Damiano. . . . Before this we had dwelt in another place but for a little while only."[2] The "other place" Clare so briefly mentions was the alien lands of a Benedictine monastery and of a group of penitents where her biographer simply notes "her soul was not at rest."[3]

The first of these, the wealthy convent of San Paolo, was two miles from Assisi in the marshlands of the Isola Romana. But it was not far enough away. Clare's relatives quickly learned where she had fled and stormed into the cloister demanding her immediate return to sanity and the family circle or should one say, to the ordinary and accepted? But the way of the ordinary was never to be Clare's. Her way was Christ and some day she would write: "The Son of God for us the Way and that Way our blessed Father Francis has shown us."[4]

Obviously, Clare's family divined that, although she was temporarily in an acceptable environment, she had no intention of becoming a Benedictine. To that they would not have been so violently opposed.

What was it then that they suspected of her? When her father and his brothers strode angrily into the splendid monastic choir, they confronted Clare clinging to the altar cloth, dressed not in the dignified black of a Benedictine but in an undyed habit of lazzo, the coarse cloth woven by the serfs of the countryside. The rope girdling her waist only emphasized the garment's bulky fit. Bare feet and a shapeless veil completed her strange ensemble. In the elegant sanctuary, Clare looked as incongruous as earthenware amid Oriental porcelain.

By nobility of birth and quality of education, Clare was equal to any of the nuns in the monastery, but she quickly felt herself out of place among them. Their manner of living, so minutely regulated and strictly hierarchical, dismayed her. Why had Francis taken her there?

Probably Bishop Guido advised it for several reasons. No woman as yet belonged to the Poor Brothers and just how they would fit into the way of life of the young mendicant community was a question neither he nor Francis nor Clare herself could answer at this juncture. Prudence dictated that she be placed where scandal could not mar the purity of her gift to God and also where she could learn what feminine religious life entailed. Then, too, there was the Offreduccio clan to reckon with. Her father had four brothers, all knights of the feudal aristocracy. Uncle Monaldo, the eldest, was lord of Coriano and head of the family. The other brothers, Paolo, Ugolino, and Scipione, could be counted upon to help in any family trouble and Clare's defiance of her father's marriage plans would be cause for united action. Little wonder that medieval monasteries, particularly those of women, resembled fortresses and were often surrounded by armed guards!

Bishop Guido did not need the gift of prophecy to foresee trouble, but perhaps he had chosen to minimize its potential when he had asked the Lady Abbess of San Paolo to take in this unusual candidate. The nuns were thoroughly upset by the invasion of Clare's family the day after her arrival. And one can hardly blame them. Armed knights and retainers burst through the doors of the monastery choir where Clare had fled for refuge. Claiming the same right of sanctuary which a benevolent Church granted to all suspected criminals in a violent and vengeful age, she turned to face her father and uncles with a courage that matched their own. Knowing that words are useless in such situations, Clare swept her veil off and revealed her shorn hair. The thick blond tresses that are one of the beauties of Lombard womanhood were no more.

As far as medieval standards were concerned, she was mutilated beyond any possibility of rehabilitation. Favarone knew that his daughter had won. He left, wrathful but defeated. However, the incident so unnerved the nuns that about a week later

Francis removed Clare to the community of recluses of Sant' Angelo de Panzo on the slope of Monte Subasio. Above this monastery are situated the caves that have come to be known as the Carceri. Did Francis, during his hours of solitary prayer there, gaze down the mountainside to the place where his first spiritual daughter was struggling to define a new style of religious life for women?

It was at Sant' Angelo that Agnes joined Clare after another secret flight from the Offreduccio palazzo. The family ire reached boiling point and the Offreduccio brothers, after feigning conciliatory politeness, gained entrance to the monastery and dragged young Agnes bodily from the premises. Again Clare's courage and prayer prevailed. The burly knights found they were unable to lift the body of the fifteen-year-old girl from the ground where she had fallen. Agnes rejoined Clare, bedraggled but probably otherwise unharmed.

Left unmolested but not at peace, Clare and Agnes struggled with the contrasting ideals of the highly formalized culture of the Benedictines and the loosely organized penitential life of the Beguine-like group of Sant' Angelo. Clare may have found the long hours of intricate psalmody of the Benedictines out of harmony with her instinctive attraction toward simplicity while the less structured group prayer of the anchorene community may not have held for Clare the richness of the Church's liturgical life which she is known to have prized. Clare's plan of a single form of life for all the sisters within the community, choir and lay, may have been modeled on her experience at Sant' Angelo. These early weeks, spent in different forms of religious life, proved fruitful by helping Clare sort out what most corresponded with her dream of the simple and poor gospel life proposed by Francis.

In the kitchens and workrooms of the Benedictines, Clare and Agnes saw the harmonious blending of simple labor and deep prayer a life which expressed the situation of poor persons who had to work for their daily bread. She would one day call work a "grace." Despite her growing awareness that she was not called to the Benedictine life, Clare found much to admire and remember in the time-tested wisdom of the basic Rule of St. Benedict. The monastic rhythm of alternating work and prayer, the concept of community chapters where all the sisters had a voice, the stability of cloister; these and many other values Clare would take with her, although she would remodel their forms, infusing her own spirit into them.

Happily, the day arrived when Francis called at Sant' Angelo to tell Clare that Bishop Guido approved his plan to establish her at San Damiano. The time of preparation had ended. What lay ahead was known only to the Heavenly Father.

Now the cold stone under foot shocks Clare out of her reveries. She descends thoughtfully into the dim nave of San Damiano. As she does so, Francis' prophecy of six years earlier becomes a reality.

In that anguished year of 1206, Francis had been searching sincerely but blindly for direction in his life. He had stumbled down into the sunken nave of San Damiano and had been drawn to the compelling image of the Crucified that hung above the altar. Dust and droppings had lain thick about him; doubt and confusion had crowded his mind when suddenly all had been changed by the wholly unexpected command: "Go, Francis, and rebuild my house, which as you see is falling in ruin."[6] This word of his Lord directed Francis' groping quest into a single-minded devotion to stone and mortar. Sometimes he has been accused of naivete as if he saw only the literal meaning of that enigmatic word from the Crucified. But in a century that expressed the vitality of its faith by erecting cathedrals of surpassing splendor, church-building was a sublime privilege. Francis seemed to see this humble chapel as a symbol of the very bride of Christ.

Francis' gifts as a mason were sufficient to fit the pinkish-gray stone of San Damiano's facade together so that they remained solid and weatherproof. He had been at work high above the ground when suddenly he had sung out in French, the language of his moments of ecstacy, "Come, my brothers, and help me build the monastery of San Damiano, for here will dwell ladies whose good name and holy life will glorify our Heavenly Father throughout his holy church."[7] At that time Francis had neither brothers nor companions of any kind. No human expectation could have urged this lone herald of the Great King to announce that a court of holy ladies would be established here to stand in waiting before his Lord. No, nothing on earth could have possibly foreseen such an incredible occurrence. It was as Clare said with wonder later "in great joy and *in the illumination of the Holy Spirit* he prophesied concerning us what the Lord later fulfilled."[8]

Six years had elapsed between prophecy and fulfillment. During that time Francis had found men coming to him who asked to share his life and poverty. How joyously and gratefully he had welcomed them! With brothers at his side his long loneliness began to ease. But his was a heart which needed more than masculine comradeship to be fulfilled. He dreamed and desired a marriage with a beautiful lady, his lovely Lady Poverty.

To his wonder a courageous young woman from the nobility of Assisi caught the fire of his dream. It was as if Lady Poverty, the mystical bride he courted and defended, had assumed flesh and blood. When Clare had begged him to show her how to follow Jesus as he did, he suddenly recalled that far-off moment of exaltation under the sun when he had sung as he worked on San Damiano. Solemnly he had revealed to Clare the revelation he had received so inexplicably. To her it became a confirmation from heaven of her divine call.

Ever afterward Clare glowed with gratitude for this mark of predilection in her regard. Her call, her vocation! That was a gift which ever claimed her gratitude. Daily she incarnated the burning sentiments that would initiate her last Testament: "Among the many graces which we have received and continue daily to receive from the liberality of the Father of mercies, and for which we must give deepest thanks to our glorious God, our vocation holds the first place. Indeed, because it is the more perfect and the greater among these graces, so much the more does it claim our gratitude. Therefore the Apostle says, 'Know your vocation!'"[9]

"Grace," "gift," "give thanks"! These words abound in Clare's writings and must have often flowed from her lips. And what was this vocation she sought to know ever more deeply? In 1212 it was only a mystery to which she must surrender herself.

On this May day, the life of the Poor Ladies was yet to be lived. It did not exist until Clare and Agnes stepped into empty San Damiano. Before them lay a future which would be revealed only as it unfolded day by day. It was as if they stood on the edge of a field of new-fallen snow looking for the path. Francis could not make it for her. All he could offer was the advice: "Walk across the field and there will be a path."

Something new and untried beckoned Clare. And she had the courage and joyous recklessness to follow it. She pledged herself to "most high and inviolable poverty." To secure this, she and her sisters sought a *privilege* of living in perfect poverty in such a way that no one could force them to accept possessions of any kind! Personal poverty of an individual monk or nun was nothing new. But it was utterly new and unheard of that an entire community, and of women no less, should seek to live entirely without property. To do this after the example of Francis and his friars was Clare's dream and unshakeable resolve. Reluctantly but admiringly, the highest authority in the Church would one day confirm it.

To Clare it seemed perfectly comprehensible that the Father who clothed the lilies of the field and fed the birds of the air would also provide everything necessary for her and her sisters—if she gave him the opportunity to do so. This was not so obvious to others, but time would prove that Clare was totally, gloriously right. She and her sisters would demonstrate by daily example the magnificent challenge and promise of Jesus: "Do not lay up for yourselves an earthly treasure . . . remember where your treasure is, there your heart is also. . . . I warn you then, do not worry about your livelihood, what you are to eat or drink or use for clothing. Is not life more than food? Is not the body more valuable than clothes? Your heavenly Father knows all that you need. Seek first his kingship over you, his way of holiness, and all these things will be given you besides."[10] In May of 1212, this was still to be proven.

Now blinking in the transition from noonday brightness to the gloom of the nave, Clare pauses within the door of San Damiano. Francis tugs her sleeve and guides her toward a sanctuary lamp that burns before a suspended Crucifix. Toward what is he directing her? To "Jesus Christ and him crucified."[11] She intuits the deep meaning of this short walk. She has but to fasten her gaze on the compelling eyes of the crucified One and experience their look of infinite compassion; she has only to mark the lowly yet glorious majesty of the naked, blood-stained figure and she finds the wealth of her life.

It is not a great work of art, this painted Christus wrought in the Umbro-Romanesque style. But for Francis and Clare it will become an image which will influence their entire lives. For Francis, it had become miraculously alive; for Clare, it would become mystically so. This painted figure of Christ stands out in such high relief from its background that it almost seems to hover in front of it. Above the calm, sad face is depicted a small figure of the Glorified Christ in an attitude of energetic supplication to the Father whose hand is seen outstretched in benediction. The entire theology of redemption hovers before Clare's wide eyes.

Medieval life was fraught with symbolism. For the man or

woman of the thirteenth century, abstract ideas were accessible through concrete images. Clare will find the heart of her vocation in the Church imaged in this remarkable Crucifix. Through compassion she will be called to remain close to the Crucified like John, Mary, and the holy women here depicted below the outstretched arms of the Savior. One day she will write: "Contemplate the ineffable charity which led Him to suffer on the wood of the Cross and die thereon the most shameful kind of death. Therefore, that Mirror, suspended on the wood of the Cross, urged those who passed by to consider, saying 'All you who pass by the way, look and see if there is any suffering like my suffering.' Let us answer him with one voice and spirit as he said: Remembering this over and over leaves my soul downcast within me. From this point . . . let yourself be inflamed more strongly with the ardor of charity!"[12]

To what goal will such impassioned love drive Clare? Only to tears? Or to identification? "Transform your whole being entirely by contemplation into the image of the Godhead Itself so that you too may feel what his friends feel as they taste the hidden sweetness which God himself has reserved from the beginning for those who love him."[13]

"The Son of God," she would write in her final days, "made himself our way." She was not speaking metaphorically but with powerful realism. Her woman's heart had met and responded to living love. Jesus was not simply an admirable example to be imitated but a vital life force that daily challenged and changed her. Celano would write: "Clare strove to become like the poor Crucified One by the most perfect poverty so that nothing might separate her in her love for the beloved or hinder the course of her union with the Lord."[14]

Will even this be the ultimate of her aspirations? She will seek and be drawn ever more deeply into the mystery of Christian exchange. What she will live, she will someday write to a soul-sister: "I consider you as a co-worker of God himself and a support of the weak members of his ineffable Body."[15]

Now as Francis brings Clare to the altar and the Crucified, she accepts the rigors of responding to a Love of infinite dimensions. In the glow of the sanctuary lamp which Francis himself had rekindled, his "Little Plant" is to take root. Not only will the living Lord of the Tabernacle be her divine sustenance and protection but she in her turn will become a flame of immolation which will brighten this once desolate sanctuary.

Prologue Endnotes

1. Ps 114:1, 4.
2. Testament of Clare, #9.
3. Legend of Celano, #10.
4. Testament of Clare, #2.
5. Rule of Clare, Ch. III #1.
6. 2 Celano 10.
7. Testament of Clare, #4.
8. Ibid., #4.
9. Testament of Clare, #1.
10. Mt 6:19, 21, 25, 32, 33.
11. 1 Cor 2:2.
12. Fourth Letter, #23–27.
13. Third Letter, #13–14.
14. *Legend*, IX, 14.
15. Third Letter, #8.

I A Rising Age

During centuries of slow ferment, Christianity had gradually leavened the cultures of both East and West, commingling them until in the thirteenth century they burst forth renewed with prodigious vitality. Beauty and war, poetry and commerce, brutality and spirituality—all blossomed in grand profusion.

It was an age of turmoil, change, and challenge. The year 1200, when Francis Bernardone was in his eighteenth year and Clare di Favarone her sixth, opened on a scene of amazing complexity. The rising medieval world was decked in a tapestry glowing with colorful figures and strong, violent patterns of ambition and arrogance. Characters such as Frederick II, known as "Stupor Mundi," and Pope Innocent III, whose will ruled the world (under God, of course), dominated the stage of Europe. Although far from a unity, the European continent was becoming more and more an entity.

War was an accepted fact of life for all: for the nobility who instigated it; for the knights who made it their profession; and for the common folk who routinely have borne the burdens of heavy taxation, devastated lands, and disrupted trade. The tides of war embroiled not just the larger countries we recognize today but the innumerable small duchies, principalities, and city-states which dotted the continent claiming fierce loyalty from their citizens.

Italy did not exist except as a peninsula divided into spheres of influence which constantly jostled each other, making and breaking alliances as the uneasy balance of power shifted. Powerful dukes of Burgundy, Spain, and Germany profited by

13

this continual surge to inject their might wherever they deemed it opportune. Thus they often became temporary masters of large sections of the Italian peninsula. The Papacy, an influential power in its own right, depended on astute alliances to keep this balance from threatening its own privileged status.

Popes constantly resorted to foreign powers to uphold the Church's position amid the restless city-states that pushed and crowded the traditional borders of papal domains. Whenever they could do so without fear of immediate reprisal, these ambitious duchies gladly annexed various portions of this rich mid-section of the peninsula. Little sense of unity bound the large urban centers and seaports together. To be a Venetian or a Roman was far more important than being an Italian. Thus wars were inevitable and endemic.

The geographical fragmentation of Italy was matched by the extraordinary physical vigor of the people which not only enabled them to survive such manifold miseries but to build an impressive civilization at the same time. Amid the struggle with pestilence, famine, and war, this people produced some of the greatest artistic works the world has ever seen.

Taking over the new Gothic architecture which had arisen in France, these vigorous Italians transformed it into an airy elegance which expressed their southern temperament. The Italian painters, musicians, and sculptors enhanced their houses of worship with creations of unsurpassing beauty. The thirteenth century can be characterized by LIFE in capital letters.

North central Italy, where Francis and Clare were born, was composed of many small communes that chafed under their German overlords who had moved in during the turmoil of the previous century. As their population and trade grew, these cities began to challenge the local barons who governed them in allegiance to some foreign power. Assisi followed this same course and in 1198 successfully stormed and razed the castle of Rocca Maggiore which had flaunted its German-guaranteed authority over the heights of the city. All the nobility of the city were forced to flee for their lives, many seeking refuge in the rival city of Perugia, twelve miles across the Umbrian valley. Among them was the great family of the Offreduccio. Thus Clare, at the age of four, experienced the terrors of civil strife and the trauma of exile. At the same time, Francis first tasted the heady wine of war and thought he found it to his liking.

Bitter conflict ravaged Assisi until a temporary truce was arranged in 1204. This struggle for power was not between the lords and the downtrodden serfs of the countryside, but rather it was between the aristocratic families and the rising burgher class of merchants and artisans of the city. The feudal families, the "boni homines or majores," lived mainly in the neighborhood of the cathedral of San Rufino. The palazzo of Favarone di Offreduccio stood on the square that fronted this reconstructed church with its attractive new bell tower. All the town houses of these upper-class citizens were designed with great towers, not for beauty but for defense. These towers were leveled when the populace rose in rage and destroyed the Rocca.

The teen-age sons of the wealthy cloth merchant, Pietro Bernardone, responded to the summons of the consuls who declared Assisi a city free to rule itself. The day when iron and fire won the commune a temporary period of civil liberty found them participating wholeheartedly. With stones taken from the leveled towers, they worked with a will to construct a stout wall about their city. Perhaps it was this project of civic defense which taught Francis the art of masonry he later employed on walls of a very different sort.

In 1202 Perugia, aided by the exiled Assisian nobles and by an alliance with Foligno, challenged the Assisian coalition and decimated it. The commune as a self-governing entity disappeared and the nobility were "invited" back to their native city. The insurgents were forced to pay heavy indemnities and rebuild the homes and towers they had once torn down.

This Perugian victory only aggravated the perpetual feud between the two cities. With only a valley between them, they were dramatically separated by their allegiance to either the Papal States or to the independent duchy of Spoleto. Perugia was a papal city, proud to shelter the pope and his entourage whenever such refuge was needed. Assisi, on the other hand, paid allegiance to the imperial powers. Basically, however, each city was seeking its own aggrandizement.

Although these frequent conflicts were devastating and brutal, they were exciting and brought a certain color and drama into everyday life. The "joyful bellicosity" of the medieval Italian has been noted, and it would seem that, by and large, the participants in these raids and counterattacks enjoyed themselves. This may help to explain why Francis' words of peace would sound so revolutionary to his hearers only a few years later.

In Clare's family, according to Pietro di Damiano who had been a neighbor during her girlhood, there were "seven knights, all noble and powerful."[1] As a boy, Pietro must have been a witness of the comings and goings of these impressive men of Clare's household. Clare grew up in the same highly charged atmosphere of chivalric warfare as Francis; its thirst for power and prestige, its passion and its pain, forming the backdrop of her young life.

Crusades were being preached with soul-stirring eloquence by monks and prelates. The Papacy thus thrust itself into the jostling quest for power that rocked and racked all of Europe. Through a brilliant "senate" of hand-picked cardinals, Innocent III (elected in 1198) began to dominate both church and state policies with his astute genius. In Europe he restored the independence of the full Papal States, thereby establishing himself more firmly as a powerful ruler of "temporalities" as well as "spiritualities." He rallied the armies of France, England, Spain, and Germany to the Cross as he proclaimed and successfully launched the Fourth Crusade in 1202.

Although the stated objective of the crusaders was the liberation of the Holy Land from unholy Saracen rule, the men were more concerned about reopening the trade routes between East and West than in routing the Moslems. A blatant materialism mingled with idealistic motivation, and few men sensed the basic incompatibility of their motives. Negotiations with the Saracens, rather than a policy of their extermination, accomplished the desired commercial revival but frustrated Innocent's plans of annexing Jerusalem to Rome as a Latin-rite diocese.

The expansion of commerce that resulted from the increased flow of goods across the continent and the Mediterranean was gradually undermining the status of the very men who had made it possible, the ruling class of lords and aristocrats.

The population of Europe began to move from the countryside into the cities. As a result towns grew both in size and importance and wealth ceased to be defined solely in terms of possessions. Coinage became the medium of exchange replacing barter of goods and services.

Elaborate public buildings and municipal defenses were built, as well as the wondrous cathedrals. For the first time, huge banking houses specializing in conversion of a wide variety of coins appeared in all the larger cities. Despite this show of prosperity, lives of most people were short and miserable by our standards. Men and women matured early and died young as plagues swept the dank, unsanitary streets of crowded slums and as wars disrupted the precarious economy of budding commercialism.

Things were only a little better in the countryside which at that time was still thickly forested, especially on the mountainous slopes of Italy. There wolves, bears, and wild boars abounded, and during the cruel winter months even city walls did not always provide adequate protection against the starving packs. Also, roaming the land and haunting mountain passes were human predators—political exiles, unemployed mercenaries, or simple bandits and murderers—who gained their sustenance despoiling any travelers or pack trains hapless enough to fall into their grasp.

A description of Rome in the thirteenth century illustrates the prevailing state of urban life in this rough-and-tumble age:

> Rome, the capital of Christendom, the most famous city in Europe, was only a den of robber barons. Miserable mobs lived in squalor among the ruins of the Eternal City. Rome was still surrounded by the third century walls built by the Emperor Aurelian. Inside the walls were huge open spaces where goats and cattle grazed. The massive ruins of ancient splendors constantly grew smaller because their stones were used by the Roman barons to build their towers and fortresses. By the thirteenth century, there were said to be five hundred towers, each a monument to the pride and habitual pugnacity of the noble families. The barons who fought each other for power within the city owned huge estates and many castles in the surrounding countryside. Brutal, barbarous, and arrogant, they made Rome ring with the clash of arms and spattered the streets with the blood of their enemies and their followers.
>
> The people of Rome, who considered themselves the worthy heirs of the patricians of antiquity, were famous for their villainous rapacity, their dishonesty and their addiction to violent rioting. They lived by providing food and lodging to pilgrims at extortionate rates and were despised as scum by their contemporaries.[2]

Assisi, a smaller city still tied to a more rural economy, probably did not match the degradation of Rome but the same elements of misery and violence throve within her walls as well. When the young Francis made his first pilgrimage to Rome, perhaps in the summer of 1205, his ideals of the Holy City were probably not as jarred as we might think. He was used to city life, born and bred in it. In fact, he reveled in it.

Yet he was also a sensitive young man, recently disillusioned in his dreams of secular glory but still seeking glory of another type. He recoiled from the niggardliness of the pilgrims at the tomb of St. Peter and sought to express his contempt by a lordly gesture of flinging his whole purse of gold coins onto the tomb. Then he joined the rough gang of beggars at the door of the church, trying to discover whether the illusive glory he sought could be found in begging for alms rather than in bestowing them with royal largess.

A priest, visiting the city some years later, wrote: "How can you enjoy safety in this city, where all the citizens and clergy are at daily strife for and against both opponents? The heat is insufferable, the water foul, the food coarse and bad; the air is so heavy that it can be grasped with both hands and is filled with swarms of mosquitoes; the ground is alive with scorpions; the people are dirty and odious, wicked and fierce. The whole of Rome is undermined and from the catacombs, which are filled with snakes, arises a poisonous and fatal exhalation."[3]

Only the hardy could survive the physical as well as spiritual jolts of a devout pilgrimage! Francis did survive, with his faith not only intact but deepened as it became detached from appearances. This insight would culminate in his kissing a leper in whom he saw his Lord, an act which set him free forever of bondage to exterior circumstances.

Not all the Christians of that era, however, possessed the vigor of Francis' faith-vision. Many scorned the Church for its secular involvements and despised the frank power-seeking of the hierarchy. Others deplored the ostentation and vice, often coupled with appalling ignorance, frequently found among clerics. Some critics fled to hermitages to concentrate on personal perfection. Others joined the evangelical groups springing up in nearly

every Italian city, particularly in Lombardy. There the Humiliati began to clash openly with the Church, as did the Waldenses
in Lyon.

Superstition and semipaganism still lurking under the surface
of Christian life produced strange cults that were quickly con-
demned. Yet in the majority of people, Catholic faith flourished
even where sin abounded. Insofar as they knew the official doc-
trines, nearly everyone believed them and faithfully fulfilled the
minimum prescribed duties of religion. Church practices
framed their lives from cradle to grave, giving them not only
color and drama, but, above all, meaning and hope.

Men and women might violate the teachings of the Church
but they rarely doubted its sacred origin, the sanctity of the
papacy and the sacraments, the nearness of heaven and hell, and
the value of the kindly intercession of the saints. Miracles were
commonplace and expected. The spirit-world was uncommonly
near, both the angelic and the demonic. The abundance of gro-
tesque gargoyles adorning the facades of churches and the innumerable images of saints and angels within attest to this. The
thirteenth century man or woman seemed incapable of looking
upon the world in a purely secular fashion.

In an age when evil was blatantly evil, good was extremely
good. Medieval Italy was notable not only for its ruthless and
merciless figures but also for its holy men and women, many of
whom received acclaim as saints while still alive. Francis and
Clare did not have to look farther than their own city to discover
examples of both.

Urban life, however, was more than just political struggles
punctuated by religious feasts. It was an intensely social affair.
Privacy was unknown and undesired. Houses were, for most of
the citizens, cramped and crowded. People spent as much time
as possible in the streets, enjoying the handsome piazzas and
spacious courts that were becoming a feature in the expanding
urban centers. They congregated there daily, meeting friends,

insulting enemies, reveling in the pleasure of seeing and being seen. It was here that news was circulated, including not only local gossip but also the affairs of the mighty in Church and Empire. Naturally enough, these gracious piazzas also provided opportunities for courtship, as the young men ogled the girls who passed, properly chaperoned, but not so closely that secret signs and love notes could not be exchanged.

Everyone knew everyone else—and about everyone else's affairs. In a fourteenth century book praising Pavia, then a city of about 50,000, we read: "They knew each other so well that if anybody inquires for an address he will be told it at once, even if the person he asks for lives in a quite different part of the city; this is because they all gather twice daily either in the court of the commune or in the cathedral piazza."[4]

Such gatherings were colorful affairs, for the rich fabrics from the East were becoming the daily apparel of the wealthier classes. Europe's own looms, too, were producing a marvelous variety of materials, skillfully patterned and dyed. Pietro Bernardone's frequent journeys to the great cloth fairs of France enabled him to bring back to Assisi cut velvets in elaborate patterns from Genoa, costly silks of brilliant color manufactured in Almeira, delicate fabrics from Tartary, and wondrously soft woolens from Languedoc. The art of satin-making reached its perfection in this century. Costly textiles such as baldachin, woven of gold and silk threads, were in great demand to adorn churches and enhance divine services.

Both men and women of the upper classes habitually wore sumptuous garments. The members of the rising middle class emulated them and at times surpassed them in their display of lavish clothing. Thomas of Celano remarked of the young Francis that he "liked to dress in fine and flowing garments" made, no doubt, from the rich stuffs stocking his father's shop.[5] It was customary to advertise one's wealth and social position by one's style of dress.

The aristocratic classes began to resent this show of extravagance by their social "inferiors." Often sumptuary laws regulating the wearing of clothes and jewelry in public were imposed. This was ostensibly to limit waste and extravagance (a Papal Legate in Tuscany banned ladies' trains of a cubit and a half) but in reality it was an attempt to prevent the lower orders from dressing more grandly than their betters.

Rich or noble men wore scarlet tunics, fur robes, an abundance of gold chains and rings and usually a flowing overgarment called a *guarnocca*. Frequently, this was lined with bright silks or fur and decorated with gold embroidery and clasps of silver.

Gowns of both men and women came in many colors, most of them bright and showy. On a Sunday morning one could see rose, bright blue, scarlet, green, and crimson garments in the piazza before San Rufino, cathedral church of the noble quarter. These garments were fastened by buttons of precious metal and girded with silver, gilt, or enamel belts. The worshippers carried purses woven of silk and metallic threads. Women frequently adorned their heads with chaplets set with jewels.

A contemporary description of the ladies of Faenza, a city of northern Italy, reads: "They wore on their heads a chaplet of gold and silver thread; had the necks all bare without any ornament to the point were the bodice begins. The veste itself was girt above the flanks with a golden girdle, often adorned with gems. Some had the bodice adorned with gold and the rest of the dress was purple or crimson silk, with open sleeves hanging halfway down the leg and usually reversed over the shoulders, as were also frequently the sleeves of the chemisette, which were open, allowing the bare arms to be seen. The arms were artificially whitened and were adorned with ornamental chains or bracelets of gold."[6]

Although each Italian city had its distinctive colors and style of dress, we may assume that such elaborate styles prevailed in Assisi as elsewhere. Clare's family, described as "the most noble in the city of Assisi, both on her father's as well as on her mother's side," would surely have indulged in lavish finery. "Their home was one of the greatest in the city and the life of her family very sumptuous" continued the same witness, Johanni di Ventura.[7] Thomas of Celano mentions Clare's "soft and costly garments."[8]

For most of the people, beauty and pageantry entered their lives mainly through the annual round of church festivals. Outside of these, people found pleasure in tournaments, fairs, hunting and falconry, horse racing, and in the performances of wandering minstrels. Indoor amusements consisted of games of dice and chess.

In this vocal and lively milieu where wars raged, heretics ranted, and thoughtful persons almost despaired, God was quietly at work, preparing two souls who would rise to a stature that would surpass even that of the majestic cathedrals then being raised all over Europe. They loved deeply every nuance and shade of their world. They were affected by all that occurred and were greathearted enough to embrace it with Christ's transforming love, a love which would waken it to the Kingdom already growing in its boisterous midst.

Chapter I Endnotes

1. Cause of Canonization, Witness 19, #1, found in Nesta de Robeck, *St. Clare of Assisi* (Chicago: Franciscan Herald Press, 1980).
2. Orville Prescott, *Lords of Italy* (New York: Harper and Row, 1972), pp. 26–27.
3. Ibid., p. 27.
4. Ibid., p. 28.

5. 1 Celano, #3.
6. Prescott, *Lords of Italy*, pp. 28–29.
7. Cause of Canonization, Wit. 20, #2, 3.
8. Thomas of Celano, Legend of St. Clare of Assisi, #4, found in *The Legend and Writings of Saint Clare of Assisi* (St. Bonaventure, N.Y.: The Franciscan Institute, 1953).

II You Will Give Birth to a Light

For some reason, a reflective mood has settled on Sister Ortolana. She glances at the bright flowers which are flourishing in pots about the courtyard and smiles with satisfaction. Her smile is caught and returned by Sister Cecilia who leaves her place among other sisters to sit beside Ortolana. The sisters are enjoying an evening recreation in the court of San Damiano. Their needles and spindles flash through intricate needlework while lively conversation sparkles among them.

Ortolana enjoys the youthful fun of the gray-robed sisters and gladly contributes her share. Her eyes stray to her daughter, absorbed in conversation and as radiant as the evening sun whose light is bathing the courtyard. Suddenly, Sister Cecilia breaks into her thoughts. Ortolana smiles again and remarks that she has just recalled something which occurred over thirty years before. It is as fresh in her mind as if it had happened only this morning while she was kneeling before the Crucifix in the chapel.

Perhaps it is Francis' recent death which caused her to recall how profoundly he had been influenced by words spoken from that very Crucifix. She, too, she confides to Sister Cecilia, had once heard the Crucified speak. . . .

The coolness of San Rufino was welcome that July day in 1194. But Ortolana was scarcely aware of it as she knelt before the Crucifix in the shadowy interior. Despite her full garments, it was evident that the Lady Ortolana was close to the time of confinement, her first. The countenance of this woman in her

25

twenties is strong but drawn with fear. Her fine hands are clasped tightly as her lips move in silent prayer.

Madonna Ortolana, wife of Favarone di Offreduccio, knight of Assisi, is judged to be a valiant woman by medieval standards. She has done things which very few women of her day dared to undertake. Three times she has set out from her home to go on pilgrimage. Along with her kinswoman, Pacifica Guelfuccio, Ortolana has journeyed to the distant sanctuary of St. Michael on Monte Gargano in Apulia, has traveled to Rome to honor the Apostles and, most remarkably of all, has braved the dangers of a long sea voyage to the Holy Land. In doing this, she has completed the round of pilgrimages referred to in medieval parlance as "Deus, Angelus, et Homo" (God, angels, and men), and her fellow townspeople honor her for this accomplishment.

Friar Thomas of Celano echoed their sentiments when he wrote of her: "What more need be said? By the fruit the tree is known and because of the tree the fruit is praised. The abundance of divine favor preceded in the root that in its little branch a wealth of holiness might follow."[1]

Lady Ortolana, true to her name which means "good gardener," desired to enrich the roots of her faith by seeing for herself the places which her Savior had hallowed by his earthly presence. To do this she probably joined a band of pilgrims which followed the crusaders to the Holy Land for it would have been unthinkable and foolhardy for a woman to travel such a difficult way alone even "for reasons of prayer and devotion."[2] Perhaps her crusader husband was already in Palestine and had sent back word that negotiations had opened Jerusalem to Christian pilgrims again. If this supposition is valid, the time may have been about 1192, at the close of the Third Crusade. The crusaders had conquered St. John of Acre by force of arms but access to the Holy Land itself was negotiated by a treaty which guaranteed safety to pilgrims but left control of Palestine largely in the hands of the Saracens.

No details are given of Ortolana's trip but it is not difficult to reconstruct its main features from what is known of medieval pilgrimages. A person who proposed to journey to the Holy Land prepared for it as seriously as if he were facing death, as well he might be! Before leaving home, one was advised to put affairs of both body and spirit in order. All debts were to be paid, amends made for any injustices, alms given to atone for sins and, if one were in charge of a household, due provision made for its care during one's absence. The journey would be long and costly and usually ship captains demanded payment in advance for they could not be certain that a given pilgrim would be returning.

Pilgrim ships as well as crusader vessels had to take advantage of the best seasons for sailing, often leaving a commercial port such as Venice in late spring and endeavoring to return before the winter storms began in November. Grim hardship was the lot of all those hardy enough to brave the seas. Not only the length of time spent aboard the rolling and cramped ships but also the poor provisions, lack of fresh water, and the primitive state of sanitation harassed the devout pilgrim.

Lady Ortolana must have approached the unfamiliar world of sea, soldiers, and ships by nerving herself and her companions with the remembrance of the special pilgrimage blessing which they had received from the bishop prior to leaving their native city. Perhaps a group from Assisi traveled together, leaving their homes after an impressive farewell ceremony and Mass in the Cathedral of San Rufino. Although the crusaders were, in a broad sense, also pilgrims, the traditional pilgrimage spirit was somewhat deflected in their case from its original character. Motives considered proper for a pilgrimage were the fulfillment of a vow, the seeking of a special favor from God, or the performance of a penance imposed for confessed sins.

Lady Ortolana's pilgrimage most likely took place before the birth of her first child in 1194. This is implied by Thomas of

Celano's statement: "For although she was bound by marriage ties and burdened with the cares of a household, she . . . went on devout pilgrimage beyond the seas and visited the Holy Places which the God-Man had hallowed by his sacred footprints, returning home at length with great joy. . . . When finally Ortolana was with child. . . ."[3] Could one of the objects of this devout lady's pilgrimage have been to implore God for the blessing of motherhood? We do not know.

Knights and their company wore the Cross conspicuously on their clothing while the pilgrims were distinguished by a penitential garb, a broad-brimmed hat, a wallet slung across one's back, and a staff, usually iron-tipped. All such groups were inevitably accompanied by persons of less exalted motives. By the twelfth and thirteenth centuries, only the production of a testimonial letter from one's bishop enabled a person to escape being classified as an adventurer or pilgrimage profiteer.

Once arrived at the port city, the travelers would have to await favorable weather for sailing, sometimes a matter of weeks. When the moment arrived, the ship captain would have the trumpets sounded and from various parts of the city the passengers would converge on the dock. Small boats would convey them to the waiting vessel, along with their chests, barrels for water and wine, mattresses, and whatever provisions they could afford to supplement the monotonous ship's fare.

Once on the galley, the ladies of the company might be assigned a berth in a low-ceilinged compartment just under the tarred decks. This may not have been such a privilege when the sea was rough and quite likely those who spread their mattresses on the floor were safer. At times these rude bunks were scarcely a foot and a half wide and seldom long enough for a person to lie at full length.

In addition to the perils from storms, bad food, and shipwreck, galleys were frequently harassed by marauding ships of infidels who gladly sold captured Christians as slaves in the markets of the Moslem East. When crusaders were on board, they would display their battle shields in prominent rows along the sides of the ship to forewarn any pirates that the ship carried armed men.

Pilgrim and crusader ships could stop only at whatever ports along the route were in Christian hands. Access to Palestine was frequently safest by way of Egypt, so after passing Cyprus, ships would put in at St. John of Acre. From there, crusaders and pilgrims transferred to smaller boats which carried them up the Nile delta to Damietta.

Setting out from Egypt, the pilgrims would travel overland through the bleak region of the Negev, the lay folk and clerics on mules, the accompanying soldiers on horseback. When at last Jerusalem, the longed-for city, appeared white and glistening in the distance, they would do as pious Jews had done for centuries. They dismounted on the "mons gaudii" (the height of joy) to sing the traditional pilgrim song of joyous thanksgiving:

> I rejoiced when I heard them say:
> "Let us go to the house of the Lord."
> And now our feet are standing
> Within your gates, O Jerusalem.
> . . . .
>
> For the peace of Jerusalem pray:
> "Peace be to your homes!
> May peace reign in your walls,
> In your palaces, peace."
>
> For love of my brethren and friends
> I say: "Peace upon you!"
> For love of the house of the Lord,
> I will ask for your good.[4]

Fervent indeed was their prayer for the peace of the Holy

C ty. Pilgrims were only tolerated by treaty, and crusaders might come only under the shelter of "safe-conduct" passes. The atmosphere surrounding the Holy Places was far from tranquil. Claimed by the three major religions of the world, Jerusalem seethed and smouldered under the eastern sun.

The party from Assisi may have stayed with the Knights of the Holy Sepulcher, or they may have put up at one of the hostelries provided by the recently founded confraternities whose purpose was to assist pilgrims. Perhaps they were welcomed by members of the Altopassio, a confraternity founded by their countrymen from neighboring Tuscany.

Once in Jerusalem the pilgrims would have sought out the Via Dolorosa, following the crooked and crowded way in compassionate remembrance of their Savior until they reached the site of Calvary. There stood the Church of the Holy Sepulcher, the holiest of holy places in Jerusalem. The crusaders had erected a Romanesque church on the spot which united three older, desecrated shrines, those of the Resurrection, the Rock of the Crucifixion, and the Crypt of the Finding of the Holy Cross. Ortolana and her companions could have entered through the double doors of the main building which, while impressively wide, were deliberately low to prevent men from riding through on horseback with the intention of sacrilege or pillage. Immediately to their right was the reputed site of Calvary, though very little of the rock itself was still there. Some distance to the left was the graceful rotunda which covered the Holy Sepulcher itself. A crypt, reached by descending stairs from the main building, contained a subterranean sanctuary dedicated to St. Helena, legendary finder of the True Cross.

When Lady Ortolana and her fellow travelers visited the shrine, however, the Wood of the Cross was not there. It had fallen into the hands of the Moslems when they had defeated the Christian army defending Jerusalem in 1187. A treaty in 1221 which ended the Fifth Crusade stipulated the return of this most precious of Christian relics. When the time came for its surrender, however, no trace of it could be found. All that now remains of it are pieces which had been sent to other churches prior to this catastrophic loss.

Mount Sion, the highest spot in Jerusalem, the ancient Rock of David, was crowned by a church said to be built at the site of the Last Supper chamber. This splendid basilica, also erected by the crusaders, gave entrance to an ancient house where a large upper room had been venerated as the Cenacle since the earliest days of Christianity. Certainly, the pilgrims approached this hallowed place with deep reverence.

But possibly the spot which most stirred Ortolana was Gethsemani, where the gnarled olive trees seemed ancient enough to be the very ones which witnessed her Savior's most anguished hours. Here at least one could feel one saw the same things which Jesus himself had seen. Here an aura of agony seemed to linger about the gray-white rocks shadowed by the bent trees. All-night vigils were common at such places so perhaps Madonna Ortolana spent the dark hours of a night at prayer among these twisted trees.

Ortolana stored her memory with the emotions and impressions these scenes made upon her. Drawing upon them later not only nourished her own devotion but enabled her to give vivid detail to the familiar gospel narratives she explained to her growing daughters. St. Jerome's words on the value of a Holy Land pilgrimage would have found echo in her heart: "Just as one understands the Greek historians better when one has seen Athens . . . so we also understand Scripture better when we have seen Judea with our own eyes, and discovered what still remains . . . of ancient towns. . . . That is why I myself took care to travel through this land. . . ."[5]

No doubt the pilgrims' itinerary included a trip to Bethlehem where old Jerome himself had found a place where he could live in peace. The Grotto of the Nativity bore faint resemblance to the original stable that had sheltered the poor couple from Nazareth but Ortolana's devout imagination could have easily clothed it with Luke's simple but graphic details. Again with Jerome, she could have felt she was seeking "a city which one already knows by what one has read of it in the Holy Scriptures. One enters the cave of the Savior, weeps at the Sepulcher . . . kisses the wood of the Cross, ascends the Mount of Olives. . . ."[6]

Lady Ortolana had sought to find her Savior himself in his earthly homeland. Instead, she found a new dimension in her faith life, a sense of compassionate relationship that intensified rather than satisfied her longing for something more. Returning home "at length with great joy," she would have proudly carried with her the emblem of a bona fide pilgrim to the Holy Land, a palm branch from Jericho.[7] Thus she would have merited the name of "palmer" applied to returning pilgrims. But the distinction of being a pilgrim, even to the Holy Land, did not seem to have relieved Ortolana's searching heart. She still suffered a sense of restlessness, of spiritual quest. And this pressing search for the divine she was to pass on to her first-born daughter.

Now even her high courage falters, and Ortolana earnestly pleads with "Christ Crucified to bring her safely through the perils of childbirth."[8] And these perils are by no means small. Many are the women who die in childbirth or its aftermath. Even should the mother survive, the life of the child is hardly assured. The number of infants who die during their first year of life is heartbreaking. Women bear many children with the hope that some of them at least may attain adulthood. A mother's heart, as well as her body, is repeatedly assaulted by the rise and fall of hope that accompanies the many births and frequent deaths. A woman hovers anxiously over the cradle during the first precarious months. Perhaps this time her love and suffering will not end in tears. The dangers which Ortolana had faced on the high seas were not greater than those to which she is now exposed. Her prayer grows more intense.

Gently, sweetly, a voice breaks into her consciousness. It seems to emanate from the Crucifix: "Fear not, woman, for you shall bring forth without danger a light which shall greatly illumine the world."[9] Bewilderment overcomes Ortolana at this unexpected response to her anxious prayer. But the deep peace which enfolds her heart does not permit her to doubt that the words are from heaven. The message, though unexpected, has a strangely familiar ring.

Thomas of Celano may have chosen to heighten the essential import of the message Ortolana received by casting the words into a biblical mold. He thereby sought to enrich them by the powerful associations that the scriptural overtones would evoke. He had an impressive predecessor in this type of evocative prose. St. Luke himself had rendered the inexpressible message given to a young maid of Nazareth by using allusive Old Testament phrases and rhythms.

"Fear not, woman!" "Fear not, Mary. . . . Do not be afraid, Joseph, son of David." How often had not Ortolana heard that word of peace read out from the Scriptures! As she pursues this remembrance, her wonder increases. She had heard, "You shall bring forth without danger a light." Centuries earlier a girl in Galilee had heard a similar announcement: "You shall give birth to a son" and a wise old man in the temple had called him "a light which shall greatly illumine the world."

Like another Mary, Ortolana ponders these words, cherishing them in her heart, questioning their possible meaning, waiting in hope to see their fulfillment. As a seal of her faith, Ortolana chose that her blond baby girl be named Clare (light or brightness) at her baptism "in the hope that the brightness of the light thus promised might in some way be verified after the good pleasure of the will of God."[10]

Twice more would Ortolana give birth to daughters, Catherine, whom history would know as Agnes, and Beatrice. These children would enter and fill with joy the large palazzo of Favarone Offreduccio. But being the mother of three lively girls was not the full extent of Lady Ortolana's responsibilities. She had a large estate and household staff to oversee and, if we can believe the allusions made by witnesses, she often bore this responsibility alone. Her lord, Favarone, seemed to be at home so seldom that one witness, whose home was divided from that of the Offreduccio's only by the piazza, declared she had never met him! Thus, the town house, the summer residence in the country, plus the farms, olive groves, and vineyards which comprised the wealth of the family, came under Ortolana's astute management.

Madonna Ortolana's concern embraced not only her estates, her home, and its frequent visitors but also the ever-present poor who swarmed the streets of Assisi. She had only to step outside the massive stone doorway of her palazzo to see the beggars sitting before the cathedral across the piazza. According to an unwritten code of beggary, certain places of advantage before cathedrals and churches were claimed by the same individual for years on end. No beggar would dare usurp the customary place of another. On just what basis this order was established and maintained is not evident, but this "code" predates Christianity and still exists today wherever beggars commonly congregate.

No doubt, Lady Ortolana's generosity was known and appreciated by this "brotherhood of the streets." Almsgiving was highly esteemed as a means of expiation for sin, and beggars felt they filled a necessary place in the Christian scheme by providing their more fortunate fellowmen the opportunity to practice this salvific virtue! Ortolana, we may believe, accompanied her alms of money and food with a respect which saw the person of Christ in these less fortunate of her townspeople. She quite likely knew and greeted them by name, being as familiar with their faces as she was with the rest of her neighbors on the cathedral piazza.

The good works which Thomas of Celano and Ortolana's fellow citizens praised may also have included personal visits to hovels along the devious lanes crowded within the city walls. Ortolana fearlessly sought out and tended to the needs of all the sick poor who were brought to her maternal attention. The food, herbs, and clothing she provided were indeed appreciated but it was the gentle tenderness of the giver which won the affection of those who received them. Where medical knowledge failed, the skilled and compassionate hands of this gentlewoman found innumerable ways to provide a bit of comfort and ease to suffering bodies. Clare was later to display a thoughtful and enlightened concern for the sick, employing skills learned, most likely, at her mother's side. The "deep compassion for the afflicted" which all the sisters praised in their abbess was but the natural inheritance of a daughter of Madonna Ortolana.[11]

The wealth of her house and her honored position in Assisian society did not prevent Ortolana from giving "as much of her time as possible to divine worship and the works of piety."[12] From her earliest days little Clare must have trotted across the piazza beside her mother to attend services at San Rufino, especially on feast days which were celebrated with pomp and pageantry, so fascinating to a little child. She may have accompanied her mother on walks after the noonday siesta to the dim peace of one of the many other churches whose belltowers pricked the skyline of Assisi.

On a Marian feast they may have slipped through the Corinthian columns of Santa Maria sopra Minerva which faced the Piazza del Commune. This ancient edifice in classic Greek style was erected in the first century to the honor of the goddess Minerva. It suffered a "conversion" when Assisi became Christian during the third century and was rededicated to the Mother of God. Or they may have chosen to wander down the Via San Paolo which leads from the same piazza to the simple church of San Stefano with its slit windows barely lighting its interior.

The former cathedral, Santa Maria Maggiore, the abbey

church of San Pietro, or the church of San Giorgio where the chapter resided and a Latin school was maintained for the youngsters of Assisi, could also have been the destination of these daily strolls. Perhaps on a pleasant day Ortolana would turn her steps through the Porta Nuova and descend the steep track outside the city walls to the ruined but still venerated chapel of San Damiano. An old priest made his residence there and would gladly accept a stipend to say a Mass for Madonna and her little daughter.

Sudden laughter swirls around her, and Sister Ortolana bemusedly lifts her hand to the coif and veil which bind her head. She smiles companionably at Sister Cecilia who is still listening with rapt attention at her side. Many years later Sister Cecilia will recount some of these precious details about the early life of her mother in Christ.

Chapter II Endnotes

1. Legend of Celano, #2.
2. Cause of Canonization, Wit. 1, #4.
3. Legend, #1, 2.
4. Ps 122:1, 2, 6–9.
5. St. Jerome, Praef. in lib. Paralip.
6. St. Jerome, cf. Épist. 46.
7. Legend, #1.
8. Ibid., #2.
9. Ibid.
10. Ibid.
11. Cause of Canonization, Wit. 3, #3.
12. Legend, #1.

III   Sun Beyond the Mountain

Citizens of Perugia are awakened each day by the sun rising behind Monte Subasio. Across the Umbrian Valley to the east of their city stands the broad bulk of this outlying peak of the Appenine Range. On its nearer flank is perched Perugia's arch rival, Assisi. In September of 1203 an unusually large number of Assisians are residing in Perugia, though not all of them by choice. How many of them who may have turned to look wistfully across the valley toward the dawn and their own city we do not know. But we can be sure that some hearts were counting the sunrises until they would once again be sheltered in the shadow of this great green eminence.

This morning crisp air with an autumn tang in it is flowing through the cracks of a shuttered window. As it strikes his face, Francis Bernardone stirs uncomfortably, then wakens fully. Another day, another day in prison. Quietly he rises from the mat laid on the floor and moves carefully to avoid disturbing the other young men sprawled about him.

He walks to the window, then hesitates. If he opens the shutters the chill air will penetrate even more keenly and rouse everyone to grumbling irritation. But Francis yields to the habit of the past ten months of opening these shutters and looking through the barred window to the east. He lifts the latch and as the heavy doors swing back, he breathes deeply, gratefully.

A perfect morning! Though the valley and the plain beyond are shrouded in a rising mist, the outline of Monte Subasio is sharply defined against a rosy glow. The sun is still hidden but the clearness of the brightening sky tells Francis the day will be

cloudless. He waits and watches, his heart torn between praise of
the sheer beauty of the dawn and yearning for the mountain of
his home.

As the brightness slowly spreads, the gloom of the mountain
face is dispersed. The jagged peak is tipped momentarily by a
fiery glow. Suddenly the sun shoots a ray through a lower notch
and the watcher sees it flash off the highest bell tower in Assisi.
The white outlines of Assisi's stone buildings appear one by one.
Francis' heart stirs with love for his city, a love which prolonged
absence has deepened and matured.

He looks with grim satisfaction at the gutted ruins of the Rocca Maggiore rising on the heights above Assisi. He is glad to see
it still in shambles. Aimlessly, his eyes wander about the outskirts
of the city as the growing daylight brings more details into focus.
There are more ruins to be seen and gloated over. The "minores" of Assisi had had their hour of triumph over those traitorous
feudal lords of theirs. Francis can make out the damaged castles
of Sasso Rosso, Rocca San Angelo, Corccorano, and Bassano, all
country estates of the nobles which Francis and his fellow citizens had gleefully plundered and burned. Above all, the sight
of the ruins of the fortress tower of San Savino on the plain
brings satisfaction to his soul. For Pietro Bernardone had raged
incessantly over the tolls exacted by the robber barons of this
castle from all the merchants who had to pass it on the main
commercial route. That humiliation had come to an abrupt end
in 1198 when the commune had arisen, taking advantage of the
temporary absence of their German overlord. This count, concerned by the weakening of the power of the Hohenstaufen
dynasty after the death of Emperor Henry IV, had sought to
strengthen his authority by switching allegiance to the forceful
new Pope, Innocent III. When Conrad hurried off to the papal
court to surrender his duchy to Innocent as a papal fief, the
citizens of Assisi had risen in an armed body and stormed the
Rocca. Taking its great stones, they built up their city walls and

towered gates and proclaimed Assisi an independent city. Proudly Francis salutes the red and blue banner of his city which he can see snapping in the brisk morning air.

But not all the ruins he sees make Francis' heart exult. He is troubled to see, here and there among the trees, the crumbling walls of a chapel or the caved-in roof of a wayside shrine. The rising sun picks out old San Damiano, crumbling beside the steep hillside track that dropped outside the walls of the city.

A frown creases Francis' brow as he remembers that the thick foliage further down mercifully conceals the lazaretto of San Lorenzo. Horror and disgust mingle as he gazes at the unseen reminder of his personal nemesis. He cannot stand lepers. Even here in prison the thought of them tortures him.

Although they live on a green hillside under the free sky, they are, Francis knows, imprisoned more strictly than he. Feudal society had only one "treatment" for leprosy, that prescribed by Moses—segregation. Lazar houses dotted remote country places all over Europe. Here the feared outcasts dragged their rotting limbs and decaying countenances to find what comfort they could in one another's misery.

Occasionally, Knight Hospitallers came to bring food and straw for bedding. Long before their horses and loaded carts came into the vicinity, the residents of the "hospital" were warned to get as far from sight as possible. Some of the wretches, whose disease was too far advanced to allow them to seek the shelter of the woods, huddled in the darkest corners of the building while their benefactors threw bundles of straw into the doorway along with supplies of food. As these noblemen rode swiftly off, the living skeletons of men and women crept back to the dubious gifts. While some fought with each other over the best of the food, others stared dully, despair gnawing at their hearts more cruelly than the disease ravaging their body.

Francis takes a deep breath and shifts his eyes. Nearer to view is the tiny St. Mary of the Angels, nearly hidden among the trees. He remembers passing it in November 1202, when he and his comrades-in-arms had marched out of Assisi to engage Perugia in battle. That detested rival had not only given willing refuge to the feudal aristocrats driven from their palazzos in Assisi but had also agreed to assist them in regaining their property and rights. When news of Perugia's military alliance with Foligno reached Assisi, tempers flared anew. Assisi sought and obtained arms and soldiers from neighboring Bevagna, Spello, Nocera, and Fabriano. The commune spurned Perugia's ultimatum to restore the self-exiled noblemen's property and make restitution for damages. War was declared amid general enthusiasm.

When a medieval Italian city prepared for war, all men between the ages of fourteen and seventy might be called to arms. Only an indispensable few stayed at home to guard the walls and keep the local shops and industries in operation. The majority of citizens fought on foot as unskilled infantry. They wore mail shirts and steel caps and wielded spears and pikes. More prosperous citizens, such as the Bernardone family, fought on horseback arrayed in the elaborate equipment of a knight. These haphazard armies were little concerned with strategy and only occasionally with tactics. Such lack of foresight proved the Assisians' downfall.

Francis recalls with lifting heart the great day of the assembling of the troops. After a shrill blast from trumpeteers on the walls and amid a deafening clangor of church bells, the soldiers gathered in the great piazza for a grand parade. Here and there colorful banners of the various merchant and craft guilds snapped in the breeze. The volunteers from the other cities marched proudly behind their town emblems. In the midst of the men was an enormous wagon drawn by oxen, the *carroccio*. This was surmounted by masts flying the colors of Assisi and was the rallying point of civic pride. It must be defended at all times by the troops.

The grand adventure did not last long. The armed Assisians

took the initiative and marched out in the direction of the bridge San Giovanni. Just as they reached a wooded hill, Ospedale di Collestrada, the Perugians burst upon them. They had secretly crossed the Tiber at a point where it bent from view. Suddenly war was no longer the gallant enterprise it had been but a bloody and humiliating skirmish with men of superior training and equipment. Francis was taken prisoner along with many of his compatriots.

Once in Perugia, his refinement and courteous manners earned him the privilege of being imprisoned with those noblemen of Assisi who had sided with the commune. Even so the extended confinement was anything but pleasant, and no one knew how long it would continue. It seemed unlikely that anyone would be released before a truce between Perugia and Assisi was arranged, an event which seemed far in the future.

As the sun rises higher over the shoulder of Monte Subasio, a beam suddenly flashes out, striking Francis on the head and shoulders as does the sword of king dubbing a valiant soldier a knight. Francis lifts his face to the full glory of the sun.

Behind him the men are stirring, most of them out of temper as usual. One of them is completely exasperated upon seeing Francis standing at the window with such a cheerful face, and he "reproaches him as a fool for looking happy while in prison. Francis replies mildly, 'Is that what you think of me? The day will come when I shall be honored by the whole world.'"[1] Laughter greets this announcement, and not a few of the men wonder where Francis gets this supreme assurance of his importance. After all he is only the son of a cloth merchant, albeit charming and wealthy.

Francis himself wonders. He is twenty-one, well-endowed with money and friends, but do these add up to the grandeur to which he feels called? All he knows is that a conviction of future greatness seethes and bubbles in his heart. Because of this he believes in himself and his destiny.

In the meantime he turns to the immediate task of pacifying

his companions who have little to do but gripe and bemoan their misery. Because he can find no greater challenge within the four walls of the prison cell, Francis focuses all his charm and good spirits on the most uncharming of his fellows. In time he achieves a kind of rehabilitation of the boorish man. He even reconciles him with the other men who had planned to ostracize him in outrage at his arrogance.

Elsewhere in Perugia a nine-year-old girl awakens. She slips from her well-blanketed bed in the Peroscio palazzo and draws aside the draperies which cover the window. She shivers as the chill strikes her but does not step back. She is looking for the mountain. Happily she notices that the sky is already bright with that special clarity which makes all the colors of the landscape stand out in vivid beauty.

Clare pushes back the heavy mass of her blond hair and gazes across the valley in blissful enchantment. A slow pageant of light is coloring the dark bulk of Monte Subasio. It has been one of Clare's daily delights to watch for the sun as it tips the jagged peak of the mountain with living flame. Once, she recalls with a shiver, the flames had been very real indeed. The Rocca Maggiore, symbol of authority and order, had blazed like a torch lighting up the night with a lurid glow. She was only four when her family had had to flee from the rioting citizens of Assisi, but the horror of it still lived in her memory. It is hard now to remember much about their home in Assisi.

Clare has happier memories of the life she has lived the past five years in Perugia. The Peroscia family had hospitably opened their home to the Favarone Offreduccios when they chose to remain in voluntary exile from their native city rather than give in to the outrageous demands of the "minores" to have a greater say in the conducting of the city government. To return before these rebels were brought to their knees would mean death.

Even the family estate at Corrano, which Uncle Monaldo held

as head of the Offreduccio clan, was for a time deemed unsafe for the younger members of the family. Although it was situated on the very borderline between Assisi and the territory controlled by Perugia, the riotous uprising of 1198 had not spared it. In the beginning the self-exiled nobles had expected that a truce would soon be arranged, reparations paid, and they would return to their accustomed position and homes. But peace had been long in coming. In fact, even now in 1203, it seemed as remote as when the civil strife had commenced for memories were long and tempers still boiled at the least provocation.

Lady Ortolana steps up quietly behind her eldest daughter and lays a soft hand on her shoulder. "What are you looking at this chilly morning?" she chides affectionately though she easily guesses what is attracting her girl's interest.

"Do you think we will *ever* go home again, Mama?"

"Figlia mia, who is to say? Yet I feel we will return someday but just when . . . ?" Madonna Ortolana shrugs her shoulders. "What do you want to do when we are back in Assisi? Climb to the top of Monte Subasio?" she teases, for she has often seen Clare turn her eyes toward the inviting peak.

"Aren't mountains supposed to be climbed?" asks Clare.

"Sometimes," Ortolana replies thoughtfully, "sometimes they are. But they can also just be there for God's sake, . . and for the sake of our spirits. It is good to see something that is so strong, so sure, so unshakeable. Then you can lean your soul on them as on the shoulders of our great Father in heaven." After a silence she adds, "Sometimes there are caves in the mountains."

"What good are caves, Mama?"

"No good or a lot of good, I would say. It depends on what you are looking for. Caves are good places to hide from sudden storms when it is needful. They are also dark and damp and lonely. But if one is ready for it one can find the living God in their depths. Many saints have found him thus. We can meet God in the mountains, Clare. And not just on the peaks or in the caves. You can't see it from here but there is a community of recluses, Sant' Angelo, on the other side of Monte Subasio. There holy women praise God day and night. Even now as the sun is rising over the top, their voices are rising in psalms of praise," reminisces Ortolana with a strange longing in her voice.

"Mama, do you think we can go there someday?"

"Yes, God willing. But right now let us praise the Lord ourselves." Obediently, Clare follows her mother back into the room and takes her place at Ortolana's side. Her mother takes up a large illuminated psalter and opens it in her lap, spreading it wide so Clare's bright eyes can follow the Latin words that her fingers point out. A combination reading lesson and morning prayer begins:

> I lift up my eyes to the mountains
> from where shall come my help?
> My help is from the Lord
> who made heaven and earth.
>
> The Lord is your guard and your shade;
> at your right side he stands.
> By day the sun shall not smite you
> nor the moon in the night.
>
> The Lord will guard you from evil,
> he will guard your soul.
> The Lord will guard your going and coming
> both now and forever.[2]

Clare and Ortolana both involuntarily glance back through the window toward Monte Subasio, now bathed in the morning sun.

Life in exile for the Offreduccio families has not been altogether unpleasant. Although Favarone and Ortolana must have missed the freedom that the management of their own house would afford, they are comfortably ensconced in Perugia by members of their own class who may have been distant relatives. Benvenuta di Peroscia testified that she had "dwelt together [with Clare] in the same house" when they were children.[3]

Uncle Monaldo's name appears on a list of noblemen in Perugia who helped to foment the feud with Assisi and to arrange the alliance with Foligno which caused the disastrous defeat of the Assisian military. It is likely that Favarone's other three brothers, Paolo, Ugolino, and Scipione, had also moved their households to Perugia. To these relatives on her father's side, Clare could add her mother's kinswomen, Bona and Pacifica Guelfuccio, whose lives were always closely linked to Clare's family. It is likely that Bona filled the role of duenna to Ortolana's girls and later, as events proved, she became an accomplice in their secret enterprises.

To Bona we owe the knowledge of Clare's secret benefactions to the poor, even as a little girl. Clare contrived to send some of the food, which it was thought she ate herself, to the poor; and Bona testified later that she "had repeatedly been the bearer of it."[4] Whether Lady Ortolana was aware of this artful maneuver of her daughter, we do not know. It is probable that the unusually large appetite of her little girl did not escape her notice but she may have secretly approved this evidence of Clare's compassion and condoned the little subterfuge.

All those who knew Clare as a child remarked on the great kindness that characterized her as well as the integrity and humility she evinced. Celano expressed his admiration in typical poetic fashion: "Hardly had the little Clare seen the light of day than she began to shine in the darkness of the world and become resplendent in her tender years by her modest upright conduct. . . . She gladly 'stretched out her hand to the poor' and from the abundance of her house 'supplied the wants of many.' And that her sacrifice might be more pleasing to God, she would deprive her own little body of delicacies and secretly send them out by messengers to quicken the hearts of the poor. Thus 'from her infancy mercy grew with her' and she had ever a tender heart that had mercy on the miseries of the miserable."[5]

The kindness and compassion of this child drew others to her, and, while in Perugia, she formed friendships so deep that in later years her childhood companions formed the nucleus of her bold experiment at San Damiano. In addition to her sister Agnes, about three years younger than Clare, Benvenuta de Peroscia and Philippa di Gislerio, a daughter of another exiled Assisian family, became her playmates. Together they strolled the streets, visiting churches, seeking to evade the vigilance of their elders, and causing heads to turn their way when they burst out in merry laughter.

But Clare did not move in an all-feminine society. In the typical Italian extended family her cousins would have been as close as first-degree kin. It is possible that as tempers cooled somewhat, the Offreduccio clan began spending the hot summer months at the country estate of Corrano. There Clare and Agnes would have lived in the same house with their cousins: Francis, son of Uncle Monaldo; Bernardino, Paolo's boy; Monaldo and Martino, Ugolino's two; and Rufino and Paolo, Uncle Scipione's sons. Two of these boys would be closely linked to Clare in later life.

Her cousin, Rufino, would be among the first of the young men to cast their lot with Francis Bernardone. It is possible that he was instrumental in bringing about the first meetings between Francis and Clare. Martino's name would be so closely allied to Clare's through his two daughters who entered San Damiano that some later biographers would mistakenly list him as her brother.

Clare's days were filled, not only with good times with her cousins and friends, but also with being trained in the many arts necessary for a girl of her station. Ortolana and Favarone decided that their daughters should learn to read and write Latin, a skill which would enable them to keep up with the intellectual developments of their age. The beauty of composition and cogency of logic which characterize Clare's writings attest to the quality of the education she had received. Clare probably also studied the basics of arithmetic which she would need in order to keep her household accounts and to barter shrewdly in the markets.

In addition, Ortolana would have taught her daughters such skills as spinning, weaving, and embroidery. No doubt she showed them the distinctive "Assisi stitch" used to give bright borders to table linens and petticoats. Perhaps she also set them to the task of making altar linens and vestments, for in later years Clare excelled in this.

The young girls would also have been gradually initiated into the complexities of managing a large household staff of maids and servants. A medieval home was almost sufficient unto itself, supplying all the family members and staff with clothing, shoes, bedding, and medicines, as well as food and wine made from the family fields. The mistress of the household was responsible for overseeing all of this. Perhaps Ortolana also sent her girls to the market place from time to time so they might learn the honored art of bargaining.

According to Thomas of Celano, Clare was early attracted by religion. He wrote: "With a docile heart she learned from her mother's lips the rudiments of faith and as the Spirit worked within and formed her into a most pure vessel, she became known to men indeed as a vessel of grace."[6]

Prayer seems to have appealed to Clare for it promised to answer an obscure hungering for God which haunted her awareness. Her first lessons in prayer were those imparted by Ortolana, not so much in words as by her example. Lady Ortolana centered her home around the things of God to which she obviously attached supreme importance. Her quiet strength amid the trials of exile, the frequent absences of her husband, and the heart-rending divisions which plagued her native city derived from her serene confidence in God.

Clare's first prayers were repeated after her mother's. As she grew older, pious practices were suggested to her, and she found delight in them. Celano wrote: "Holy prayer was her constant companion and, as she was often diffused with its fragrance, she began little by little to lead a life of seclusion. Since she had no chaplet on which to tell her Paternosters, she would count her little orisons to the Lord by means of a heap of pebbles."[7]

Ortolana watched Clare carefully and wondered if this budding piety would be just a childish fascination with something new, or if it indicated some hidden calling to a life of growing intimacy with the Lord. She did not worry overmuch when Clare showed a taste for solitude at times, for she knew her girl.

Everything that Clare did, she did wholeheartedly and with amazing intensity. She played with abandon, studied her lessons with absorption, labored over her needlework until she perfected it, and, above all, loved everyone she met with unbounded affection. No wonder that she also prayed with such fervor. Nothing was too small to claim Clare's undivided interest, no challenge too large to daunt her. In fact she seemed to thrive on difficult things and to thrill in the sheer test of trying out her developing skills.

Clare displayed as much enthusiasm for the colorful tournaments held in their castle courtyard as she did for the rich pageantry of a Papal Mass. It is likely that during the five or six years the family spent in Perugia, Pope Innocent III and the Papal Court visited the city on more than one occasion. In the early 1200s, the popes led a rather roving existence, moving from town to town as political expediency, weather, or invitation prompted them.

Perugia was Guelf, that is, willing to support the Papacy as opposed to Assisi which declared itself Ghibelline in allegiance to the empire. In theory, empire and papacy were at one, but in practice this was seldom so. In gratitude to the loyalty of the Perugians, the great Innocent would have chosen to spend some weeks in their city from time to time. Thus Clare and her family would have had the opportunity to assist at some of the elaborate papal functions and to hear for themselves his justly famed oratory. Innocent was a master of the art and could magnetize his hearers with his forceful, imaginative rhetoric.

Pope Innocent III was then in his prime, a vigorous man in his early forties. Despite his shrewd handling of worldly affairs, he had little faith in secular methods to achieve the goal he had set for his reign, the purification and reform of the Church. He knew too well that such a conversion would not be effected by decrees or diplomacy. So he looked carefully at the evangelical movements of the day. He sorted through the conflicting reports about them with his keen legal mind. Where he found evidence of genuine gospel living, he did not hesitate to revoke a previous edict of condemnation. Thus it was that in 1201, Innocent had reinstated the Humiliati and later tacitly reconfirmed another reform group, the Poor Men of Lyon.

Innocent's intuitive sense of the changes taking place in the world of his day caused him to understand that any return to the gospel must be accomplished by new means. He looked for courageous men who would voluntarily renounce the values and wealth of the world so as to preach by their lives the love and compassion of the Savior who lived among the poor, ate with the outcasts, and spoke of a Father who loves all his children. Did he express any of these convictions to his hearers in Perugia? We do not know. There would come a day, however, when his piercing eye would meet the fire in those of a young man from Assisi and see there the torch which could light the reforming fire he dreamed of. But that day still lay in the future. No one could foresee that the paths of a prisoner in a Perugian tower and of an intense child of the nobility would cross that of this greatest pope of the Middle Ages.

Ortolana, watching Clare grow in age, prayed that wisdom and grace would accompany her. She never forgot the prophecy that had preceded her child's birth but wisely did not try to foresee its unfolding. She waited, prayed, and watched the dawns succeed each other on Monte Subasio. As the sun fired the peak of the mountain of her home, Ortolana longed for the day when peace would return to the beautiful Umbrian countryside. Like Dante at the end of the century who also was a political exile, she too had "proved how salty tastes another's bread, and how hard a path it is to go up and down another's stairs."[8]

Clare would always be marked by the experiences of being an exile. She would grow to womanhood, formed by the beauties of her native land and the sad realities of what man could do to man even in the name of good. She saw great castles thrown down but did not fail to notice that the mountains of God endured.

Chapter III Endnotes

1. Legend of Three Companions, #4.
2. Ps 121:1, 2, 5–8.
3. Cause of Canonization, Wit. 2, #2.
4. Ibid., Wit. 17, #1.
5. Legend of Celano, #3.
6. Ibid., #3.
7. Ibid., #4.
8. Dante, *Divine Comedy: Paradiso*, Canto XVII.

IV   Glowing Embers

All Assisi is astir one day early in 1206. Shopkeepers draw bolts across their doors and street vendors drop awnings over their wares to join the throng converging on the square before Santa Maria Maggiore, the old cathedral. The plain façade of this Romanesque church, relieved only by a rose window, stands contiguous to the bishop's palace, now the center of attention this sunny winter morning.

Carts and mules stand abandoned by owners who mix with the populace pouring from doorways and courtyards. Knights, peasants, merchants, noble ladies, and their maids are all turning their steps in the same direction. Perhaps Lady Ortolana and her older daughters are among them for the Favarone family have returned at last to their native city. This is no ordinary scandal stirring the town today.

Francis Bernardone, former leader of the young bloods of the city, is being hailed before the bishop on charges of robbery and contempt of paternal authority by his father, Pietro. Everyone knows this wealthy burgher. Quite likely Lady Ortolana herself has patronized the Bernardone shop to purchase the fine stuffs she requires to outfit her family. Possibly, she and Clare had even dealt with Pietro's personable elder son who waited on customers with the courtesy of a prince.

This young man advertised his father's wares supremely well, for, says the Legend of the Three Companions, "In all things Francis was lavish, and he spent much more on his clothes than was warranted by his social position, for he would use only the

51

finest materials." It is added that "his natural courtesy of manner and speech accorded well with his noble attire."[1]

"When Lady Pica heard the neighbors commenting on her son's extravagance, she responded, 'What do you think my son will be? Through grace he will become a son of God.'"[2] Many laughed at her fond blindness. Yet how formative can be a mother's belief in her child!

For now, Francis, the former dandy whose garments were a splash of color anywhere, goes about clad in a hermit's tunic. He may sing as loudly and lustily as before, but it is religious, not romantic, ballads that he spins out on the air. Townspeople have not failed to note the change. Apparently it stemmed from the nearly fatal illness he suffered after his father had ransomed him from the Perugian prison in late 1203. After recovering, he would go off into the hills in moody silence and return with restless, burning eyes.

Madonna Pica watched him with anxious concern. Francis confided to her only that the world had strangely changed while he was ill. His friends' laughter now sounded banal, and their pleasures seemed foolish. Unhappy with himself, unhappy with his life, and more unhappy still with the future laid out for him by his ambitious father, Francis turned from the city to the solace of the mountainside.

Even here the sunlight and green slopes he loved mocked rather than consoled him. In the dark emptiness of his spirit, he began to seek the kinship of the caves dotting the ledges of Monte Subasio. He tried to pray seriously for the first time in his adult life. Attempting to exercise inner faculties unaccustomed to being controlled, Francis felt taunted by his own soul, that strange spirit within him that tormented and teased him in turns.

In the womb-like darkness of the cave, Francis set his will, the only part of his soul with which he felt contact, to seek out a light by which he could see. But the light he sought could not be conjured up by will power. It could arise only from some deeper strata of his spirit, areas where until now Francis had never consciously walked. Dimly he felt that if his soul was being emptied, it was only so it could be filled. What or who would fill it, he did not know. Clinging to this desperate hope, he agonized in the darkness.

During those two years of painful transition, Francis had not escaped the tongues of the gossips. Some mocked him, some pitied the parents of this eccentric boy, a few recalled the prophecies surrounding his birth. The more thoughtful observed that if he were moving in the direction of many self-styled reformers, he was beginning by reforming himself most thoroughly.

Country folk volunteered that he was frequently seen around abandoned churches or at the lazaretto. Clare heard the gossip and with her instinctive urge to defend the weak, she felt an almost maternal compassion for this hapless young man, so easily cut up by malicious tongues. And now he is being hailed before the gaping populace in a public trial at the bishop's palazzo, and by his own father! Her sensitive heart recoils. She may have seen an earlier episode when street urchins had pelted Francis' small figure with mud and filth.

> Shouting out that he was mad and demented; they had thrown the mud of the streets and stones at him. When the noise and the shouting of this kind concerning Francis had been going on for a long time . . . the report of these things had come finally to his father. When he had heard the name of his son mentioned . . . he had risen immediately, not indeed to free him but rather to destroy him. He had laid hands upon him and had dragged him shamelessly and disgracefully to his home. Thus, without mercy, he had shut him up in a dark place for several days.[3]

When Pietro left for yet another cloth fair, Madonna Pica had quietly opened the prison, fed her son a good meal, and sent him off in warm clothing, her prayers following. Lady Ortolana could sympathize with Pica's torn heart.

"What will Bishop Guido make of the case?" muses Clare, as the crowd carries her toward the large residence. Bishop Guido, the spiritual pastor of Assisi, was also a temporal lord of some magnitude. In this respect he was no worse, and in some ways better, than many of his contemporaries in the episcopate. The Church's prestige was considered to be enhanced by large ecclesiastical holdings. Guido, in point of fact, is said to have owned nearly half of Assisi.

Despite this concern with temporalities, he exhibited a genuine sympathy for the poor and often championed their rights in opposition to prestigious members of his own flock. Bishop Guido was a fighter and his forte seems to have been the law courts. His tenure in the episcopacy was characterized by endless litigation.

Some future day, when he and the Podestà will successfully divide the city into rival camps and civil strife is imminent, a dying son of Assisi will sing of the beauty of forgiveness. The heretical Podestà, excommunicated by Guido, and the pugnacious bishop he boycotted will listen deeply moved by the liquid melody extolling brotherly communion. Publicly, they will embrace, spiritual father and errant son, each craving pardon of the other.

Today, however, another father and son are not to be reconciled, much to the hurt of both. Bishop Guido's love of the dramatic led him to glory in the pomp and ceremony surrounding his office. But it also had opened his heart to an appealing young man who had come to him with a strange request; he desired counsel concerning genuine gospel living and true poverty. The Bishop perceived the stirrings of the Spirit in Francis Bernardone and extended ecclesiastical protection to him.

Francis availed himself of this privileged state for when his father summoned him to appear before the civil court, he responded that he was exempt from its authority. Then Pietro had recourse to the Bishop's tribunal. Guido "sent word to Francis that he must appear and answer his father's indictment; and he replied to the messenger; 'I will willingly appear before the Lord Bishop who is the father and lord of souls.'"[4] Francis now faces the most harrowing test of his emerging vocation.

Pietro! How Francis loves him . . . and how he fears him! This genial, indulgent father, the idol of his childhood, is now the nemesis of his manhood. How exquisite the ties that bind them and which also force them inevitably into opposition. Although Francis has successfully overcome his nauseating repugnance and in kissing a leper experienced "sweetness of body and soul,"[5] he quivers in anguish at the thought of confronting his father. But unless he does so, he will never be free.

Francis and Pietro, it would seem, are too much alike to misunderstand each other and too different to agree with each other. Both are men of outstanding gifts, marked for achieving any goal they set for themselves. The tragedy of their relationship is the sharp divergence of their aspirations: Pietro has set his heart on building a fortune, and his son desires total poverty; Pietro has striven to make the name of Bernardone famous, and his son wishes to see only the name of Jesus exalted; Pietro has founded his hopes on worldy success, while Francis opts for the folly of the Cross. These two men, each great in his own way, torture one another's heart.

Over this, Madonna Pica agonizes. She loves both her men. She understands them both. And in her heart she forgives them both. Like many another woman, she silently bears the pain of seeing her great loves oppose and wound one another. Few realize that the deepest wound of all is in the hearts of these valiant women.

Quickly, the crowd fills the square before the bishop's palazzo. Bishop Guido emerges through the arched doorway. Storming up to him, Pietro waves his arms, violently denouncing his unworthy son. Other voices shout out in approval or contradiction but all are suddenly hushed by a penetrating but calm voice.

"My Lord Bishop," begins Francis, "not only will I gladly give back the money which is my father's but also my clothes." Going into the Bishop's room, he strips himself of his garments and placing the money on them he stands naked before the eyes of all present and says, "Listen all of you and mark my words. Hitherto I have called Pietro Bernardone my father, but because I am resolved to serve God I return to him the money on account of which he was so perturbed, and also the clothes I wore which are his; and from now on I will say, 'Our Father who are in heaven' and not Father Pietro Bernardone!"

His father rose up burning with grief and anger, gathered up the garments and money and carried them home. Those present at the scene took the side of Francis because Pietro had left him without any clothing, and moved with pity, they started to weep over him. The Bishop, seeing Francis' fortitude of spirit, was in admiration of his fervor and constancy, and gathered him into his arms, covering him with his own cloak."[6]

Lady Ortolana, with Clare and Agnes at her side, leave the square in thoughtful silence. At length Ortolana comments that young Francis has found a second father in Bishop Guido. Clare's reflections are unknown to us but perhaps she notes that Francis had deflected the blow of being disowned by Pietro by himself disowning his father. Here was a man who could not bear being unloved and so had transformed a deep hurt into a blazing parable of supernatural love.

Rumors which enter the Offreduccio palazzo from time to time give Clare even clearer evidence of Francis' deep grief over this break with his father. "Pietro persecuted him and judging his service of Christ to be madness, he hurled curses at him everywhere. Therefore the servant of God called to his aid a certain low-born and quite simple man, and putting him in place of his father, he begged him that when his father hurled curses at him he should on the contrary bless him."[7] Again the exorcising of grief by transforming it into reason for gratitude.

Clare had grieved with Francis and for him, but she also remembered the pain and passion mingled in Pietro's eyes as he had brushed by her after the "trial." She feels less compassion, however, for Angelo, Francis' brother, when she heard of his taunts. "On a certain morning in winter time, (Angelo) saw Francis at prayer clothed in poor garments and shivering with the cold. He said to a certain fellow townsman: 'Go tell Francis to sell you a pennysworth of sweat.' But hearing this, the man of God was filled with gladness and answered smiling: 'Indeed I will sell my sweat more dearly to my Lord.'"[8]

During the ensuing years, gossip about Pietro's mad son had grown rather than diminished. He had adopted a sort of hermit life but from time to time some supposedly sane citizen left all he had or gave it to the poor in order to join him. Pilgrims in 1209 reported that Francis and a group of these men, each more ragged than the other, had traveled to Rome and talked with the great Pope Innocent. Gradually, a certain tone of respect crept into the voices of those who spoke of these "Lesser Brothers" as they now styled themselves.

Clare has much more to do than ponder the development of Francis Bernardone's strange career. As the eldest daughter of a wealthy family, her social obligations begin to take up more and more of her time. Clare has to take her place beside her mother in managing the large household. Childish games soon give way to more sedate pursuits while Clare's natural vivacity is curbed to meet the requirements of a well-bred lady.

Increasingly, Agnes becomes Clare's intimate and confidante.

This gentle, deeply loving girl provides both foil and check to Clare's more dominant and creative personality. The two girls share their dreams and moods, the wonder of what it means to be approaching womanhood and the profound, almost wordless, experience of maturing religious awareness. Church festivals for them are more than simply opportunities to dress in their finest gowns and display their patrimony of family jewels. Agnes and Clare have both imbibed the deep piety of their mother, and it is beginning to bear fruit in their receptive souls. A spiritual bond, deeper even than that of blood, grows up between them.

Outwardly, Clare's manner of living does not differ from that of the other girls of her age and class. We may reasonably suppose that the normal delights of a young woman pleased Clare also. She dressed in the rich and colorful fashions of the day, not just to please her parents but also because she herself found real pleasure in lovely materials and well-cut gowns. In a few short years Francis, still the draper's son, will ask that Clare solemnize her spiritual betrothals by dressing as beautifully as a bride. Few of the many who admire this lovely girl suspect that Clare "wears a very harsh white garment under her other clothes."[9]

Witnesses attesting to the manner of life Clare lived during her teen years emphasize her unfailing compassion for others and her practical charity. Bona Guelfuccio, who lived with her, told that Clare "was kindhearted and attended to all good works."[10]

All households in Assisi were open to the streets and little passed therein that was not soon noised about the neighborhood or further, if it was sufficiently scandalous. Sunny windows, doorways, and open courtyards were favorite places for the women to sit and do their sewing or weaving while chatting with passersby or household members. Unmarried girls easily found a pretext to perch at some convenient window or balcony during the daily strolls of the young men of the city.

Thus Bona's statement that "Clare was a prudent girl who

always remained at home" is completed by her addition that "she kept herself hidden for she did not wish to be seen and so she contrived that those who passed by the house should not see her."[11] Clare was far from shy and capable of acting with bold decision as the future would reveal. But at this time in her life she was unwilling to attract the attentions which could so easily have been hers.

What did she look like, this budding scion of Assisi's nobility? Messer Ranieri de Bernardo de Assisi declared under oath that she was "of beautiful countenance."[12] A contemporary description of Clare when she was about sixteen states: "[Her] face was oval, her forehead spacious, her color dazzling, and her eyebrows and hair very fair. A celestial smile played in her eyes and round her mouth; her nose was well fashioned and slightly aquiline; of good stature, she inclined to stoutness but nowise in excess." Here is a description of a tall and shapely girl whose sparkling eyes and radiant color bespoke health and goodness. Can we blame Favarone for dreaming that she would "marry magnificently in accordance with her rank to some great and powerful lord?"[13]

Perhaps Favarone, who had fathered three daughters, can be forgiven for looking forward to stalwart sons-in-law who would someday stand at his side and share his love of arms and war. Practical concerns dictated this as only reasonable. Clare was ripe for marriage by medieval standards and Agnes displayed charm and promise also. The little one, Beatrice, who seems to have been an "autumn" child of Favarone and Ortolana's marriage, would no doubt follow her sisters under the expert tutelage of Lady Ortolana. Favarone contemplated the future with pleasure, quite certain he would have the choice of elegible youths of wealth and rank.

To Favarone's total astonishment and irritation, Clare responded to his plan to select a husband for her with a coolness that intimated possible rejection. This was not to be tolerated!

Even though urged strongly by "her father and mother and relations," Clare "could in no way be induced to consider a betrothal."[14] Not only was Favarone disappointed and angered, so were most of Clare's relatives. Forty years later we have this frank and somewhat amusing admission from Messer Ranieri de Bernardo, probably a cousin by marriage. I "often urged her to consent but she would not even hear it spoken of, and the more I spoke, the more she urged me to despise the world!"[15]

Days of turmoil, tears, and threats followed, and the usual peace of the Offreduccio palazzo departed. One by one, separately, and in groups, Clare's extended family pressed her to accept one of the many advantageous offers of marriage available to her. Messer Ranieri stated that his wife was related to Clare's family and, being on familiar terms with the Offreduccios, was often present at these sessions. Neighbors, too, added their voices to the hubbub swirling around the lovely but stubborn girl. One of them, Pietro de Damiani testified "that being her neighbor he knew no one could ever persuade her to take heed of worldly things" of which an attractive marriage alliance was chief.[16]

Thomas of Celano summed up the struggle and Clare's strategy thus: "When her family wished her to enter a noble marriage, Clare would never consent but feigning she would wait, commended her virginity to God."[17] For what was she waiting? If Clare were entertaining thoughts of becoming a nun, why didn't she simply say so? Two excellent houses of Benedictine nuns were thriving in the vicinity of Assisi. With her dowry and education, she would have been eagerly accepted by either.

But mystifyingly, Clare said nothing. She seemed to be absorbed in her works of charity which had expanded beyond her childhood gifts of delicacies surreptitiously taken from her plate, to alms gladly given "to her utmost possibility."[18] Another familiar friend of her family, Johanni de Venturi, noted: "The life of her family was very sumptuous, nevertheless she, who was served with the food of a great house, would set it aside to send to the poor."[19]

This same witness remarked "that he saw her fasting and praying and given to works of piety." Later he concluded "that from the beginning she had been inspired by the Holy Spirit."[20] Yet another of the ever present neighbors attested: "She was esteemed most virtuous by all."[21] Because of all these marked forms of piety, it is conjectured that Clare may have been a "home penitent," a member of the widespread penitential movement of her times. Clare's charity began at home with delicate attentions to family members, servants, and the ever-fluctuating stream of relatives and neighbors. Her natural charm made her supernatural charity most attractive. It was noticed only afterwards that "when she was sitting among those of the household, she always wished to speak of the things of God."[22] It must have required considerable tact to gently deflect her companions' conversation from the time-hallowed custom of exchanging choice bits of gossip. Something of Clare's gift of persuasion, as well as her piety, is revealed here.

"Such was her life of virtue and sacrifice in her father's house, such were the first fruits of the Spirit, such her first essays in holiness. Thus, all unknown to herself, she began to be praised by her neighbors, and as the true fame of her secret acts became known the report of her goodness was noised about among the townpeople. As a box of spices, even when closed reveals itself by its sweet odor, so did Clare by the fragrance of her virtues, even though hidden from the world." eulogizes Thomas of Celano, her admiring biographer.[23]

This "sweet fragrance" which so subtly perfumed her actions and gave them a graced ease emanated from secret depths in Clare's spirit. There appears to have been a striking continuity of the action of the Holy Spirit in Clare Offreduccio's life so that her later association with Francis and her espousing of his ideals was already foreshadowed by the lifestyle she had chosen to lead in her father's house.

If Clare so steadfastly refused to give even the least consideration to an earthly marriage, it was not because she failed to
appreciate its goodness and beauty. Rather she had developed
such a high ideal of what marriage could be that she sensed
that it could never be realized in a wholly human relationship.

Poised on the threshold of womanhood, Clare obscurely recognized that someone had already solicited her heart, someone
to whom in the stark clarity and directness of childhood she had
already given her pledge. Her father's proposals of marriage
partners served to bring more acutely to Clare's awareness the
claims of this first lover. With him a troth had been made, and
Clare freely and knowingly chose to honor it, feeling somehow
that the integrity of her very self demanded this fidelity. It is
highly doubtful that she could have expressed this deep conviction in so many words even though it was fully formed and
powerfully operative by the time Clare reached her mid-teens.
She knew that she belonged solely to the Lord. It was as simple
as that and as total.

Only many years later would Clare express in poetic phrases
the ecstasy, the honor, and the privilege that she knew were hers
in this divine romance. Writing to a princess who was struggling
to avoid a royal marriage in order to become a Poor Lady, Clare
exclaimed:

> For though You, more than others, could have en-
> joyed the magnificence and honor and dignity of the
> world, and could have been married to the illustrious
> Ceasar with the splendor befitting You and His Excel-
> lency, You have rejected all these things and have
> chosen with Your whole heart and soul a life of holy
> poverty and destitution. Thus You took a spouse of a
> more noble lineage, Who will keep Your virginity
> ever unspotted and unsullied, the Lord Jesus Christ:
>
> When you have loved [Him], You shall be chaste,
> when You

have touched [Him], You shall become pure;
when you have
accepted [Him], You shall be a virgin.
Whose power is stronger,
Whose generosity is more abundant,
Whose appearance more beautiful,
Whose love more tender,
Whose courtesy more gracious.
In Whose embrace You are already caught up.[24]

These words were written after Clare had tasted the truth of
them. But they were already accepted in faith as Clare stood
firm in her refusal of an earthly marriage. They express what
Clare must have felt at this time and highlight some dominant
features of her spiritual life. A spontaneous femininity shines
throughout the passage. The bridal theme delights Clare's romantic and ardent nature. Obviously, she esteems the goodness
of the human marriage her correspondent was declining and
says so clearly. For any woman, Clare considers marriage as
fitting and becoming. Yet she is aware of a freedom which allows
a woman to clear-sightedly choose a "Spouse of nobler rank"
than any earthly man possesses. Although such a choice involves
a renunciation of some natural goods, it implies no denigration
of them. Of what value is a choice that rejects only what it despises or holds unworthy?

Clare highly appreciated the natural pleasures and goods of
life and was profoundly grateful for them. She would one day
urge her sisters to "praise God for every beautiful green and
flowering plant you see; and for every human being you see and
for every creature, always and in all things, God must be
praised."[25] Not MAY be praised but MUST be praised! The way
of life she was destined to co-create with God and Francis is
described by Celano as one "where there was great pursuance of
all that was beautiful and good."[26]

Whether Clare was tending the flowering plants in the inner

court of her father's house, going with alms to the hovels of the
needy, or visiting an empty church fragrant with worship, she
diffused the subtle power of her pledge of the penitential life
which was already becoming a life-giving force within her.
Like another Maiden, surprised by the invitation of the Spirit,
Clare surrendered her whole being to his invasion. Mystified
but trustingly she waited under the overwhelming shadow for
the next step of her way to be revealed.

The Lord who claimed Clare's heart was not an abstract deity
hidden in light inaccessible but a very near, very vivid presence
she encountered with every sunrise and embraced in every sun-
set. The moon and stars revealed his splendor, the myriad
flowers and grasses, his largess. All creatures, great and small,
lived by his abounding life. Above all, she tingled to meet him in
every hand stretched out to her, whether it was the lily-white
fingers of a noble lady or the grubby, broken hand of a street-
corner beggar.

Clare discovered that the Lord was not only "out there" but
also welling up within her. She blushed to realize that, if she was
reaching out for him, it was only because he had first become
enamored of her. Echoing through the chambers of her heart,
she heard the pleading, triumphant voice of the divine lover
who has fallen in love with the daughters of earth. "I passed by
you and saw that you were now old enough for love. So I spread
the corner of my cloak over you to cover your nakedness; I
swore an oath to you and entered into a covenant with you; you
became mine, says the Lord."[27]

From his secret dwelling within her spirit, Clare could feel this
yearning lover reaching out to others. Would she assist his infinite desire to manifest his love? So powerful a surge of compassion swept her up and beyond herself that Clare knew without
doubt that it arose from depths deeper than her own spirit, from
the very wellsprings of divinity, from a God who was courteously, if insistently, asking her to become a channel for his immense embrace of all created things. Clare felt at once so great

and yet so small. The cosmos could not contain her yet the tiniest wildflower overwhelmed her.

So poised Clare on the threshold of maturity. One thing only was lacking to her. Until that was revealed, she hestiated and groped her way in shadows. In the dimness of the world, she glowed like a fiery ember waiting the stirring of the Spirit to burst into flame.

Not far outside the gates of Assisi, the sunbrowned hand of her future guide was rekindling the sanctuary lamp before the Crucifix in old San Damiano.

Chapter IV Endnotes

1. Legend of Three Companions, #2.
2. Ibid., #2.
3. 1 Celano, #11, 12.
4. Legend of Three Companions, #19.
5. Testament of Francis, #3.
6. Cf. Legend of Three Companions, #20.
7. 2 Celano, #12.
8. Ibid., #12.
9. Cause of Canonization, Wit. 20, #4.
10. Ibid., Wit. 17, #4.
11. Ibid.
12. Ibid., Wit. 18, #2.
13. Ibid., Wit. 19, #2.
14. Ibid.
15. Ibid., Wit. 18,. #2.
16. Ibid. Wit. 19, #2.
17. Legend of Celano, #4.
18. Cause of Canonization, Wit. 18, #3.
19. Ibid., Wit. 20, #3.
20. Ibid., Wit. 20, #5.
21. Ibid., Wit. 19, #2.
22. Ibid., Wit. 18, #3.
23. Legend of Celano, #4.
24. First Letter to Agnes of Prague, #5–10.

25. Cause of Canonization, Wit. 14, #9.
26. Legend of Celano, #36.
27. Ezek 16:8.

V The Flame is Kindled

Melody swirls through the night-shrouded woods. From all sides liquid song pours from throats of myriad nightingales. Clare stops entranced. Why has she never heard such a midnight chorus before? Why? Because she has never been on her way into the woods at this hour.

It is nearly twelve, the night of March 18, 1212. Palm Sunday is drawing to a close and the Paschal moon is approaching fullness. Even now its creamy radiance streams down the roadway leading out of Assisi's western gate, the Porta Pietro. Clare di Favarone and her closest confidante, Pacifica Guelfuccio, emerge from its shadowed portico, hesitate only a moment, and then step swiftly onto the whitened pathway.

Many months of clandestine meetings and surreptitious exchanges have preceded this night. Clare wonders anew about just how this high adventure began. How or when did she begin to suspect that her destiny was to be intertwined with the strange career of Francis Bernardone?

Rufino, Uncle Scipione's son, may have stimulated her interest in the message and life of this controversial young man. Last year Rufino had earned the ire of the family by daring to join Francis where he was camped with his brothers at St. Mary of the Angels. This usually quiet cousin may have spoken to Clare of his unbounded enthusiasm for the ideals which Francis had embraced. Clare was impressed. Possibly she and Rufino were quite close for they had shared the years of exile in Perugia together as well as having spent many summers at the family castle of Coriano. It would seem clear that in their religious ideals they had much in common.

What Clare did not know was that Rufino had been equally enthusiastic when speaking to Francis about his cousin, Clare. She had requested Rufino to find out if Francis would be willing to give her some counsel. Her steadfast refusal of marriage without any explicit reason for her stand was becoming an embarrassment. Some deep intuition stirred Clare with the presentiment that the direction of her future might be parallel to that of Francis. Celano described their early mutual admiration thus: "Hearing of the now famous name of Francis, who like a new man had restored by new virtues the way of perfection forgotten by the world, Clare at once desired to hear and see him. She was moved thereto by the Father of spirits, whose first promptings each had followed although in different ways. And no less did Francis, impressed by the fair fame of so gracious a maiden, desire to see and speak with her. . . ."[1]

Numerous obstacles stood in the way of the fulfillment of this desire, however. Not the least of them being that a beautiful eighteen-year-old daughter of the nobility dare not be seen speaking to a vagabond friar in his early thirties. The scandal such an adventure would arouse could keep Assisi's gossips delightfully busy for weeks! Her reputation, along with his, was at stake.

Clare was not one to be daunted by difficulties, nor was Francis a man to turn back once he had divined the will of his Lord. Celano notes: He "being wholly eager for spoils and having come to depopulate the kingdom of this world, would fain somehow 'deliver' this noble prey 'from the wickedness of the world' and restore her to his Lord."[2]

He visited her. How? When? Where? We do not know, but carefully he arranged to be where she could also be without arousing comment. We know that during the Lent of 1212 Francis was invited to give a series of sermons (or more precisely, exhortations to penance) in the cathedral of San Rufino. Situated on the same piazza as the Offreduccio palazzo, this was the parish church of Clare's family. Doubtless she attended these talks, as did most of Assisi.

Audaciously, Clare also managed to visit Francis "so arranging the times of (her) visits that this divine pursuit might not be known by man or objected to by public gossip. Only a lone trusted companion accompanied the girl when she left her paternal home to hold secret meetings with the man of God, whose words seemed to her afire with God and whose deeds beyond the power of man."[3]

The "lone trusted companion" was none other than the good Bona Guelfuccio, the ever-willing accomplice in all Clare's more daring enterprises. Besides assisting Clare in her secret gifts to the poor when a little girl, Bona had become a faithful auxiliary to her charitable works in later years. When Clare's interest in and concern for the brothers first kindled, it was again to Bona that she had turned. She "gave me money with the command that I should take it to those who were working in St. Mary of the Portiuncula in order that they might be able to buy some meat," recalled Bona years later.[4]

Although this gesture on Clare's part indicated her practical concern, it also reveals that at this time she did not fully grasp the manner of life that Lady Poverty exacted of Francis and his brethren. He, who later legislated that his brothers were never to accept money as alms, very likely refused the gift that Bona proferred in Clare's name, gently but firmly explaining his convictions regarding alms and adding that as long as the brothers were well, they did not eat meat.

Such a reply, far from ruffling Clare's feelings, stimulated and challenged her. Something within her leapt high at the prospect of such an ideal of poverty, an ideal that queried the roots of the newly emerging social order.

Bona's cooperation proved invaluable as her later testimony

indicates: "I repeatedly accompanied the Lady Clare to talk with Francis and they did this secretly in order not to be seen by her family."[5] Scarcely had Clare looked into the smoldering depths of Francis' eyes when the glowing embers within her breast leapt into flame. So complete and radical was the transfiguration of her soul by the illumination of his words that Clare ever afterwards called it her time of conversion. She was not turning away from a life of wantonness and sin, but the wavering doubts about the future direction of her life were so completely resolved that she never once turned aside from the way Francis revealed to her. Her North Star had arisen and the compass needle of her spirit detected and followed it unerringly.

"The most high celestial Father . . . deigned to enlighten my heart by his mercy and grace to do penance after the example and teaching of our most blessed Father Francis," she would write later of this decisive encounter.[6] From then on nothing in this world or the next appeared quite the same to her. Francis had thrown back the varied veils of deception that generally shroud this world in murky gloom. She saw created things as they truly are: ephemeral but bearing the splendor of their creator.

Francis "exhorted her to contempt of the world, vividly showing her how vain was earthly hope, how deceptive worldly beauty. . . ."[7] Yes, Francis who loved everything his Father had made knew them to be but signs pointing beyond themselves to him whose beauty they reflected in such myriad profusion.

With a tenderness only a lover has, Francis spoke of his beloved; and to Clare it seemed as if she beheld the very countenance of Christ alive with love for her. Her whole being thrilled as that ardent lover of Jesus rhapsodized on his favorite fascination, the endless and totally unmerited love of God for his human children.

Francis grew nearly ecstatic as he "manifested to her the sweetness of the nuptials of Christ and persuaded her to keep the pearl of her virginal purity for that blessed Bridegroom whom love made Man."[8] Clare recognized that she was listening to a man speaking from personal experience, and she needed little urging to allow her soul to consent utterly to all he said.

Francis may have gazed at the eager, lovely girl before him with both satisfaction and compassion. He divined the great "yes" welling up in her spirit, and from the depth of his own experience, poignantly intuited the tremendous price to be exacted before that innocent "yes" became the consummated "Fiat" of the vowed and crucified nun. But he did not shrink from his role of "loyal bridesman" of Christ. If Clare were willing, he would lead her to the altar and to the Cross.

It must have been difficult for Clare to conceal from those about her the fire consuming her spirit. A way was opening before her, a guide of fire and tenderness stood by her side and "a glimpse of the joys of heaven was opened to her, the sight of which made the world seem mean indeed, the desire of which made her almost faint away, while the love thereof made her long for the nuptials of heaven."[9]

The mystifying bar, which had prevented Clare from committing herself to a betrothal despite family pressure and also kept her from joining any community of nuns, suddenly clarified itself. An amazing pattern emerged from the seemingly disparate threads of her life and revealed what a long, patient, and careful preparation had been given her by an all-wise Father. In her own way, Clare was a natural "Franciscan," beginning with her embrace of the penitential life while still at home which blossomed into a lifestyle conjoined with that of Francis' lesser brothers. Without the least deviation, her life had followed a direct line which stretched from childhood to the day of her death. Grace built beautifully upon her natural qualities and character.

The torch was held aloft by Francis; it was for Clare to become the flame.

Now Clare discerns points of light flickering and dancing among the newly leaved trees of the woods. Mid-March is too early for fireflies. Her heart lifts as she realizes these are the torches of Francis and his friars who are coming to meet her. The melody in her heart joins the chorus of nightingales. It blends with the refrain from the morning's celebration in the cathedral: "Hosanna to the Son of David. Blessed is he who comes in the name of the Lord!" How perfectly the spirit of the liturgy matches the mood of her heart. Francis has chosen well.

For as Lent had progressed, Clare had felt an urgency pressing her on, and "with great fervor of heart [she] betook herself to the man of God for counsel on her conversion, as to what was to be done and how she was to do it. Francis commanded that on the feastday, she should dress and adorn herself in her finery and go with the rest of the people to the blessing of the palms. Then, on the following night, she should 'go forth outside the camp' and 'turn her worldly joy into mourning' for the Passion of the Lord."[10]

Such was the plan and it delighted Clare. The execution of the plot, however, would not be so simple. Although we have no explicit proof, the facts suggest that Bishop Guido had been informed of what was afoot and had given his approval. Perhaps when Francis had first confided to him his desire to admit women into his "way of life and poverty," the good bishop had registered skepticism about the wisdom of such a development.

Was Francis as mad as so many sensible people labeled him? But no, Guido was forced to conclude, he was hopelessly sane with that uncomfortable sanity of a man who takes the gospel simply as it is written.

Cautiously Guido may have inquired, "Do you have anyone specific in mind?"

Francis, nodding and with a glow brightening his face, could have responded in words used by Celano not too many years later: "Your lordship, I do. 'She is of noble parentage, but she is more noble by grace; she is a virgin in body, most chaste in mind; a youth in age but mature in spirit; steadfast in purpose and most ardent in her desire for divine love; endowed with wisdom and excelling in humility; Clare by name, brighter in life and brightest in character.'"[11]

The Bishop may have been surprised to learn that it was the daughter of the highest echelon of local society whom Francis had "enticed"; yet if he knew her and her family at all well, a moment's consideration would have sufficed to convince him that if any woman in Assisi could carry such a risky calling through to a successful establishment it would be Clare di Offreduccio.

Francis undoubtedly had explained to Guido about the many talks he and Brother Philip had held with Clare. With a humble wonder in his voice, he had related that she had "committed herself wholly to his guidance, considering him to be, after God, the director of her steps. Now her soul depended on his admonitions, and she received with a ready heart whatever he spoke to her of the good Jesus. She was already weary of earthly finery and ornament and 'counted all things as dung' which the world esteems that she 'might gain Christ.'"[12]

Convinced of the viability of the project, Guido had exercised his prerogative as pastor. Yes, Francis could receive Clare at a time and place he could arrange at his own discretion. In the name of the bishop, he could cut her hair and receive her vows, but this should be done in a church with a priest present. Afterwards, however, Francis was to take the girl to an established community for a while until the inevitable gossip would have subsided. Guido also agreed that old San Damiano might eventually be a suitable place to install Clare and the other . . . "Poor Sisters," would it be?

"Poor *Ladies*, my Lord Bishop," Francis had responded, aglow with the privilege of "delivering this noble prey from the world and restoring her to his Lord."[13]

Clare "delayed not long in her consent."[14] Her companion, Bona, had gone to Rome to keep Lent but Pacifica Guelfuccio fell in readily with Clare's secret plans. In fact she revealed that she was quite willing not only to accompany Clare but even to join her whenever it would be possible. Clare was delighted. Their homes were only separated by the piazza so their frequent conversations aroused no comment. Since Pacifica often accompanied Clare when she visited the poor,[15] it was not difficult for them to slip out together to meet Francis at some prearranged place.

At length plans were completed, even to the careful choice of the bride-like attire Clare would wear when she made her last appearance in the midst of her family. She and Pacifica had cut and sewn in secret the homespun lazzo the brothers had given her to use for a habit. A simple black veil had been designed and, with some laughter, a rope measured and cut to fit about Clare's waist.

"When Palm Sunday came, Clare, radiant in festive splendor among the crowd of women, entered the church with the others," records Thomas of Celano.[16] The most solemn week of the Church year opens with the moving memorial of Jesus' triumphal entry into the Holy City. All of the upper-class citizens of Assisi flocked to the cathedral of San Rufino to receive a palm branch from Bishop Guido himself and to take part in the great procession. Naturally, the girls and young women appeared in their newest and most becoming fashions.

No one considered it strange that Clare di Favarone appeared more lovely than ever. Perhaps some surmised that a fortunate young nobleman had finally won her favor and a marriage announcement would soon be forthcoming. Clare in her richly embroidered gown, maybe of ruby or crimson silk, glowed with a tremulous joy characteristic of a girl in her first love. A light veil, held in place by a discreetly jeweled circlet of beaten gold, framed her face and highlighted her lustrous hair. Her open sleeves, artfully reversed over her shoulders, emphasized the grace of her figure and movements. Perhaps an enameled belt encircled her waist repeating the warm colors of a flower-embroidered bodice.

All the girls and women stood together on one side of the church with the men on the other. Palm Sunday is traditionally one of the best attended services of the year and March 18 in the year 1212 would have been no exception. Persons who seldom darkened a church doorway the rest of the year were on hand to receive their palm branch and to enjoy the spectacle of the noble congregation turned out in its elegant best.

Clare's feelings on this memorable morning are not explicitly known to us. An incident, preserved by Thomas of Celano, indicates that they may have been quite turbulent. The distribution of the palms had begun, with the clergy receiving theirs first. The faithful flowed into the central aisle and moved slowly toward Bishop Guido sitting on his episcopal throne at the edge of the sanctuary. Each one knelt as he took his palm branch, kissing it and then the hand of the bishop. The young girls were the last to come up but as they moved forward, Clare remained in her place head down. She seemed quite unable to join the group. Was she groping for composure this last time she would attend services with her mother and sisters?

Bishop Guido, aware of the plans for the coming night, noticed her absence. His questing eyes found her isolated figure in the nave. Rising from his throne, he went down the steps and pressed a palm into her cold hand. With a fatherly gesture he rested his hand in blessing on her veiled head. Perhaps he whispered a word of encouragement as Clare bent to kiss his ring, clinging slightly to his strong hand.

As the long service continued, Clare recovered her poise. She stood, palm in hand, with the rest of the congregation for the impressive narration of the Passion by the large body of clergy in the sanctuary. The pain in her own breast enabled Clare to empathize with her suffering Lord in a personal communion hitherto unknown to her. In her mind's eye, Clare saw him stumble, cross-laden through the city gate of Jerusalem, going forth from the beloved city to die by the choice of his own people.

Inspired words flamed through her spirit: "Therefore Jesus died outside the gate, to sanctify the people by his own blood. LET US GO TO HIM outside the camp, bearing the insult he bore. For here we have no lasting city. . . ."[17] What she was about to do would, she well knew, scandalize Assisi and bring unforgiving disgrace upon herself and her family. Tears trembled on her lashes and she clasped the palm more tightly. What she must do, she must do. Into her darkened heart stole the words of Jesus: "The world must know that I love the Father and do as the Father has commanded me. Come, then! Let us be on our way."[18] She lifted her chin and brushed the back of her hand across her eyes.

Somehow the day had passed, and Clare had managed to display her usual bright spirits. Relatives and neighbors had streamed in and out, fotunately diverting Ortolana's thoughts from Clare's strange behavior at Mass that morning. Perhaps their young house guest, Christiana di Suppo, distracted Agnes, too, so no embarrassing questions were asked. Amid the general festivities, Pacifica Guelfuccio slipped in and exchanged a meaningful glance with Clare. Yes, all was well. Tonight before the moon rises they would meet in the street.

The Offreduccio palazzo, like all the great houses of the city, had two doorways opening onto the street. There was the wide and ornate main entrance through which all the ordinary traffic of the house passed. Off to the side and placed higher in the wall was a narrow, arched doorway, the dread "porta di mortuccio," doorway of the dead. This was opened only to allow the dead to be carried out, feet first, from the family home. Those who went out this door never returned. A superstitious fear surrounded this exit and no living person ever used it.

Christiana said that at that time it was "blocked up with heavy wooden bars and a stone column to prevent it from being opened."[19] It was through this dread doorway that Clare chose to leave her father's house. As soon as the palazzo was quiet for the night, she made her way to it. "With a strength that astonished her," records Celano, "she broke it open with her own hands."[20] Christiana remarked that "all who saw that opened door next morning were astounded that such a feat could have been performed by any girl. It would have taken many men to remove those obstacles."[21] But the strength of Christ had taken possession of Clare, and, as she jumped lightly down into the street, Pacifica was startled to hear her soft laughter.

Still smiling now, Clare almost dances toward the flickering torches in the woods. She feels light with a wondrous freedom. The songs of the night are at one with the song in her blood. Is this what it means to be totally poor? to "desire nothing in this world but Jesus Christ and him crucified?" From now on Christ will be her wealth, her sole and only treasure. Her whole being thrills as she realizes that though she has left her father's house and all worldly security behind "all things are hers and she is Christ's and Christ is God's."[22]

Suddenly, Francis, his deep eyes as luminous as the torch he carries, steps out of the woods in front of her. One of the friars thrusts a taper into Clare's hand. She holds it high, her eyes reflecting its glow and her lips parted with expectancy. She seems all aflame herself, still gowned as she is in the shimmering silk of the morning. Francis smiles approvingly.

His clear strong voice rises above the trills of the night birds as he begins the royal wedding psalm:

> Hear, o daughter, and see; turn your ear,
>   forget your people and your father's house.
> So shall the king desire your beauty,
>   for he is your lord, and you must worship him.
> All glorious is the king's daughter as she enters;
>   her raiment is threaded with spun gold.
> In embroidered apparel she is borne into the king;
>   behind her the virgins of her train are brought to
>   you.

> They are borne in with gladness and joy;
>   they enter the palace of the king.[23]

So singing Francis conducts Clare and Pacifica through the woods. It seems to Clare that all her senses are alive with heightened sensitivity to the exquisite loveliness of the night. With delight she breathes in the fragrance of the rich verdure around her and exalts in the silken touch of the night breeze on her cheek. She catches a glimmer of stars through the branches overhead at the same time as she hears the shimmer of the stirring leaves.

Suddenly the "palace of the king" rises before her. The tiny chapel of St. Mary of the Angels appears in a clearing surrounded by mud and wattle huts. "There," says Thomas of Celano, "the friars who were keeping vigil at the little altar of God received the virgin Clare with lighted torches."[24] Clare's heart skips a beat as she realizes they had had enough confidence in her calling and her courage to decorate the chapel to celebrate her nuptials. Fresh green boughs adorn the entrance and wildflowers twine about the candles burning on the altar. In the torchlight she notices the beaming faces of Brother Leo and Brother Sylvester, the priests, of Brother Philip who along with Francis had encouraged her, of Brother Rufino, her cousin, of Brother Bernard, and so many others. . . .

Clare slips to her knees. As she does so, Francis lifts the gold circlet and veil from her head, and her fair hair tumbles down. Quickly, Clare unclasps her necklace, removes her bracelets, and slips off her rings. Gravely Francis takes the glittering jewels and hands them to Pacifica. Then Clare steps into the shadows where Pacifica throws the rough gray tunic over her head. Her embroidered dress drops to the ground as she pulls the livery of Lady Poverty about her. Stepping nimbly out of her satin slippers Clare walks barefoot back to the altar step. The moment is at hand.

Does Francis' hand tremble as he picks up the shears, or is it only a trick of the moving flames? Tenderly he lifts the thick locks of Clare's hair from her neck and the scissors bite in. Soon a gleaming heap lies on the altar. A coarse black veil is bound about Clare's shorn head. As Francis hands a candle to her, it seems to him that all the glowing beauty of her former attire is now burning within her.

Brother Sylvester, the priest, moves forward to stand beside Francis as the bishop's delegate for this unique profession ceremony. The book of the Gospels lies open on the altar. A hush fills the tiny chapel.

Solemnly Francis questions, "Daughter, what do you seek?"

Preparing to make her reply, Clare places her two hands between his. But Francis gently lays them on the altar before the Tabernacle. In the silence of the night, Clare responds in a clear voice: "I want only Jesus Christ and to live by the gospel, owning nothing and in chastity." The directness of these stark words expresses the dominant trait of Clare's character. Having perceived her goal, Jesus Christ, and the surest means, gospel living in complete poverty, Clare simply commits her whole being with no reserve.

The pledge given in such dramatic circumstances would never be revoked. Her steadfast loyalty to Francis' ideals would make her his most faithful follower. Her capacity for sacrifice and persistent struggle, her love and trust, would eventually lead her to the heights of holiness. The call of God, transmitted to Clare through Francis, is absolute. She would stand by Francis to the end of her life, complementing and completing his ideals with keen feminine insight. In her person she would incarnate Lady Poverty whom the knight errant Francis would revere and serve with courteous devotion.

Thomas of Celano completes this account of the initiation of a new way of life for women in the Church by noting how appropriate it is that it took place in the Portiuncula. "This is that place in which the new legion of the poor under the leadership of Francis took its happy beginnings, that it might be clearly evident that the Mother of Mercies had brought forth both religions in her inn. When Clare had received the livery of holy penance before the altar of the Blessed Mary and as a humble handmaid had been espoused to Christ as if before the bridal bed of that holy Virgin, Francis straightway led her to the church of San Paolo where she was to remain until the Most High should provide something else."[25]

Now Clare follows Francis out of the chapel reveling in the freedom of her simple garments. Perhaps Pacifica turns back toward Assisi taking with her the cast off clothing and shorn tresses of the former Clare di Favarone. Who would blame her if her heart quavers as she negotiates the hour's climb up the slope to the city gate? Until she can rejoin Clare, Pacifica will remain at home. But she has a heavy task ahead of her, a proof of her loyal friendship. She it is who will have to confront Ortolana's distress and the Offreduccio brothers' rage. Ruefully she wonders who will need the more courage this day.

An hour's walk in the opposite direction brings Clare and Francis to the Benedictine monastery of San Paolo in Bastia. The bishop had requested the nuns to admit her into their cloister for a time, quite probably because that community enjoyed special Papal protection and sanctions against anyone who would molest the peace of the nuns. Clare would need this.

It is early morning when they arrive and gray light is filtering through the trees. In response to Francis' summons, a door in the fortress-like wall is cautiously opened. When it is explained who is calling at such an early hour, the portress swings the heavy door back to admit Clare.

Francis watches the gray-clad, barefoot girl cross the threshold and experiences a pang of apprehension. She suddenly seems so young, so unprepared for what lies ahead. Will she be able to hold fast to an as yet untried manner of living?

He turns back toward the Portiuncula, and as he does so he sees the first rays of the sun tipping the church towers of Assisi with living flame. On the other side of Monte Subasio the cross atop San Damiano is silhouetted against the brightening sky.

Chapter V Endnotes

1. Legend of Celano, #5.
2. Ibid., #5.
3. Ibid., #5.
4. Cause of Canonization, cf. Wit. 17, #7.
5. Ibid., Wit. 17, #3.
6. Testament of St. Clare, #7.
7. Legend of Celano, #5.
8. Ibid., #5.
9. Ibid., #6.
10. Ibid., #7.
11. 1 Celano, #18.
12. Legend of Celano, #6.
13. Ibid., #5.
14. Ibid., #6.
15. Cause of Canonization, Wit. 1 #4.
16. Legend of Celano, #7.
17. Heb 13:12–14.
18. Jn14:31.
19. Cause of Canonization, Wit. 13, #1.
20. Legend of Celano, #7.
21. Cause of Canonization, Wit. 13 #1.
22. I Cor 3:23
23. Ps 45:11, 12, 14–16.
24. Legend of Celano, #8.
25. Ibid., #8.

VI The Hearth

Suddenly Clare realizes that he is gone. Only a few minutes ago she had felt his strong, gentle hand under her elbow guiding her forward in the dim light of San Damiano. Francis said nothing as she and Agnes knelt on the rough, cold slabs before the Crucifix suspended over the altar. Seeing her absorbed in prayer in this place where his own vocation was revealed, Francis silently withdraws. As the loyal bridesman of Christ, he feels he has fulfilled the trust laid upon him.

Clare sighs softly and experiences a slight chill of apprehension. Francis has left her alone just when she is hoping he will stay and help her to map out the life to be lived in this new house of God. Will it always be like this—that just when she hopes to lean on his strength, he will be gone?

Francis has left her, but she is not alone. Clare turns again to the Crucified One looking down so compassionately on the two gray-clad girls kneeling in the empty chapel. Her panic subsides as she begins to delve deeper into the hard but essential lesson that alone will ensure the stability of her life.

"The Son of God became for us the Way (Jn 14:16) and that Way our blessed father Francis, his true lover and imitator, has shown and taught us by word and example,"[1] Clare would write many years later concerning the grace of this moment. Her intuition discovers Christ as her way, not through intellectual discernment but through the experience of her heart. A person who becomes more intensely real to her day by day solicits her love. To such love she yields completely, knowing that it will daily challenge and change her.

The only explanation for her calling is found in who Christ became for her. To another young woman who is about to enter the Poor Ladies, she will one day write: "Be strengthened in the holy service which you have begun out of burning desire of the Poor Crucified...."[2]

This "burning desire of the Poor Crucified" naturally inclines Clare to seek after Lady Poverty. Celano explained it thus: "Clare strove to become like the Poor Crucified One by the most perfect poverty so that nothing might separate her in her love for the Beloved or hinder the course of her union with the Lord."[3]

With deep satisfaction Clare now allows her gaze to stray over the smoke-darkened stones behind the altar. The low vaults of the nave, stained from dampness, speak eloquently to her that this chapel is a poor person's offering of praise to the Lord. It is not even hers to offer! It is on loan from the bishop. Clare exults with a fierce joy. How great this joy of freedom which enables her to "run after Christ unburdened by any possessions!"[4]

During the weeks just spent at Sant' Angelo, Clare has "caused the paternal inheritance which had come to her to be sold and has given the proceeds to the poor, keeping nothing of the money for herself."[5]

Beatrice, Clare's younger sister, would later attest that Clare "sold her own heritage and part of the heritage of Beatrice herself."[6] It seems likely that what Clare disposed of was property which would have formed part of her dowry. Although some witnesses speak as if Clare did this while still at home, it is difficult to understand how she could have done so without arousing the suspicions of her family about her future plans. Not until it became manifestly clear to them that Clare would never marry would they have permitted her to take such a drastic step. Christiana di Suppo, who, while living with Clare's family, "saw and heard" all that transpired, later disclosed that Clare's "own relations would have given her more money than others (doubtless hoping to keep the family estates intact). Clare, however, would sell nothing to them, and preferred to sell to others in order that the poor should not be defrauded. She sold all that came to her by inheritance and distributed the money to the poor."[7] This seems to be an example of Clare's sense of social justice, of the need she felt for the wealthy to make restitution to the poor of the land, to those being mindlessly exploited in feudal society.

Freed at last even of her dowry, often a medieval woman's sole assurance of security and respect, Clare "brought [Christ] as her dowry [only] two gifts, the gifts of poverty and the vow of chastity," as Pope Innocent IV so wonderfully phrased it. She "chose to be the bride of Jesus Christ the Poor One."[8]

Happily, Clare begins to survey this dwelling which her Lord, through Francis, has provided for her. Clare's glance falls on Agnes kneeling so sweetly beside her, and she breathes forth another prayer of gratitude. While at Sant' Angelo, "Clare had offered from the fullness of her heart . . . an earnest petition that as she had been of one heart and soul with her sister in the world, so now they might be of one mind in the service of God. She prayed therefore most urgently to the Father of mercies that the world would pall on Agnes whom she had left at home. . . . For they were attached to each other by a deep mutual love, so that their recent separation was painful to both."[9]

Clare's prayer was heard, for, being "moved by the Divine Spirit, [Agnes] hastened to her sister. She opened to her the secrets of her heart and declared that she wished to give herself wholly to the service of the Lord. Clare joyfully embraced her, saying: 'I give thanks to God, most beloved sister, that he has heard me, for I was full of solicitude for you.' "[10]

As Agnes turns to Clare, their eyes meet, and laughter bubbles up from their hearts. Together they duck through an arched doorway to the left of the apse. It leads into the stone building adjoining the chapel which Francis intends to be the dwelling place, the "locus" of the Poor Ladies, just as the Little Portion of St. Mary's is for the brothers.

What do the first two Poor Ladies see? A roughly finished but sturdy stone building, probably exceedingly dirty and tenanted by various other creatures of God, ranging from bats and rats to twittering swallows nesting under the eaves.

Much of that original monastery remains, a symbol in stone of the poverty, strength, and trust which gave form to the life of the early feminine followers of Francis Bernardone. Beyond the arched doorway is the tiny choir, dimly lit by a small, deeply recessed window. The dark wood of the primitive stalls, though lovingly polished, is rough hewn and unskillfully joined. An alcove opposite the door is considered by some to be the place where Francis had hidden from his father's wrath. Soft shadows play over the uneven stone floor. Here the first sisters must have recited most of their psalms from memory. An oil lamp fastened to a standing lectern probably provided the only light for the readings during the Night Office.

In contrast to the austere choir, the courtyard is a triumph of light and color in the bright Umbrian sunshine. Flowering shrubs and potted plants flourish in the sheltered warmth. A well stands in the middle of the court with chain and bucket hanging ready as if to supply that medieval luxury, pure fresh water. The Poor Ladies drew from its cool depths one of the staples of their frugal diet.

An arcade runs along the inner part of the court. In its shadows one glimpses yet another arched doorway. This leads into a large, vaulted room with rough tables and benches fastened into place along its walls. The first refectory of the Poor Ladies bears a vague resemblance to the chapel. Here repasts were taken, as sacred in their own way as the Divine Banquet of the Eucharist. The sisters learned to receive their daily bread as a gift from heaven, blessed by their Father and broken among themselves with deep gratitude and sisterly love.

Throughout the main floor, gray flagstones lie in irregular patterns, now so worn down that in places the floor seems to undulate in the flickering sunlight. The bare feet of the first

Poor Ladies helped to wear them smooth, as did also the scrub brushes they must have wielded with energy.

Opposite the inner door of the little choir is a steep and narrow flight of steps which leads to the second floor. Halfway up is a small room which according to legend, was dedicated to Our Lady when St. Francis obtained the Great Pardon for the Portiuncula. At the top of the steps is a low doorway through which daylight streams. It leads to an alcove situated between the walls of the chapel and the convent. This hidden terrace would become Clare's special delight, her place of prayer, her garden of praise, her mountain solitude.

The little retreat affords a broad view of the Umbrian plain and of the Appenines in the hazy distance. From the flank of Monte Subasio on which San Damiano stands, the rich Spoleto valley spreads in gentle ripples. Looking southward, Clare could make out the dusty-pink road winding on toward Rome, the silvery glint of the Topino River and the pattern created by fields, vineyards, and olive groves.

She could have observed both the mighty and the lowly of her people riding or trudging along the dusty lanes. The largeness of vision afforded by this niche in the chapel wall helped to create a spaciousness in her spirit, a broadness of heart such as the brothers learned by tramping the roads of the wide world. The daily events of the monastery were overshadowed and proportioned by more universal concerns. The same God who saw the seed scattered by the hopeful Umbrian peasant also guided the destinies of kings who came over the mountains with their invading armies.

The dormitory of the Poor Ladies lies just under the exposed beams supporting the gently peaked roof. Here, too, the floor is of inlaid stone, a floor on which Clare and her sisters slept with nothing but a straw mat between them and the cold flags.

In these first days Clare devises a "mattress" of dried vine twigs and uses a flat rock from the river bed as her pillow.[11] She and her sisters will sleep side by side under the rafters, and as the community grows in number, the very nearness of so many snoring, wheezing, coughing, or dreaming sleepers may well have been as penitential as the thin pallets and crinkly straw pillows they lie on.

The monastery of San Damiano is neither strikingly gracious nor spacious. The arrangement of windows and doors reflects utility at the expense of symmetry. Yet an aura of gentleness clings about the pinkish-gray stone and umber roof tiles. The oft-repeated curve of the Roman arch in doorframe and cloister walk softens the austere lines of the building and subtly suggests mobility in harmony with stability.

The small complex of chapel and convent most likely was surrounded and sheltered by trees. Somber cypresses, some olive trees, perhaps a few beech and oak. Since Francis would decree that his friars were to plant many trees on any site where they dwelt but should enclose it only with a thick hedge, perhaps he and his brothers contrived this simple arrangement for the Poor Ladies also. No doubt some ground was set aside for a kitchen garden which besides vegetables would produce the herbs and bright flowers Clare loved so well.

Clare and Agnes explore their new home with eagerness mingled with gratitude. They have brought little with them but choose to depend on what their Father in heaven will provide.

Francis and his brothers quickly make it their concern to care for the sisters by sharing the fruits of their begging tours with them. As soon as the citizens of Assisi hear of the destitute little monastery on the hill below their city, they are disturbed to think that yet more "holy beggars" will be making demands on their charity. Clare, contrary to Francis' practice, gratefully accepted money as alms as well as gifts in kind whenever these were offered.

Perhaps the brothers also begged the boards and unmatched planks to construct the rude choir stalls and the plain tables and benches used in the refectory. Gradually, the place begins to appear lived in and cared for, but in no way does it resemble the grand structures that formed what was considered a proper monastery.

There is small need of bolt and lock to discourage robbers, for what little there is in the house offers no appeal to potential thieves. This, too, is according to Francis' ideals. "If we have possessions," he once remarked, "we will need arms to protect them. If we carry arms, how can we be men who wish peace?"[12]

San Damiano, small and obscure, is still redolent with the presence of Lady Poverty. Clare lovingly embraces the ideal which Francis has revealed to her. For him, poverty is a great lady whom he will serve with knightly devotion. He will defend her good name, make her excellence known to a world that despises and fears her, and restore her to the place of honor she once held in the Church.

For Clare, with typical feminine instinct, poverty is not so much a lady that she will serve but a companion of Christ whom she will become. Someday she will write: "O God-centered poverty whom the Lord Jesus Christ . . . condescended to embrace before all else!"[13]

Little San Damiano soon became the ideal haven of Lady Poverty. It was not long before the face and form of this allegorical Lady took on the features of Sister Clare, not only for Francis but also for the brothers who, in the early days, came often to San Damiano. They brought provisions begged in the city or gave needed assistance in making the crude dwelling a more habitable, if not a more comfortable, place.

"Like a nursery that had been planted by the brothers, they [the Poor Ladies] were the joy and edification not only of the Order of the Brothers but of the entire Church. When he [Francis] thought of them, his spirit was always moved to pity because he knew that from the beginning of their conversion they had led and were still leading an austere and poor life by free choice and out of necessity . . ," tenderly recalled Brother Leo when writing out his memories of those early joy-filled days.[14]

Peace, poverty, and prayer Clare seeks to implant in this little place to which Francis has led her. What will cause these to flourish, however, is not her austerity so much as her joy. Her delighted laughter often lilts through the stone passages of San Damiano. She and Agnes find something to rejoice over in every circumstance of these idyllic first days when Lady Poverty seems to perch on the open window sills and wander happily through the unfurnished rooms.

In the attic above the chapel Agnes and Clare arrange their "beds," if they can be called such. Perhaps Clare, with concern for her younger sister, insists that Agnes use a straw pallet instead of the vine branches she favors for herself. The two sisters are not long alone. Pacifica Guelfuccio joins them as soon as she learns they are installed in San Damiano. Other young women also come, many of them sent by Brother Francis or Brother Philip. Instead of being dismayed by the precarious experiment in gospel living initiated by Francis and Clare, they are challenged, attracted, and irresistibly drawn by it.

Benvenuta of Peroscia, Clare's close friend from the days of the Perugian exile, joins the small group in September. As the number of sisters increases, Clare and Agnes pass on to them what they have learned from the monastic and penitential lives but only as much as serves to give stability and substance to the exhortations which Francis himself frequently imparts to them. He comes often and it was probably he who gave the gray lazzo habit to many of the first sisters.

As her group becomes more and more a true sisterhood, Clare begs Francis to give them also, as he had his brothers, something in writing to guide them. Francis, to whom Clare had "voluntarily promised obedience with the few sisters whom the Lord had given her," regards Clare with profound admiration and would rather allow her to develop her own rule of life.[15]

Yet he is aware of his responsibility. Once when questioned by his brothers, Francis replied gravely: "Not to have called them would not have been a wrong; not to care for them now that they have been called would be the greatest unkindness."[16]

The life which the young sisters are pursuing at San Damiano is far from easy. They share "privation, poverty, hardship, toil, humility, and contempt from the world."[17] The sisters often fast simply because there is nothing in the house to eat. At times even the brothers can beg nothing more than turnips for themselves and, in the beginning, the sisters had to depend on the charity of the brothers. Clare's allusion to humiliation and contempt from the world can be seen as a reference to the wild gossip and strong disapproval which surrounded her first steps in religious life. Very few of the worthy citizens of Assisi were willing to support this unorthodox and unrealistic venture in gospel living. If these girls, many of them pampered daughters of the nobility, wish to profess poverty, then let them taste it in its stark and harsh reality.

Francis observes all this but notes something striking. Clare recalled fondly: "As he and his friars often saw for themselves that . . . we accounted all these as great delight, he rejoiced in the Lord."[18] The Poor Ladies, despite the hardships that they endure, always seem to be overflowing with joy. It radiates from their faces. The lightness of their steps on the bare stones betrays it. The lilt of laughter in their voices bears witness to its presence in their hearts. Francis can even detect it in the melodious murmur of the sisters as they pray the canonical Hours. He loves them for it.

"Moved by love, he wrote for us a form of life,"[19] Clare attested later. Only a portion of this first "Forma Vitae" is preserved for us, but it probably never was a lengthy or detailed document. Pope Gregory ix, when writing to Agnes of Prague referred to it disparagingly as merely "a draught of milk." To Clare, however, it is exceedingly precious. In it Francis gives play to the native poetry of his spirit, something he rarely allowed himself to do in his other legislative writings. Likely enough, he did not give the Poor Ladies much more than the gospel texts he had given his brothers only a few years earlier in 1209. Details of daily living did not concern him overmuch except in matters of divine worship and where poverty was concerned.

The fragment we still possess expresses what Francis (and Clare) perceived as the essence of the vocation of the Poor Sisters at San Damiano:

> Since by divine inspiration you have made yourselves daughters and servants of the most high King, the heavenly Father, and have taken the Holy Spirit as your spouse, choosing to live according to the perfection of the holy Gospel, I resolve and promise for myself and for my brothers always to have that same loving care and special solicitude for you as [I have] for them.[20]

Clare carefully enshrined this text in the heart of her Rule and it is also found in her Testament. She added that Francis "faithfully kept this promise and wished it always to be kept by the friars."[21]

The other point of this first Form of Life concerned poverty, but we do not possess the explicit text from this period. It is probable that parts of it are scattered throughout Clare's redaction of her Rule. All we have is her affirmation that when Francis wrote his few words for the Poor Ladies, he was especially concerned that they "should persevere always in holy poverty."[22]

Response to a call from on high, espousals to God, gospel living, and holy poverty form the essential constituents of the life Clare wishes to develop at San Damiano. From their observance flowed the hallmarks of what would one day be designated typical of Franciscan spirituality: gratitude, humility, and joy. Together they were the outward manifestation of personal and passionate attachment to Jesus.

Within this broad ambient, at once so free and so demanding, Clare simply allowed the life of her community to develop. At some later time, she will put on paper what the sisters are living, but at this point Clare is content to wait and see how the Spirit will direct them.

All the Hours of the breviary were prayed daily by the sisters, including the midnight office of Matins. Austerity in clothing marked the community and all the sisters went barefoot. This must have been a particularly trying form of penance during the winter months when the north wind blew chill off the shoulder of Monte Subasio, often carrying with it sleet and snow. The stone floors of San Damiano would become as icy as the frozen roads.

Even when food was sufficient, Clare was so abstemious "that the sisters were made sad and lamented over it. [Pacifica] shed tears over it several times."[23] She said later "that the sisters were amazed that Clare's body could continue to live."[24]

Clare, in the exuberance of her first love, probably felt no particular need of food, and perhaps she discovered, as have many others, that prayer thrives when the stomach is more empty than full. She found it quite easy to go without food entirely on Monday, Wednesday, and Friday. Even on the other days she ate very little. Benvenuta told "that during the Greater Lent and that of Saint Martin's Summer (Nov. 11 to Christmas) Clare always fasted on bread and water except on Sundays when she drank a little wine if there happened to be any."[25]

This was Clare's practice for several years, and she did not escape the consequences of this harsh treatment of her body. It is doubtful that she allowed any of the other sisters to imitate her example, except infrequently. The most authentic sign that this extreme, even imprudent fasting, proceeded from yearning love is Philippa's testimony that "notwithstanding all this, Clare was always joyous in the Lord."[26]

Thomas of Celano describes her mortification with both brevity and humor: "Thus the days of her meager fare and the days of her strict mortification followed one upon the other in such wise that a vigil of perfect fast was ended by a feast of bread and water!"[27]

Benvenuta, who was with Clare almost from the first days testified: "She treated her own body with such asperity that she was content with one habit of lazzo and one cloak. And if it ever seemed to her that any sister had a habit that was shabbier than hers, then she took it for her own, giving hers to the sister in exchange."[28] This practice is reminiscent of Francis' attitude for he frequently gave away his tunic or cloak to any beggar that came along in exchange for the poor man's rags.

Beneath her rough habit, Clare carefully concealed a hair shirt made of boar's hide which she wore with the bristles next to her skin. She tried her best to keep this garment secret from her sisters, but in the close company of San Damiano very little could be kept hidden for long.

Benvenuta explains why Clare sought to hide this practice from the others. She "wore it in most hidden fashion in order that the sisters should not reprove her for doing so."[29] Apparently, the sisters felt free enough with Clare to express their concern quite strongly. Clare's sister Agnes was about the only one who actually saw the garment of boar's hide, and quite possibly it was her reproofs that Clare wished most to avoid.

Later Clare adopted a cilice of horsehair fastened by strings about her waist. Another Agnes, who entered the monastery when still a child, spied this intriguing garment and begged to be allowed to try it. Clare lent it to her but, remarks Celano, "she so quickly succumbed to such harshness that after three days she gave it up more readily than she had cheerfully asked for it."[30]

This loan to Agnes by Clare was an exception, for Benvenuta bears witness that "though she afflicted her own body with these hairshirts, she was most merciful with the sisters, for whom she would not hear of such penances, and most willingly gave them every consolation."[31]

Pacifica notes that Clare "greatly loved the poor," a love which did not confine itself to spiritual works of mercy only.[32] Although there is no evidence that Clare left San Damiano and visited the poor in their homes as she had formerly done, it is clear the poor, especially the sick, made their way to her small convent.

Quite probably Francis and his brothers sent many of these suffering ones to the tender concern and skilled hands of Sister Clare. Lepers came to have their sores bathed and bandaged and to experience the rare grace of being treated lovingly as members of the human race. Distraught parents brought their ailing children to the gray-clad sister who always seemed to calm the little ones and to sooth away their fevers.

Clare had learned much about the arts of healing from her mother, and she gladly put her skill at the service of those who came to her. But it did not take these simple people long to realize that the power and tenderness in her hands flowed from a compassion rooted in the veins of prayer. While Clare washed out sores, bandaged hurt limbs or provided draughts to bring down fevers, her lips often moved in silent supplication. When her patients took their leave with her promise of "I will pray for you." ringing in their ears, they felt assured of divine help.

Prayer occupied the first place in Clare's plan of life. The day at San Damiano was organized about the set times for liturgical prayer to which Clare attached great importance. But these formal hours of prayer did not quench her ardor for ever-deepening communion with her Lord. Very soon she discovered how conducive are the night hours for intimate converse with God. Sister Pacifica asserts "that often Clare passed the nights in vigil and prayer."[33] She added that she "would lie for a long time most humbly prostrated on the earth."[34]

Clare was certainly no stranger to the practice of prayer when she came to San Damiano. But it was within the strong, austere shelter of its walls that her soul found its haven in which to expand and deepen. The fruits of this profound prayer were not long in appearing.

All of the sisters noticed that when Clare returned from prayer "sweetness came from her lips while her face shone more radiantly than usual."[35] One sister could only say that then "her words were of an indescribable gentleness."[36] Celano describes it thus: "When she returned with joy from holy prayer, she brought with her burning words from the fire of the altar of the Lord, which enkindled the hearts of the sisters."[37]

Clare regarded Francis as the superior of San Damiano and felt that she and the other sisters were living together under his direction. No one was abbess of the community, although she knew that the sisters looked to her for guidance in following Francis' counsels. Clare gave as the Spirit inspired her but always with deep humility and respect for the grace of the Lord at work in her sisters. Clare sought to have her relationship with her co-sisters be that of a "handmaid with her mistress," a point she would stress in her Rule. If she sought any privilege at all, it was simply the right to be the servant of all her sisters.

Kindness, gentleness, and compassion were traits of her character which had made Clare beloved while still living in her parents' home. These same qualities grew in scope and depth as her relationship with the Lord became more intimate. After her death, the sisters were asked about what it was like to live with Clare. One after another spoke of how much they were affected by her "great kindness," her "aimiability," her "gentleness and compassion."

The Rule of the Poor Ladies would not be definitively approved until two days before Clare's death, forty-one years in the future. But the sisters had only to observe Clare to know in fullest measure what God was calling them to be. She neither dictated regulations, stipulated directives, nor prescribed any sanctions. There was no need for such. Clare was their model simply by keeping her eyes fixed on Jesus as Francis had revealed him to her.

In those early days, Francis came frequently to San Damiano where his spirit was always refreshed in this serene dwelling place of Lady Poverty. Clare seemed to comprehend his ideals more acutely than the closest of his brothers. She was discovering and living with vibrant joy what she would one day express to another young woman who was about to embark on the Franciscan adventure: "O blessed poverty who bestows eternal riches on those who love and embrace her! O holy poverty, to those who possess and desire you God promises the kingdom of heaven and offers indeed eternal glory and blessed life!"[38]

That "blessed life" already flourished at San Damiano. Francis experienced profound content with his "Little Plant" for he intuited that she, almost alone of all his followers, would never deviate from his ideal or disappoint him in the least. "Little Plant." In the Middle Ages the word "plantula" also meant "foundation." Upon such a foundation as Clare, Francis knew a great edifice could securely rest.

From this lowly beginning would soar a cathedral of praise composed of living stones, women living solely for the glory of God and the nurturing of his Church. Daughter of the Church that Clare was, she realized keenly that the quality of her life would have far-reaching consequences. She and her sisters were chosen by God through Francis to create a work of beauty, not in stone and mortar, marble and glass, but in ceaseless prayer and joyous penance. Their edifice was to glow with a thousand lives silently burning on the altar of holocaustal love.

Chapter VI Endnotes

1. Testament of Clare, #2.
2. First Letter, #13.
3. Legend of Celano, #14.
4. Ibid., #13.

5. Ibid., #13.
6. Cause of Canonization, Wit. 12, #3.
7. Ibid., Wit. 13, #11.
8. Bull inaugurating Cause of Canonization.
9. Legend of Celano, #24.
10. Ibid., #24.
11. Cause of Canonization, Wit. 1, #7.
12. Legend of Three Companions.
13. First Letter to Agnes of Prague, #17.
14. Legend of Perugia, #45.
15. Testament of Clare, #7.
16. 2 Celano, #205.
17. Testament of Clare, #8; and Rule, Ch. VI, #2.
18. Testament, #8.
19. Rule of Clare, VI, #2.
20. Ibid.
21. Testament, 14.
22. Testament, #10.
23. Cause, Wit. 1, #7.
24. Ibid., Wit. 1, #8.
25. Ibid., Wit. 2, #8.
26. Ibid., Wit. 3, #6.
27. Legend of Celano, #18.
28. Cause of Canonization, Wit. 2, #4.
29. Ibid., Wit. 2, #7.
30. Legend of Celano, #17.
31. Cause of Canonization, Wit. 2, #6.
32. Ibid., Wit. 1, #3.
33. Ibid., Wit. 1, #7.
34. Ibid., Wit. 1, #9.
35. Legend of Celano, #20.
36. Cause of Canonization, Wit. 4, #4.
37. Legend of Celano, #20.
38. First Letter to Agnes of Prague, #15, #16.

VII   Firebrands of Europe

Swallows glide about the half-razed towers of the Rocca Maggiore above Assisi, and larks soar over the newly tenanted San Damiano this spring of the year 1212. While Clare di Favarone begins to blaze a new path for women in the Church, extraordinary men and women in other parts of Europe are rising up whose lives will cross, clash with, or complement hers. The thirteenth century is engendering both saints and sinners in its vibrant milieu, persons whose one common denominator will be greatness. As the rising cathedrals summon artists and builders to superlative achievements, the challenging intellectual and spiritual arenas are evoking triumphs of another order.

Innocent III stands forth, according to his own conception of the divine order, as the first man of his age. He not only astutely directs the extensive machinery of the Church but also engineers the raising up and deposing of kings and princes. He exercises extended rights of semikingship over England's princes, creates the kingdom of Portugal, and imposes his authority firmly on the Spanish realm. His influence is felt in Norway and Sweden, on the Baltic shores, and in Poland, while Hungary has become a papal fief. Innocent, in fact, is virtual overlord of western Europe.

United to his prodigious political acumen is zeal for the spiritual renewal of the Church and genuine compassion for all who suffer. He possesses a humility unexpected in a man of his character which is united with an almost mystical piety that has been nourished on the works of St. Bernard, Hugh of St. Victor, and St. Peter Damien. His spirituality is completed by a practical concern for the poor, the captives, and the sick for whom he sets in motion agencies to alleviate their distress. These qualities mark the finer shades in a portrait of one whom circumstances, as well as his own genius, had raised to the summit of the medieval Church. Although Innocent is sometimes mistaken and often misunderstood, he nevertheless acts in all things for God's glory.

In 1209, the same year that he had given provisionary approval to the Lesser Brothers from Assisi, Innocent had crowned the German prince, Otto IV of Brunswick, as Holy Roman Emperor. He quickly rued the act, however, for Otto not only failed to honor the solemn pledges he had made to further the interests of the Papacy but flagrantly abused his benefactor by trying to seize territory belonging to the Church. He harassed bishops and plundered monasteries. When Innocent threatened him with excommunication, his reply was preparations to march on Rome.

Obviously, Otto is unworthy of the imperial dignity, and Pope Innocent contemplates strong measures of reprisal. He who had crowned Otto would depose him. But who would be willing, and moreover, who had sufficient support, to oppose this powerful German prince? The rightful heir to the German sovereignty is young Frederick Hohenstaufen, son of Henry IV and Constance of Sicily.

When Emperor Henry had died in 1198, his legitimate heir was scarcely out of the cradle. Constance sought a safe haven in her homeland of Sicily and a sure protector of her son's rights in the newly elected Innocent III. The mettlesome child had been born in the same year as Clare, 1194, and according to some traditions, had been baptized at the same font in Assisi. He may have lived as a child in the Rocca Maggiore for his nurse was the wife of Conrad of Urslingen, Duke of Spoleto and Count of Assisi under Henry IV. When Empress Constance died, her son's upbringing had been left to a succession of tutors and courtiers who alternately spoiled or neglected him.

Brilliant but unbridled, Frederick had grown into turbulent adolescence. He had proven so uncontrollable that in 1209 Innocent had washed his hands of all legal guardianship. On his own, the boy had sought to establish his right to the crown of Sicily but without immediate success.

Disappointed in Otto, Innocent has been forced to turn his thoughts once more to the possibilities residing in the enigmatic, slippery, and immensely gifted youth. Young Frederick's failure to secure his dynastic rights in Sicily stemmed only from his lack of political support. This Innocent can easily supply but still the Pontiff hesitates. Can he command the obedience and loyalty of this strong-willed boy? Yet there is no one else available. If Frederick can be accepted by the various German princes as their legitimate overlord, Otto would be deprived not only of political allies but also of any right to the emperor's crown since this was traditionally conferred on the reigning German prince.

Otto's fortunes began to wane, and in 1211 Frederick was recognized, in name at least, as emperor of the Germanies. He immediately left Sicily in order to consolidate his claims beyond the Alps. Doubt continues to furrow Innocent's brow, and he delays in his plan to crown Frederick as Holy Roman Emperor.

Events in France have also claimed a share of Innocent's attention since his accession to the papal throne. Heresy, rampant in Southern Gaul, is spreading rapidly. Albigensianism, as it came to be called after Albi, one of its chief centers, is another revival of the old dualistic heresy which had for a time ensnared St. Augustine in the fourth century. In the late twelfth and early thirteenth centuries, Manichean beliefs had combined in a potent mixture with political expediency and commercial enterprise. They had taken hold in parts of France and northern Italy where church life and discipline had unfortunately fallen into shocking degradation.

Before anyone recognized what was occurring, the reformers who preached an amalgam of gospel poverty and impossible purity had won the allegiance of large masses of the uninstructed common folk and disillusioned nobility. Innocent first sought to counteract the influence of these men by sending out missionaries. He saw in his mind's eye a body of men inspired by burning faith and the gospel ideal, unencumbered by worldly goods and thus able to approach the poor with open arms, proclaiming the words of love and truth by their lives as well as by their words. He had first appealed to Citeaux to select some of its men who, imitating the poverty of Christ, would go forth humbly but with zealous hearts to seek out the lost and the deceived and restore them to Christ's fold.

These early missionaries had failed because they heeded only one part of Innocent's prescription for successful evangelizing—that of preaching. Their rich trappings and large retinues contrasted, to their discredit, with the austere and simple lives of the leaders of the heretics. With some misgivings and many qualifications which also went unheeded, Innocent had then appealed to the secular arm to support the new Church tribunal he had set up—to be known as the Inquisition. Once it became clear that the leaders of this new "crusade" would become legal inheritors of the lands belonging to any heretics they brought to conviction by the Inquisition, the attempt to convert them degenerated. Once a person was convicted or killed in resisting "arrest," his property was confiscated. The atrocities and massacres which followed grieved Innocent's heart exceedingly, but he was unable to control the powers he had unleashed. Why had he appealed to the force of arms in the first place?

The answer to this question is found in the "Doctrine of the Two Swords." According to St. Bernard, the two swords mentioned in St. Luke's Gospel (22:38) symbolized spiritual power and temporal power. "Both belong to Peter; one of them he actually wields, the other is at his disposal as and when circumstances require. Referring to the latter, our Lord told his apostle: 'Put up thy sword in its scabbard.' It was Peter's, surely enough, but not to draw with his own hand." In the Middle

Ages, these arguments carried considerable weight. St. Bernard was enunciating the only theory of Church authority his contemporaries held valid. On the spiritual plane, the Church, in the person of her head, the Sovereign Pontiff, enjoyed a fullness of power and therefore the right to judge all Christians (sovereign princes included) whenever they sinned. But side by side with this direct right went an indirect right to compel the obedience of all who defied him by using whatever means would be effective. Pope Innocent was acting in accordance with an approved principle when he called on Philip of France to mount a crusade on Languedoc. But he soon recognized that this kind of persuasion was not the solution to the Albigensian threat.

When a middle-aged Spanish canon, Dominic Guzman, requested permission in 1206 to preach to the heretics, Innocent gladly approved his plan. For Dominic had grasped the essence of Innocent's vision of evangelical men living poor and blameless lives, who preached the truth with eloquence, and lived that truth with integrity.

At Prouil in France, Dominic established a convent of nuns to be the center for his activities. The nuns by prayer would supplicate the power of grace that must accompany the preachers while their convent would provide a haven for women converts from Albigensianism. One of the insidious sides of this heresy lay in its connection with the chief commercial enterprise of the countryside, the weaving of fine wool. A convert lost not only social position but faced financial catastrophe as well.

As Dominic's thoughts developed, he drew up a rule of life for his men, his army of preachers. Taking the offensive in the citadel of the foe, he and a few followers threw themselves into the fray. Traveling from village to village in the vicinity of Albi and Toulouse, they fearlessly exposed errors and set forth the foundations of Catholic truth by engaging in public debates with the heretics. This was a dangerous business, and more than one preacher gave up in discouragement. Dominic himself had often to escape from a town by night or take long detours to arrive at his destination without suffering ambush.

As he watched his companions give up one after another, he often felt close to despair. How could one alone confound this fast spreading heresy? And yet, could he blame these good clerics? Life was precious, and to throw it away on an apparently futile cause was more than most men could do. Dominic prayed and fasted. Slowly a nucleus of dedicated priests gathered about him. Soon he would present to Innocent his nascent army of learned, prayerful men who would do battle with pen and oratory for the truth.

Alongside the men of this turbulent thirteenth century stands a remarkable array of valiant women whose contribution will prove to be as formative of the age as that of their male contemporaries. In Assisi, Clare is beginning to bring the flame of Francis Bernardone's ideals to a white heat by applying the bellows of contemplative prayer.

In far-away Thuringia, a four year old princess of the royal house of Hungary, Elizabeth by name, is being taken officially into the Wartburg, family seat of her future husband, seven-year-old Ludwig. By the time she will marry, Elizabeth will have developed an intense love for the poor which will urge her to open the granaries of her estates to victims of famine and to establish a hospital where she can serve the sick with her own hands. This kind of generosity, which flowered when it came into contact with the friars sent out by Francis, aroused the ire of Elizabeth's in-laws. After the death of her husband when she was only twenty-one, Elizabeth was dispossessed and driven from the family castle. She continued to devote herself to charitable works and has been hailed as the first social worker.

Another scion of royalty, Agnes, daughter of the King of Bohemia and Queen Constance of Hungary, an aunt of Elizabeth, was also betrothed at an early age. Born about 1205, she was allied to Boleslaus, son of Henry, Duke of Silesia, and of the future saint, Hedwig. The marriage never took place, for Boleslaus died before achieving manhood. Agnes thereafter was sought by a number of royal suitors but refused to accept any of them. She had heard of the new way of life for women being initiated in Assisi.

In France Blanche of Castile is acting as regent for her son, Louis, whom she is bringing up with such integrity and piety that he will one day be honored as a saint and a son of Francis. One of Blanche's daughters, Isabelle, will be responsible for establishing a house of Poor Ladies in France during the lifetime of Clare and of entering it herself. Even after Louis came of age to take up the government of his country, he permitted his mother to continue her regency for some time. He recognized that her wisdom and skill were bringing his kingdom to an unprecedented state of internal peace.

Not all the great women of this century are from palaces, however. In Liége, a young nun named Juliana had a vision in 1209 that would result in the establishment of the feast of Corpus Christi before the end of the century. Francis' love of France stemmed from his belief that this people honored the Blessed Sacrament most highly, and he often longed to preach there.

In Italy near Rieti, a young woman named Philippa Mareri, has retired to a mountain cave with some companions, desiring to imitate the Poverello. When she learns of the life led by Clare and her sisters, she will move into a monastery with her followers and adopt the Rule from San Damiano.

Near Padua another girl, Helena Enselmini, is also searching for a way of life which will give expression to her desire to live for God in a poor and simple way. In time her spiritual director, a Portuguese Franciscan named Anthony, will guide her to request the Poor Ladies in Assisi to send someone to initiate her into the manner of living observed there. Agnes, Clare's own sister, will respond to the call.

Women in this thirteenth century are enjoying an unusual

degree of freedom and prestige. In addition to being the inspiration of some of the greatest literature of all times, they themselves are making headway in the field of scholarship. We know that Clare and her sisters were well educated both in the church schools of Assisi and in their own home. It is most interesting to learn that in the Italian universities of the time, coeducation was admitted not only in principle but also in practice, and many women were in attendance at the universities of Bologna, Genoa, Padua, and Naples. In the University of Bologna, there were even some women professors on the faculty. One of them, Marie di Novella, became professor of mathematics at the age of twenty-five.

Other areas in which women are distinguishing themselves are hospital work and the care of the sick. Pope Innocent has issued many mandates establishing city hospitals in all the larger cities of Europe. Many of them are endowed by women of rank who give not only of their wealth but also of their time and skill. Sisters' hospitals are becoming more numerous and gradually will outnumber those controlled by men. The success of these hospitals in gradually eradicating leprosy and in keeping down the death rate from the prevalent scourge of erysipelas shows how capable these medieval women are.

In the field of the arts, many women are employing their talents in needlework, lace-making, and weaving to adorn the splendid cathedrals. It is probable that even the architectural plans for some of the great churches were executed by women as well as the designs for the blazing beauties of the stained glass windows being perfected during this period.

All over Europe the Divine Breath is breathing on embers long banked which are bursting into flame and causing the thirteenth century to be one of the most remarkable periods in the history of humankind.

VIII   Sister Moon

Night descends on the Spoleto valley gently as the twilight fades. The gates of Assisi are securely locked and gradually the city grows quiet. Even in the palazzos of the wealthy the inhabitants retire not long after the sun goes to rest. As a young moon rises, the Umbrian countryside is drowsing peacefully.

On the hillside outside the walls of the city, the little monastery of San Damiano stands silent under the stars. Only the feeble glow of the sanctuary lamp relieves the velvety blackness enveloping the cloister. Nearly all the sisters are asleep after a strenuous day.

After praying Compline, the night prayer of the Church, together, most of the sisters had retired. Some linger for a while in the chapel, among them Sister Clare. Thomas of Celano, drawing on the memories of these sisters writes: "For long periods after Compline, Clare would pray with the sisters . . . and after the others had gone to their hard couches to rest their tired limbs, she would remain watchful and unwearied in prayer, that while sleep lay hold of the others, she might 'by stealth' as it were 'catch a whisper of God.'"[1]

In these dark hours, quietness seeps into Clare's spirit as she yields herself to the silent but irresistible call of her Lord. "She opens wide the depths of her soul to the streams of divine grace" and silently savors the gift of God.[2] She surrenders the cares of the day just past and entrusts the unknown tomorrow into her Father's hands. As the night grows deeper, Clare abandons herself to the Lover who is seeking her.

Prayer in these early years may have often been just mute

yearning, a wordless longing that torments rather than satisfies Clare. She experiences keenly her helplessness, her radical inability to bridge the great gulf that seems to separate her from the "most high Lord." Words are wholly inadequate. Yet the craving of her heart must find expression. Tears spontaneously release her pent-up affection and are so sincere that "the others also are moved to weep."[3]

In time all the other sisters leave, and Clare watches alone before the altar. Her aching desire causes her to fling herself on the floor where, face to the earth, she allows the very posture of her body to express the unspeakable longing of her spirit. "She bedews the ground with her tears and caresses it with her kisses, and thus seems ever to clasp her Jesus on whose feet these tears flow and these kisses are imprinted," records her biographer.[4]

The intensity that is hers by nature, the wholeheartedness with which Clare gives herself to whatever she does, characterizes her prayer as fully as it does all other areas of her life. Her extremes in fasting and mortification are due in part to this same trait.

Although this almost ruthless drive to do nothing by halves forms the natural cornerstone on which Clare's future holiness will be built, at this early stage it is almost her undoing. Fortunately, Clare also possesses remarkable common sense and a delicate perception of the movements of grace which prevent her from becoming eccentric. The proof of this is her sunny and balanced disposition.

Not all saints in the making are a pleasure to live with, but, according to her sisters in religion, Clare was. Celano sums up their impressions: "Although severe bodily mortification usually begets affliction of spirit, quite the opposite was seen in Clare, for in all her mortification she preserved a joyful, cheerful countenance, so that she seemed either not to feel bodily austerities or to laugh at them. From this we gather that the holy joy which flooded her within overflowed without; for the love of the heart lightens the chastisement of the body."[5]

The "love of the heart" is the deep and truest explanation of all that Clare does. She is discovering the Heart of Love in Jesus that Francis' fiery zeal is illuminating for all their contemporaries. From his conviction that "the love of him who loved us much is much to be loved"[6] flows the prayer: "May the power of your love, O Lord, fiery and sweet as honey, wean my heart from all that is under heaven, so that I may die for love of your love, you who were so good as to die for love of my love."[7]

Clare is learning that what attracts this divine Lover most powerfully is not eloquent prayers but tongue-tied helplessness, not elaborate rituals but mute poverty, not a wealth of words but silent emptiness. To her helplessness, her poverty, her emptiness, the great and good Lord will bow down. He himself will cross the abyss to reach her. She remembers with emotion that once he came "despised, needy and poor (himself) into this world, that men and women who were in dire poverty and want, and suffering absolute need of heavenly nourishment might become rich in him by possessing the kingdom of heaven."[8]

Clare is so overwhelmed by this divine graciousness that she knows not whether to weep for wonder or to "rejoice and be glad. Be filled with a remarkable happiness and a spiritual joy!"[9] She does both.

The moon slowly rises as the stars wheel in their cosmic patterns. As midnight approaches, Clare rises from the floor. She lights a candle stub from the sanctuary lamp and shielding it carefully, picks her barefoot way up the steep, uneven steps to the dormitory. Her shadow wavers on the wall as she gazes tenderly over the sleeping sisters. It is the summer of 1214, only two years since she and Agnes were the sole occupants of this rough loft. But now, how many more sisters have come to share their "life and poverty!"

Sister Pacifica is here, Sisters Benvenuta, Balvina, and a number of other courageous girls who had been drawn to share in this radical experiment of gospel living in the past year. Other young women are also knocking at the heavy old door, asking with a light in their eyes to join them. Clare welcomes each one and tells them the "the Gospel words: 'that they should go and sell all their goods and take care to distribute them to the poor.' "[10] The response to this ultimatum quickly sorts out the ones who are genuinely called from those who are merely curious.

Even so, not all those who enter, stay. Some do not possess sufficient health despite their good will; others do not hold the fullness of the Catholic faith. Some girls come infected with the ideas of the Cathari who are gaining a foothold in Umbria. The number and influence of these heretics is increasing and soon the sect will gain so much tolerance that one of the Cathari will become mayor of Assisi.

Gradually, taught by mistakes and guided by intuition, Clare learns to recognize rather quickly a girl with a genuine vocation. Once Francis had sent five young women to be received into the monastery. Sister Agnes and some other sisters were with Clare when they arrived. After some brief conversation, Clare came to a decision. Sister Cecilia relates that she consented to "receive four but would not receive the fifth saying she would not persevere in her vocation even if she remained in the monastery three years. However, after being greatly importuned to receive her, she consented but the novice left after half a year."[11] This young lady was of noble rank, the Lady Gasdia, daughter of Taccholo.

Cupping her candle, Clare begins to move gently from one sleeping sister to another "silently arousing them by signs and calling them to the divine praises."[12] Some waken easily as if they have been eagerly awaiting this midnight summons. Others respond more slowly as if returning from some far journey.

Back in choir Clare lights the oil lamp fastened to the wooden lectern and rings a small hand bell, momentarily shattering the silence as its echoes resound through the stone corridors. Sister Benvenuta supplies this cryptic addenda: "Those sisters who do not get up at the sound of the bell, Clare calls by other signs!"[13]

While waiting for the sisters to assemble in choir, Clare continues her silent prayer. Her thoughts turn with concern toward Francis who has gone away again. Not long before, he had stopped at San Damiano to say good-bye, for he and Brother Bernard were setting out for Spain hoping "to preach the gospel of Christ to the Miranolin [of Morocco] and his people."[14] The possibility of martyrdom such an undertaking holds out is an added incentive and his feet fairly danced, so happy was he by such a prospect. Clare could not disguise her apprehension despite her wish not to dampen his childlike joy.

Now her concern is acute. She has heard that "his desire had borne him so swiftly along that even though he was physically weak, he would leave his companion behind and hurry ahead."[15] Clare worries that he might have fallen ill and her loving concern seeks him, reaching out for him through the dark night hours. How frightening to be ill, perhaps dangerously so, in a strange land!

Clare can sympathize with the appeal that martyrdom holds for Francis for she experiences its attraction also but she feels he is needed too sorely by his young Orders to be taken from them prematurely. God apparently agreed with Clare for we read: "When he [Francis] had traveled as far as Spain, however, he fell sick by God's designs as he had other plans in store for him. Prevented by his illness from gaining martyrdom, Francis realized that his life was still necessary for the family he had founded . . . and so he returned to tend the flock committed to his care."[16]

That was not the first time Clare had stood in the doorway of San Damiano and watched her father and guide set off eagerly in pursuit of martyrdom. Toward the end of 1212, less than six months after he had taken her to the little cloister, he and a companion had set out for Syria. The great defeat inflicted on the advancing Moorish threat by the Spanish at Las Navas de Tolosa had fired all Europe with the hope that the Moslem peril had been turned back for good.

Just about the time that Clare and Agnes were settling into San Damiano, Pope Innocent III had issued an urgent appeal to all Christendom. He called on the princes to take up arms against the Moors and ordered universal prayer and penitential processions to be held. Perhaps some of the most enthusiastic of responses was at little San Damiano where Clare, Agnes, and Pacifica implored, begged, and pleaded with the Lord on behalf of threatened Europe. When news arrived at last of the brilliant victory at Las Navas de Tolosa in July of 1212, the sisters joyously thanked God as the church bells rang out. A heavy cloud, laden with catastrophe, had lifted from the horizon of Europe, and men everywhere were stirred to new hope.

That would not be the only instance when Clare and her sisters would expend themselves in prayer and penance to avert military disaster. The little monastery would someday find itself in the very midst of a battlefield for wars ceaselessly swept the Italian peninsula.

Events stirring the world about her always claimed Clare's intense interest and practical response. Sister Benvenuta recounts that although Clare "would not speak of secular matters, neither did she wish the sisters to remember them"; she often asked the sisters to pray for "any person in the world [who] was known to have committed some action against God [and she herself] grieved with many tears" over them.[17]

In the general enthusiasm following the victory at Las Navas de Tolosa, Francis had decided to set off at once for the Moorish stronghold in Syria. However, it was late in the season for sailing and the only ship he found was soon forced by storms to turn back. It was not long before Francis came tramping up the valley to Assisi. "Will he be returning this time?" Clare wonders. Tonight as her heart fears for Francis, Clare finds that the psalms take on fresh meaning:

> O Lord, my God,
> I cried out to you and you healed me.

O Lord, you brought me up from the nether world,
You preserved me from among those going down
   into the pit.
Sing praise to the Lord, you his faithful ones,
And give thanks to his holy name.
For his anger lasts but a moment,
A lifetime, his good will.
At nightfall, weeping enters in,
But with the dawn, rejoicing.[18]

Trusting that her tears of the night will indeed turn to rejoicing in the morning, Clare retires with the rest of the sisters after Matins. As they quietly return to their interrupted slumber, Clare slips over to her place at the far end of the long, low room. Through the window opposite her, she can see the stars shining and notes that the moon is low on the horizon. Does Francis also see and salute Sister Moon from wherever he is?

Before long Clare hears the glad news that Francis and Brother Bernard are back at the Portiuncula. A weight lifts from her heart. Her joy is complete when Francis comes to visit her and the sisters at San Damiano. Clare notes that he is thinner and more tired looking, but the glow deep in his eyes is more luminous than ever. Francis is full of joy about an extraordinary gift he has been offered. Count Orlando of Chiusi, whom Francis had met at a festival honoring a new knight, has offered him a mountain! Its name is La Verna and, according to the Count, "very wild and solitary, perfectly suited for someone who wants to do penance in a place far from people."[19]

Clare shares Francis' delight for she knows of his almost mystical rapture over mountains as places of prayer and retreat. "See how our good God provides for his little sheep, my sister!" he exclaims.[20] Already Francis has dispatched two friars to see the place and if it is as suitable as the Count claims, he will gratefully accept it.

Perhaps Francis also describes to the eager group of sisters something of his travels for he had probably visited the great sanctuary of St. James at Compostela in Spain and, on his return journey, had traveled through parts of his beloved France.

While he had been gone, a number of "educated and noble men" had asked to be admitted to the brotherhood, among them one Thomas of Celano.[21] Francis received them graciously after his return and, knowing Clare's pleasure in well-turned sermons, may have sent some of them to visit the Poor Ladies from time to time. Perhaps it was at this period that Clare's future biographer first met the woman he so admires and praises in his later works.

In addition to spiritual nourishment, the brothers from the Portiuncula continue to provide their sisters in Christ with their bodily needs as well. A small hut is built just outside the garden where the chaplain can stay and also the friar-questers when it is convenient. These men do all in their power to obtain the needed alms for the little monastery but Clare apparently thought they were overzealous at times.

Sister Philippa remembered "that when the begging brothers brought back whole loaves as alms for the monastery, Clare would reprove them, saying, 'Who gave you these whole loaves?' She said this because she preferred to receive in alms broken loaves instead of whole ones," Philippa explained.[22]

One day the supply of olive oil, so necessary for cooking, runs out completely. Sister Clare sends for Brother Bentevenga who usually goes questing for them and tells him of their needs. He is willing to go but asks for some container to take with him.

Clare finds "a jug which she washes with her own hands and places it on a little wall near the entrance to the monastery. Brother Bentevenga goes to fetch it but finds it already full of oil." Apparently disturbed that someone else had procured the oil before he could get there, the good brother asks who filled it. None of the sisters can tell him. Sister Pacifica admits that she had seen Clare take "the jar out empty and bring it in full, but she does not know by whom or how it had been filled."[23] No one can get a direct answer from Clare so the mystery remained unresolved although the sisters, among them Agnes, Balvina, and Benvenuta, have their suspicions.

The sick and the suffering come daily now to the door of the monastery, for they trust in the compassion with which they will be received. As far as their own poverty permits, the sisters share what they have. While Clare tends to their bodily ills, the poor and distressed pour the sorrows of their hearts into her sympathetic ear. She can do little more than promise them the prayers of the sisters, but this is all they are seeking. Already people are noticing that God seems to be especially gracious in response to the prayers of the Poor Ladies.

One day a little boy of three or four, Mathiolo, pushes a little stone up his nostril. It lodges so deeply that no one can remove it and the child is screaming in fright and pain. Fearing that their child is in peril, his frantic parents rush him to San Damiano. Aroused by his frightened screams, several sisters hurry with Clare to the door. Clare takes the terrified youngster into her arms, murmuring softly to him. Almost at once Mathiolo grows quieter. When Clare "signs him with the cross, the stone immediately falls out of his nose, and he is healed."[24] Sister Benvenuta who related this incident later said that she saw the little boy perfectly well afterwards.

About this time Francis is experiencing "great agony of doubt." His whole soul is drawn irresistibly to prayer, for in it he often experiences communion with his Lord for which his whole being hungers. But he feels just as irresistibly compelled to draw others to share in this incomparable joy. He can come to no resolution of his dilemma and "wants very much to know which of these will please our Lord Jesus Christ most."[25]

Francis knows that among those closest to him, Brother Sylvester and Sister Clare will understand his doubts best and that they seem to enjoy a familiarity with the Lord which enables them to discern his will most clearly. "So he calls Brother Masseo and says to him: 'Dear brother, go to Sister Clare and tell her on my behalf to pray devoutly to God, with one of her purer and more spiritual companions, that he deign to show me what is best; either that I preach sometimes or that I devote myself only to prayer. And then go also to Brother Sylvester who is staying on Monte Subasio and tell him the same thing."[26]

Brother Masseo sets out and calls at San Damiano. When Clare learns of Francis' anguish, her eyes darken with sympathy for she knows just how keenly he must be suffering from this conflict. Thoughtfully, she goes to the chapel with her companion.

Brother Masseo continues up the slope of Monte Subasio until he finds Brother Sylvester and repeats Francis' request. At one time, Sylvester had seen a cross of gold issuing from Francis' mouth which extended in height to heaven and in width to the ends of the world. Immediately he sets himself to pray and soon has God's answer. To Brother Masseo he says, "The Lord says you are to tell Brother Francis this: that God has not called him to this state only on his own account, but that he may reap a harvest of souls and that many may be saved through him."[27]

Brother Masseo then returns to San Damiano where he marvels to learn that both Clare and her companion have received the very same answer from the Lord. Francis is awaiting Masseo's return with deep anxiety for he is expecting a message from his King. Withdrawing with Masseo into the woods, he "bares his head and crossing his arms, he kneels down before Brother Masseo and asks him: 'What does my Lord Jesus Christ order me to do?' "

"Brother Masseo replies that Christ had answered both Brother Sylvester and Sister Clare and her companion revealing that he wants him to go about the world preaching because he did not call him for himself alone but also for the salvation of others."[28]

As if relieved of a great burden, Francis springs to his feet and cries out, "Let us go in the Name of the Lord" and takes off with such haste that Brothers Masseo and Angelo have to run to keep up with him. The first village where he preaches is Cannara. The people flock out to meet him. Unfortunately, so do a large number of swallows which twitter excitedly in all the trees. Francis' words are all but drowned by their chatter. Suddenly, Francis raises his hand and bids the birds be still so that he might preach as the Lord has commanded him. The birds fall silent and stand about so attentively that they, too, seem eager to hear his fervent words.

When Francis turned to Clare in his doubt, she may have experienced some surprise that he whom she regarded as her teacher and guide should be seeking to know the Lord's will through her. Perhaps the incident caused Clare to define more sharply in her mind what is to be the role of the Poor Ladies in the Church and in relation to the First Order. It is clear that although Clare intends to live as fully as possible the gospel ideals that Francis and his brothers embrace, she does not envisage herself or her sisters tramping through the world along side of them.

Within the charism which inspired Francis course two complementary streams, that of contemplative prayer in solitude and that of ministry to the multitude. It was the very awareness of this double thrust which had tormented Francis. At first sight these two streams may seem mutually exclusive if they are viewed as an either/or choice. The wisdom of God's answer to Francis through Clare demonstrates that both of these streams are to be present but with varying degrees of emphasis. Francis learns to harmonize his life of solitary prayer with his preaching so that both of these elements are present at all times but one or other of them predominates.

This way of varying emphasis became the accepted pattern of his life and that of the other brothers as well. It also became a viable mode for the Order as a whole. Some members or groups within the Franciscan family engaged more directly in ministry and service to others while other segments highlighted the aspect of solitude and prayer. Both spiritual modes of living are apostolic, both are building up the Kingdom within the individual Franciscan and the universal Church.

Even in the most active of lives, prayer will be the indispensable companion and support while in the most hidden and withdrawn of lives, profound concern for the needs of humankind will be the deep motivation for seeking the Lord. This can be seen most visibly in the complementary ways of life of the First and Second Orders. They complete and sustain each other.

From the beginning, Clare instinctively felt that her personal call was to live the gospel ideals of Francis with the stronger emphasis on contemplative prayer. Yet she did this with a wholly apostolic outlook. The sisters whose lives are primarily ones of prayer are "placed . . . as examples and mirrors for other men as well as for the other sisters. The sisters whom they inspire are in turn mirrors and examples to those living in the world."[29]

The brothers' lives of preaching and ministry complete the hidden immolation of their cloistered sisters but at the same time, the apostolic power of the sisters' prayer fructifies the work of those in the field. The friars are stimulated to kindle their own ardor at prayer by the example of the sisters, while the sisters in turn are nourished by the spiritual support and guidance provided by the brothers.

This harmonious interplay is observable in the relationship between Clare and Francis throughout their lives. Francis' literal and active interpretation of the gospel life is the masculine counterpart to Clare's no less literal but receptive response typifying her feminine approach. Francis' own feminine side is educated, as it were, and released by his association with Clare. Conversely, Clare's basic femininity is brought into contact with her own masculine qualities through her relationship with Francis.

He is for her guide and illuminator, father and support. She is for him a revealer of the treasures in the depths, an inspiration, a lady and a comforter. In Clare the stark and straightforward, almost harsh demands of Francis' idealism are humanized as it were and given a certain flexibility and compassion. She can teach him how to break out of the dark moods that seize him by laughing gently at the too-great seriousness that leads to them.

A strong feminine element always existed in Francis, but he seemed to have feared it as a demonic temptress until he meets it outside himself in Clare. In her he discovers the natural and harmonious woman and learns not to fear but to value and use freely his feminine qualities. Through her he learns to establish a friendly, even reverent relationship with this once frightening and disturbing element in his nature.

In Clare, strength and drive, directness of perception and single-minded pursuit of her goal are aspects of her own masculine side which, through her relationship with Francis, she learns to use with care and discretion. She might have become a masculinized woman who sought to dominate her environment by sheer force of will. Instead, she learns to distinguish and recognize her truest feminine gifts through the discipline her masculine side imparts. She becomes more finely woman, and Francis, more fully man, through their profoundly intimate and humanly spiritual relationship.

Out of their personal experience flows the distinct but complementary forms of the religious families they founded. By embracing the more contemplative style, Clare gives expression to the feminine element in the Franciscan charism as well as in her own character. She takes what she has received from Francis but is not a slavish imitator. Instead, she is an active co-partner in unfolding more fully certain dimensions of his original inspiration.

Clare, by being true to the deepest instincts of her womanly nature, is tremendously assisting the full development of the Franciscan charism. By her life both friars and sisters are enlightened about what the Lord desires of them and are encouraged to pursue it. The contrast and complementarity of Francis' and Clare's spiritual modes of living can perhaps be best illustrated by setting two quotations from Francis side by side:

To the brothers, he says: The Lord "has sent you into the entire world for this reason: that in word and deed you may give witness to his voice and bring everyone to know that there is no one who is all-powerful except him."[30]

But of the sisters Francis prophesies: "Ladies will dwell here who will glorify our heavenly Father throughout his holy Church by their celebrated and holy manner of life."[31]

Chapter VIII Endnotes

1. Legend of Celano, #19.
2. Ibid., #19.
3. Ibid., #20.
4. Ibid., #19.
5. Ibid., #18.
6. 2 Celano, #196.
7. Prayer "Absorbeat" attributed to St. Francis in *Omnibus*, p. 160.
8. First Letter to Bl. Agnes, #19.
9. Ibid., #21.
10. Rule of Clare, Ch. II, #4 (pluralized).
11. Cause of Canonization, Wit. 6, #15.
12. Legend of Celano, #20.
13. Cause of Canonization, Wit. 2, #9.
14. 1 Cel., #56.
15. Legenda Major, #9, 6.
16. Ibid., #6.
17. Cause of Canonization, Wit. 2, #10.
18. Ibid., Ps 30:3-6.
19. Fioretti, Part II.

20. Ibid.
21. 1 Celano, #57.
22. Cause of Canonization, Wit. 3, #13.
23. Ibid., Wit. 1, #15.
24. Ibid., Wit. 2, #18.
25. Fioretti, #16.
26. Ibid., #16.
27. Ibid.
28. Ibid.
29. Testament of Clare, #6.
30. Letter to Entire Order, #9.
31. Testament of Clare, #4.

IX Clearer Leaps the Flame

Bad news always travels swiftly. Before his body is cold, all Assisi knows that the great Innocent has died in Perugia. Flags and pennants drop to half-mast while the bells of the city toll and toll. The Church of Christ is without a shepherd. The date is July 16, 1216, Clare's twenty-second birthday.

At San Damiano, the death of the greatest Pontiff of the Middle Ages is experienced as a deeply personal loss by the young abbess. Clare knows of Francis' profound love and respect for this man who had confirmed his exceptional vocation and had given him a place and a mission in the Master's vineyard. Through Francis' enthusiastic praise, Clare had come to feel that Innocent was also her father, so it was but natural that she had turned to him when she felt her own vocation was endangered.

Earlier this very year Clare had proposed a bold plan to protect her community and its unique way of life. The Fourth Lateran Council (Nov. 1215) had decreed that henceforth no new religious family could be founded unless it adopted one of the Rules already approved by the Holy See. Pope Innocent had explicitly said that this decree did not affect the Friars Minor whose Rule he had personally approved some years earlier.

But Clare felt uneasy about the status of the Poor Ladies. So far no formal Rule had been drawn up for the San Damiano community. Clare had been content to follow the Rule of the friars insofar as women could in those days. The adaptations she made were simple and obvious. This, together with the exhortations and a few "writings" of Francis, were sufficient for her.

Together with her sisters Clare sought simply "as a poor virgin [to] embrace the poor Christ."[1] Poverty thus became the one thing necessary as far as a rule for daily living was concerned. She knew that love needs no law other than itself. But Clare was wise enough to fear that worldly "prudence" might marshal arguments designed to rob her of her treasure.

Prelates and canonists could try to counter and overwhelm with "reasonableness" the simple gospel foolishness of her way of life. Clare did not wish to suffer her Lord's reproach that the "children of this world take more initiative than the children of light when it comes to dealing with their own kind."[2] She, therefore, decided to act, before she could be acted upon.

In an age when women had to depend on male support, she conceived the idea of soliciting and obtaining this protection, before it could be turned against her. It seems rather certain that it was Clare, not Francis, who led the way this time in safeguarding their tryst with Lady Poverty.

Now kneeling in prayer as the bells toll, Clare allows her mind to review those events which brought her into direct contact with Innocent and which had culminated in an exceptional document drafted by his own hand. The Privilege of Poverty, as it is called, reveals not only Clare's determination to have her way of life guaranteed but also Innocent's keen appreciation of the workings of the Spirit in her regard. The very tenor of the document, combining spiritual ideals with practical details, reveals something about the complex character of the man who had borne the burden of the Papacy so brilliantly for eighteen turbulent years.

In her Testament Clare describes her decision in these words: ". . . for even greater security, I took care to have our profession of most holy poverty, which we promised our Father [Francis], strengthened with privileges by the Lord Pope Innocent, during whose pontificate we had our beginning . . . so that we would never nor in any way depart from it."[3]

According to Celano, Innocent was astounded by the urgent appeal of the young abbess that he ensure that her monastery should always remain poor. "This magnanimous man congratulated Clare on such fervor and declared hers to be a unique proposal since never before had a like privilege been asked of the Apostolic See. And to match this unusual petition with an unusual response, the Pontiff with great joy wrote with his own hand the first draft of the privilege she sought."[4]

The Privilege of Poverty is quite an interesting document in both content and tone. It is addressed specifically to "Clare and the other handmaids of the Church of San Damiano at Assisi" for it was to this monastery alone that the concession of poverty was made. Other communities of Poor Ladies would come into existence, some very soon, but the great privilege was granted only to San Damiano. However, it seems that a few of these early communities did manage to obtain it also.

Possibly because Innocent drafted the document himself rather than going through the formal channels of the Curia, a copy of the original document has not survived. However, it is likely that the confirmation given by Gregory ix some years later is a close replica. Two forms exist which may reflect the earlier and later documents.

The images and scriptural allusions employed in the first three paragraphs of the Privilege are found so frequently in Clare's own writings[5] that one wonders if the pontiff simply restated phrases from Clare's original petition to him or if she so committed the Privilege to her heart's memory that its words and phrases recurred spontaneously when she wrote to others.

The document opens:

> As is manifest, in the desire to dedicate yourselves to the Lord alone you have renounced all desire for temporal things; wherefore you have sold all things

and given them to the poor and propose to have no possessions whatever, that in all things you may cleave to the footprints of Him who became for us the Way, the Truth and the Life (Jn 14:6).

Nor does the lack of possessions deter you from such a proposal; for the left hand of the heavenly Bridegroom is under your head (cf. Cant 2:6; 8:3) to support what is weak in your body which you have subordinated to the law of your mind and brought into subjection.

Finally, He who feeds the birds of the air and the lilies of the field will not fail you in both food and vesture, until he himself comes and serves you (Lk 12:37) in eternity, when namely his right hand will embrace you in the fullness of his vision.[6]

The desire for perfect poverty is situated in the only context that gives it value, the love of Jesus and the desire to imitate him. The Holy Father demonstrates that he shares Clare's calm trust that their heavenly Father will provide all that is necessary by freely allowing Clare and her sisters to choose a life as unencumbered as the birds of the air and the lilies of the field.

The first sentence notes that they are choosing to renounce, not just temporal possessions but "all desire" for them. This touches precisely on what alone will make their poverty holy and liberating. But something even more profound is implied. The Poor Ladies are not forcing themselves into a difficult renunciation but rather are demonstrating that they have lost the desire for earthly goods altogether because a desire for greater things has taken its place.

There is also a wise emphasis that "what is weak in their bodies they have subordinated to the law of the mind" by reasonable penance. But it is not so much what Clare and her sisters do of themselves which is important. It is what they are allowing Christ to do in them by supporting their weakness, nourishing and sustaining them in body and soul, and finally rewarding them at the heavenly banquet where he shall be their servant. This positive emphasis runs consistently throughout Clare's writings about poverty. By their choice of total dependence, the Poor Ladies are allowing Christ to be their Way, their Truth, and their Life with a concreteness that is the unique charism of the Franciscan ideal.

Paragraph four of the Privilege is the most important for it expresses in thirty-seven succinct words all that Clare asked of the Church of God and the Vicar of Christ.

> As you have thus petitioned Us, so We confirm by Apostolic favor the proposal of highest poverty, granting you by the authority of these Letters present that you can be compelled by no one to receive possessions.[7]

With this as her shield Clare felt invincible against the importunities of anyone who would seek to dissuade her from following Christ in the perfection of the Holy Gospel as Francis had revealed it to her.

Pope Innocent may have felt that living such a life of total commitment to Lady Poverty might be more than what some of the first Poor Ladies had bargained for when they had entered. Thus he added:

> But if anyone among you will not observe such a proposal, she cannot dwell among you but must betake herself to another place (i.e., monastery).[8]

Obviously, Innocent recognized the necessity of all the members of San Damiano being of one heart and mind about the form of life they had embraced. Incidentally, this prerogative of a professed nun simply to "betake herself to another monastery" reflects the precanonical status of San Damiano.

Paragraph five contains some very strong censures to be incurred by "any person, ecclesiastical or secular, (who) shall have attempted, knowingly and rashly, to contravene this page of Our confirmation. We decree therefore that it is allowed to no man to rashly disturb you or your church or to vex you with any importunities."[9] We may suspect that Innocent never before wrote censures against persons who wished to *give* endowments to monasteries!

Pope Innocent concludes his decree in a gentler mode with a prayer and blessing of singular wisdom:

> But to you all and to those who in that same place preserve love in Christ, be the peace of our Lord Jesus Christ, that they may both receive the fruit of their good work and before the strict Judge obtain the rewards of eternal peace.[10]

Now Clare silently offers this same prayer for Pope Innocent himself, struck down unexpectedly in his fifty-sixth year after a brief illness. A little more than six months have passed since his greatest achievement, the Fourth Council of the Lateran, had convened.

In November of 1215, 412 bishops (among them the Latin Patriarchs of Constantinople and Jerusalem), 800 abbots and priors, ambassadors and envoys from all the heads of state, as also innumerable theologians and clerks had met in magnificent assembly in the Mother-church of Christendom, St. John Lateran. The brilliance and pageantry of the solemn opening surpassed anything Europe had ever witnessed. Dominating the scene in bejeweled cope and tiara, Innocent had appeared as an epiphany of papal splendor.

Two years had gone into the preparations for this Council for which Innocent cherished high hopes. Two goals, the unity of Christendom and the internal unity of the Church, dominated the planning. The Holy Father hoped that by sending out a rousing summons for a Fifth Crusade, he could effectively achieve both. If all the warring princelings of Europe were united in a vast and holy endeavor, the liberation of the Holy Land, peace might ensue on the continent. And the liberal indulgences and pardons attached to participation in the Crusade might bring back to the fold of Peter many straying or heretical sheep.

Innocent's opening address began on a pensive note: "How I have longed to eat this Passover with you before suffering!" He envisaged a triple Passover: "A corporal Passover which should be marked by a liberation of the terrestial Jerusalem; a spiritual Passover whereby the whole Church should pass from vice to virtue, and finally an eternal Passover celebrating the passage from this temporal life to heavenly glory."

Despite the grandeur of this vision of all humankind marching toward the eternal Pasch, Innocent did not lose his realistic understanding of what the human race is usually capable of. With powerful and heartfelt eloquence, he invoked the striking prophecy of Ezekiel who had beheld six armed angels summoned to Jerusalem to smite all inhabitants except those marked by the Tau on their foreheads. "Who are those worthy to bear this sign of saving grace?" thundered the Pontiff. He allowed the question to hang over the heads of his listeners. Then with supreme skill, he dramatically summoned the metaphoric avengers and ordered them, in the words of Ezekiel, "Begin with my sanctuary!"

If any of the prelates who sat before him had cherished any hope that Innocent would subordinate his relentless campaign to rectify church abuses to his pressing interest in the Crusade, they lost them now. Innocent knew, as well as they, that the sheep often strayed because they lacked a vigilant shepherd. Too many bishops held their sees only as sources of revenue and were seldom, if ever, in residence in their own dioceses. At that time the duty of preaching and instructing the faithful rested primarily on the bishops although they could delegate this responsibility to qualified clerics. Some did. Others, jealous of the prerogatives, refused to allow anyone other than themselves to preach within their jurisdiction, but they themselves seldom bothered.

Many parish priests were barely literate and unable to do more than say Mass and collect stipends. Some lived openly immoral lives, inviting the scorn of their people and discrediting all priests in the eyes of the simple faithful. If the people of the land were often grossly ignorant of the fundamentals of the faith, the reason was not hard to discover.

The Lateran Council did "begin with the sanctuary" and enacted vigorous decrees regarding the education of the clergy, the duty and necessity of preaching, and attempted to do away with that bane of the Middle Ages, lay investiture. But it is one thing to issue decrees and quite another to put them into effect. Unfortunately, the wealthy and influential prelates of the Curia and hierarchy, at whom many of these reforms were aimed, found ways to prevent their implementation. Innocent's great dream of a reformed and truly holy church would not and could not be realized by issuing laws.

Almost certainly there stood, among the great throng of common folk and clerics that crowded into the back of the Lateran, the small, ragged figure of Francis Bernardone. The fierce zeal of Innocent to purify the House of God kindled a like ardor in his spirit and he longed for the day when he could see the glorious Tau traced on the forehead of all the children of the kingdom. In fact, from this time onward Francis adopted the Tau, the T-shaped cross, as his personal emblem. It became his unique signature, the heraldic device he placed over his cell door, the seal he affixed to all he wrote.

Because the Council also intended to deal with regulations concerning religious orders, it is most probable that all heads of communities as well as founders of new orders were present. Among them would have been Dominic Guzman, who had brought with him the Rule of Life he had composed for his growing army of preachers. He was disappointed to learn that no new rule would henceforth be approved unless it were based on one of the time-tested Rules from the past—that of Basil, Augustine, or Benedict. Dominic was advised to confer with his men in France and choose one of these Rules as the basis for his own Constitutions.

Francis, as has been noted, was more fortunate. His way of life had received papal approbation about six years earlier, and Innocent did not include his Lesser Brothers among those groups which were required to accept an older Rule.

According to a legend that many consider authentic, it was during this Council that Francis and Dominic first met. One night Dominic had dreamed that he and an unknown stranger were presented by the Virgin Mary to Our Lord who charged the two of them with the conversion of the world. The next day Dominic recognized the ragged stranger of his dream in the streets of Rome. It was Brother Francis. Dominic stopped him excitedly, told him of the dream and embraced him with Latin exuberance saying, "Let us be comrades and nothing on earth can prevail against us!"

Gladly Francis returned the embrace for he had already heard of the heroic work which Dominic and his men were doing in his beloved France. Quite likely both Francis and Dominic had become aware of each other through their mutual supporter and friend, Cardinal Ugolino, then the most influential man in the Curia.

We can imagine that Francis later eagerly described this meeting to Clare and her sisters, expressing his deep admiration for Dominic in whom great learning was joined with great humility and zeal for souls. An instant friendship had sprung up between the two men, so different and yet so akin in their love for Christ and his Church. Dominic was a man of great personal magnetism. He is known to have had a capacity for instant rapport, sympathy, and enthusiastic loyalty for his friends. Francis always felt honored by Dominic's undisguised admiration for him and his Order. He found in the great preacher a true soul-brother who shared his convictions about Lady Poverty and who made it the basis for his society also.

Quite possibly as a result of the rulings of this Council, Clare had to accept a charge which she had until now managed to decline. Francis insisted that she assume the governance of the Poor Ladies. Only her vow of obedience to him kept Clare from refusing a role that was plainly repugnant to her for as Celano says, she genuinely "wished to be under rather than over others and was more willing to serve rather than be served."[11] Sister Pacifica, who was present when Francis proposed the matter to Clare, assures us that only "the insistent prayers of Francis prevailed on her to accept the order and government of the sisters."[12] It was probably not just humility that caused Clare to refuse the title of abbess; it may also have been her concept of a superior as "servant and handmaid" which clashed with the Benedictine style of abbess as a person of great dignity and authority.

Although Clare had to accept the title, she exercised her native ingenuity in transforming its meaning to accord with her own and Francis' ideal that the superior should be among the members "as one who serves." Celano relates how she did this. "She never shrank from any menial task; most of the time she was the one who poured water on the hands of the sisters (at meals); it was she who made them sit down so she could serve them and she who brought them their meals."[13]

The only prerogative that Clare claimed as abbess was the right to be the handmaid of the other sisters. She designated herself in all her letters, not as "Clare, Abbess" but as "Clare, servant and handmaid," usually with the adjectives of "unworthy" or "useless." This was neither rhetorical humility nor un-healthy inferiority. Rather, Clare genuinely felt she could never do enough to express her esteem for her sisters and her profound affection for them. To serve them was her joy ... and they knew it! In this she corresponded exactly to Francis' ideal of a superior to whom he frequently applied the term "servant."

In Chapter V of the Earlier Rule which Francis composed, a Rule which most commentators consider as closest to expressing Francis' ideal way of life for the friars, he linked the words "minister and servant" not less than six times. He states his mind most clearly when he says: "Similarly, all the brothers in this regard should not hold power or dominion, least of all among themselves. For, as the Lord says in the Gospel: The rulers of the peoples have power over them, and their leaders rule over them; it shall not be like this among the brothers. And whoever among them wishes to become the greater should be their minister and servant."[14]

Elsewhere, Francis describes the office of superior as an appointment to wash the feet of the brothers.[15] That Clare took this mandate literally is attested to at least five times in the testimony the sisters gave before her canonization. Thomas of Celano in his biography dwells on the fact that Clare, as a matter of course "would wash the feet of the lay-sisters as they returned from without and then would kiss them."[16]

Sister Agnes tells that "once while washing the lay sisters' feet, wishing to kiss them as was her custom, one of the lay sisters accidentally hit her on the mouth at which Clare rejoiced and kissed the sole of that foot."[17] She added that this had occurred on a Thursday during Lent, probably early in Clare's religious life and before her long illness set in.

In medieval times foot washing was not just a courteous ritual but a strict necessity. The lay sisters who had been begging alms had walked barefoot through the muddy lanes of the countryside and the still more filthy streets of the city. All manner of refuse and garbage was habitually dumped from the windows of the town houses onto the narrow streets, there to mingle with the dung of animals.

One time when Clare was washing her feet, Agnes noted the joy radiating from her face as she tenderly bathed those soiled feet. Impulsively, Sister Agnes asked to drink the water that Clare was sloshing over her feet. When she did so, she found it to taste "indescribably sweet!" When Sister Agnes was later asked if any other sister had tasted it she said "no, for Clare had immediately thrown it away."[18]

Clare sought all possible ways to serve her sisters. Celano writes: "Only reluctantly would she give an order; she would rather do a thing of her own accord, preferring to perform a task herself than to bid others to do it."[19] Sister Pacifica, with a slight hint of exasperation, said: "When . . . Clare gave any command to the sisters she did so with much fear and humility, and nearly always she hastened to do herself what she ordered others."[20] Obedience at San Damiano needed to be spontaneous and quick if the sisters were not to find their task already done by their eager servant-mother!

One of the services that Clare especially cherished was taking care of the needs of the sick sisters. Regularly, she emptied the chamber pots from the infirmary. Sister Cecilia one day observed Clare washing them out and noted that there was even vermin in them. Perhaps Clare's smiling face startled Sister Cecilia for she asked how she could endure the odor. Clare replied that "she was not conscious of any evil smell but rather of fragrance."[21]

Sister Cecilia tried to summarize her impression of Clare as superior by saying: She "was most diligent in her exhortations to the sisters, as in her care for them and she had compassion on all who were infirm, being solicitous to serve them, submitting herself most humbly to the least lay sister, and always holding herself of no account."[22] Clare was learning to live for others so totally that she never felt she could do enough for them. According to Thomas of Celano who drew most of his information from the sisters themselves, Clare "did not love the souls alone of her daughters; she was also most thoughtful for their bodily welfare. Thus frequently in the cold of the night, she herself would cover the sleeping sisters."[23]

Clare also exercised that most difficult form of charity, namely, correcting her sisters whenever it seemed necessary for their welfare. Celano remarks: "In her cloister there was no place for lukewarmness or sloth, for a sharp reproof would stir up any languor in prayer and in the service of the Lord."[24] The manner in which Clare did this impressed itself deeply on the sisters. Sister Cecilia remembered that "she was never disturbed and taught the sisters with great benevolence and kindness, but when it was necessary she diligently reproved them."[25] Her reproofs, however, were given "with much grace and gentleness," according to Sister Angeluccia.[26]

In acting thus Clare was living out what she would later prescribe in her Rule: "The Abbess should admonish and visit her sisters and humbly and charitably correct them. . . . On her part, the Abbess is to be so familiar with them that they can speak and act toward her as ladies do with their servant. For that is the way it should be, that the Abbess be the servant of all the sisters."[27] These phrases are direct echoes of what Francis had written in his Rule about the relationship between the ministers and the friars.[28]

Even when a sister has committed some grave fault, Clare cautions the rest not to become upset or angry. The Abbess "should console those who are afflicted, and be, likewise, the last refuge for those who are disturbed; for, if they fail to find in her the means of health, the sickness of despair might overcome the weak."[29]

Thomas of Celano records that "when temptation troubled a sister or, as sometimes happens, sadness took hold of anyone,

[Clare] would call her secretly and console her amid tears. Sometimes she would throw herself at the feet of the sorrowing that by motherly consolation she might allay their grief."[30] It was Sister Agnes of Messer Oportulo who remarked that "she saw several whom Clare had thus consoled" and added that one of them, Sister Illuminata of Pisa, told her that their "mother had thrown herself on the ground at her feet."[31]

"The sisters were not insensible to such favors, and repaid her with entire devotedness," records Celano.[32] The budding religious life at San Damiano already bore resemblance to the fully formed ideal Clare would later express in her Testament: Loving one another with the Charity of Christ, let the love you have in your hearts be shown outwardly in your deeds so that, compelled by such an example, the sisters may always grow in love of God and in charity for one another."[33]

Scarcely conscious of it, Clare was inspiring her young community to live on the heights of supernatural charity with natural and joyous ease. She did this simply because she kept "her eyes fixed on Jesus" the Suffering Servant and her Lord.[34]

Clare's ideal of serving the Lord in others is actually an expression of her poverty. She was fascinated by the Great King of heaven who "made himself poor, although he was rich, in order that, by his poverty, [we] might become rich."[35] She saw this poverty and renunciation of Jesus as a way of putting himself at the service of others. "For the Son of Man also has not come to be served but to serve and to give his life as a ransom for many."[36] The fact that Jesus looked upon poverty as a means of service for others made it incumbent on Clare to do likewise.

If she praised poverty so highly, it was because she saw it not as a separate virtue but as a comprehensive disposition of the whole person. It comprised for her the quintessence of Christian charity. As a Franciscan writer expressed it: Poverty "is a renunciation of self, a total emptying like that of Our Lord's in order to be filled with the Spirit of love, the Spirit of God, and to become an instrument of grace through which this Spirit will be able to achieve the happiness of our neighbor."[37]

Poverty, humility, and service are so bound up with each other that they become a single expression of a soul striving to be like Jesus. For Clare there does not seem to be a problem of striving to cultivate individual virtues. Rather she seems to have been moved by the Spirit within her who oriented her toward service, of her own sisters first of all and, through them, of the whole Body of Christ.

Scarcely two days of mourning for Innocent III elapsed when Clare and the sisters at San Damiano are startled by a joyous peal of all the bells of Assisi. The Church of God already had a new shepherd, Honorious III, the former Cencio Savelli. The speed of his election is due in no small part to the citizens of Perugia. As soon as the death of Innocent was announced, they made it known that all the Cardinal-electors then present in their city were to be locked in for a conclave as soon as the funeral rites were concluded. They were to receive diminishing rations of food as the days went by. Under such conditions, the electors found it expedient to act with unprecedented haste. Cardinal Savelli was already an old man and was probably elected as an interim Pope until the electors would have opportunity to deliberate more freely. To the surprise of many, Honorious was to reign for eleven vigorous years.

Without doubt Francis was in Perugia during these momentous days and, according to some authorities, was even present at the death of Pope Innocent. The body was laid in state in the Cathedral of Perugia to await the funeral planned for the next day. A French prelate, Jacques de Vitry, arriving in Perugia to receive his episcopal consecration, learned that Innocent had died that very morning. He remained to attend the funeral and await the election of a new Sovereign Pontiff. What he saw shocked him profoundly. In a letter to friends back in France, he wrote: "That was the day when I really understood the nothingness of earthly grandeur. Incredibly, the preceding night, thieves had entered and stripped the Pope of everything of value he had on. With my own eyes, I saw his half-naked body lying in the middle of the church, already smelling."[38] There is a legend that Francis stole into the cathedral after this desecration and with deep compassion removed his own rough tunic to cover the nakedness of his father in Christ.

A few weeks after Honorius' election, Francis sought and obtained an audience with him. The kindly old man on the Chair of Peter won Francis' deep affection at once. Honorius was known to be a man of genuine piety as well as of compassion for the poor to whom he had given almost all of his personal fortune. Francis, accompanied by Brother Masseo, approached the Holy Father with the freedom and simplicity of beloved sons for Francis came bearing a message for the Pope from the Lord himself.

The previous night Francis had had a dream in which he begged Our Lord, through the intercession of the Blessed Virgin, that everyone who visited the Portiuncula chapel might obtain a plenary indulgence of all their sins and of the punishment due to them. Christ had directed Francis to go to the Pope to have this favor approved.

Honorious and his courtiers may have listened with some astonishment to Francis' bold request for such an indulgence was rarely given and then usually under very difficult conditions, such as going on a Crusade. Honorious must have been impressed with the sincerity of Francis who said simply that he had been sent by Jesus Christ himself. He granted the requested indulgence but limited it to one day each year, on August 2, that being the date of the dedication of the restored chapel.

It is difficult for us to realize what a stir this great pardon created among the people of the time. Francis expressed it best by announcing, "I desire to send you all to paradise!" Was it possible for the Poor Ladies to go to the Portiuncula to avail themselves of this wonderful privilege? We don't know for certain. At this time the formal laws of enclosure did not bind the San Damiano community. A few years later Francis would invite Clare to a meal at the Portiuncula and she would consent to go. But this episode has been challenged. Even if it did occur, it was noted as a great exception to Clare's usual mode.

Whether or not Clare and her sisters did actually go to St. Mary of the Angels, they most certainly knew about this marvelous privilege and shared Francis' deep jubilation. Pilgrims came from near and far so that the words of the dedication liturgy proved prophetic: "And when strangers come from distant lands to pray here, listen to them, O Lord, and send them away forgiven."[39]

The group of Lesser Brothers attracted to Francis and embracing his ideals was becoming a recognized and respected community within the Church. Recruits were flocking to him, and he received them with tender and grateful joy. Unknown to Clare, the life of the Poor Sisters, also, was becoming known farther and farther abroad. The time was at hand when Clare's daughters would begin to leave San Damiano and establish themselves all over Europe. A most valuable testimony to the impact that their hidden lives exerted on others is found in a letter which Jacques de Vitry wrote in the fall of 1216.

> [In the midst of this corruption] I nonetheless found consolation in seeing great numbers of men and women who renounced all their possessions, and left the world for the love Christ: "Friars Minor" and "Sisters Minor," as they are called.
>
> They are held in great esteem by the Lord Pope and the cardinals. They are totally detached from temporal things and have but one passion to which they devote all their efforts: to snatch from the vanities of the world souls that are in danger and to prevail upon them to imitate their example. Thanks to

God, they have already achieved important successes and made numerous conquests. Those who have heard them, say to their friends, "Come along!" and so one group brings another. As for the brothers themselves they live the life of the primitive Church of which it is written: "The whole group of believers was united, heart and soul" (Acts 4:32). During the day they go into the cities and villages, giving themsleves over to the active life of the apostolate; at night they return to their hermitage or withdraw into solitude to live the contemplative life.

The women live near the cities in various hospices and refuges; they live a community life from the work of their hands but accept no income. The veneration that the clergy and the laity show toward them is a burden to them and it chagrins and annoys them."[40]

Chapter IX Endnotes

1. Second Letter to Agnes of Prague, #18.
2. Lk 16:8.
3. Testament of Clare, #12.
4. Legend of Celano, #14.
5. See Letters and Testament of Clare.
6. Privilege of Poverty, 1–3.
7. Ibid., #4.
8. Ibid.
9. Ibid., #5.
10. Ibid., #5.
11. Legend of Celano, #12.
12. Cause of Canonization, Wit. 1, #6.
13. Legend of Celano, #12.
14. Earlier Rule of Francis, Ch. 5, #9–11.
15. Admonition IV.
16. Legend by Celano, #12.
17. Cause of Canonization, Wit. 10, #6.

18. Ibid., Wit. 10, #11.
19. Legend of Celano, #12.
20. Cause of Canonization, Wit. 1, #10.
21. Ibid., Wit. 6, #7.
22. Ibid., Wit. 6, #2.
23. Legend of Celano, #38.
24. Ibid., #20.
25. Cause of Canonization Wit. 6, #4.
26. Ibid., Wit. 14, #4.
27. Rule of Clare, Ch. X, #1, 3.
28. See Chap. 10, Later Rule of Francis.
29. Rule of Clare, Ch. IV, #9.
30. Legend of Celano, #38.
31. Cause of Canonization, Wit. 10, #5.
32. Legend of Celano, #38.
33. Testament of Clare, #18.
34. Heb 3:1.
35. 2 Cor 8:9.
36. Mk 10:45.
37. Heribert Roggen O.F.M. *The Spirit of St. Clare,* trans. Paul Joseph Oligny (Chicago: Franciscan Herald Press, 1971), p. 24.
38. Jacques de Vitry, Letter of 1216 in *Omnibus,* p. 1608.
39. 1 Kg 8:41–44.
40. Letter cited.

X   Scattering Embers

With a start, Clare realizes that Francis is studying her intently. She blushes and stirs uneasily. As a rule Francis never raises his eyes when addressing the sisters. But now he is scanning her face with an expression of troubled concern in his eyes. Most of the sisters have already left the parlor radiant with the contagious joy that always permeates Francis' exhortations. Perhaps because he comes less often now his words to them seem to have more power and fire.

Five years have passed since he first brought Clare and Agnes to San Damiano, and he is delighted and consoled to observe the growing fervor and number of Clare's sisters. He has begun to reduce the frequency of his visits to San Damiano, stepping into the background as he sees the Divine Bridegroom leading the sisters so strongly by his Spirit. Clare is proving to be a wise and vigilant mother to her sisters, leading them to embrace Lady Poverty with simple joy and humility. But in one area Clare seems to be notably lacking in prudence. Francis' visit today is the result of a talk with Bishop Guido about this matter.

Somehow Guido learned of the fasts which Clare was imposing on herself and he heartily disapproved. Could Sister Pacifica or Sister Agnes in their distress over the severity of Clare's abstinence, have appealed to him? We don't know for certain. Sister Pacifica has admitted that "the sisters were made sad and lamented over Clare's fasting."[1] Their own remonstrances had had no effect on her. Possibly in their concern as they saw their young abbess growing paler and thinner, they had turned to the fatherly Guido.

Guido, in turn, had summoned Francis and apparently told him that he, as Clare's spiritual guide, must put a stop to such extremes. "For a long time," Pacifica says, "Clare never ate on three days of the week, namely, Monday, Wednesday, and Friday. Even on the other days, her abstinence was so great that she became ill."[2]

Now Francis is troubled as he notes Clare's pallor and the hollows in her cheeks, once so full and rosy. The few remaining sisters, among them Pacifica, Benvenuta, and Agnes, now look expectantly at Francis who is groping for words to introduce the subject of Clare's penances. Perhaps he asks her to detail her usual practices. Clare does so simply, adding that since the sisters do not have to endure the hardships the brothers meet with on the road, they make up for this lack by extra fasting and penance.

Francis listens. He who had once led her to the decision to make "a temple of her body and to strive by virtue to be worthy of the espousals of the Great King"[3] now reminds her that St. Paul has written that since "your body is a temple of the Holy Spirit . . . you are not your own. You have been purchased and at a price!"[4] On firm ground now Francis charges her with disrespect for this temple. Gently but firmly he orders her, as Bishop Guido had commanded him, "to eat something every day."[5] To Pacifica's infinite relief, Francis then specifies that Clare is "to eat half a roll on those days when she was wont to fast entirely (a half-roll weighed about one and one-half ounces)."[6]

Clare's obedience is simple and complete. Sister Benvenuta later testified that from then on "she obediently took a little bread and water" every day.[7] In fact Clare took this command so seriously that until her death, it would require only a reminder that she may not pass a day without eating for her to cheerfully comply. Once a sister even roused her from a profound ecstasy with this simple injunction.

Clare's spontaneous obedience indicates how genuine were the motives that inspired her penances. All she desired was to serve her Lord and to make of herself an acceptable "sacrifice of praise." To do so by obediently eating a roll was as pleasing to her as to do so by abstaining. Bishop Guido's kindly intervention did not come soon enough or extend far enough, however, for Celano informs us that "such severity maintained over a long period of time made Clare subject to infirmities, consumed her strength and undermined her bodily vigor."[8]

Clare, in her youthful enthusiasm, had erred seriously and for the rest of her life she would bear the consequences. But she was a woman who could learn from her mistakes. The unusual moderation and thoughtful consideration for the sick, the overburdened, the very old or the very young which we find in her Rule is proof of how fully she profited from this hard lesson. God had permitted her to discover that even sacrifice must be "seasoned with wisdom." It is also possible that for one who possessed as strong and ardent a character as Clare, God chose this way to inculcate a prudence which, as a foundress, she would need in abundance. Everything that Clare later wrote and taught on the subject of bodily mortification witnesses that she did learn her lesson, thoroughly and humbly.

It is May of 1217 and the Umbrian valley is filled with the steady tramp of sandaled friars assembling for the Pentecost Chapter. From the little terrace at San Damiano, Clare can see groups of gray-robed men coming along the dusty pink roads. She marvels at the astonishing number of brothers who are gathering this year around Francis at the Portiuncula. Over two thousand of them, rumors say. And Clare knows that Francis has made no provision for them.

In the Fioretti we find a description of a typical Chapter gathering on the plain near St. Mary of the Angels. Cardinal Hugolino, witnessing the growing numbers arrive, returned to the Papal Court which was resident in Perugia, with such enthusiasm that soon "many people came to see (the gathering) from the Pope's entourage . . . and from other parts of the Valley of Spoleto. Many counts, barons, knights, and other noblemen and many plain people; cardinals, bishops, and abbots with other members of the clergy flocked to see this very holy and large and humble gathering of so many saintly men, such as the world had never seen."[9]

What they beheld was "the friars sitting about on the plain in groups of sixty or a hundred or two or three hundred . . . so quiet and meek that there was no sound or noise."[10] When Francis spoke to them he seemed in a state of exaltation which touched and uplifted all present. They were ready to obey his express command "to concentrate only on praying and praising God. And leave all your worries about your body to Christ because he takes special care of you."[11] We may wonder if a smile of delight crossed Clare's face when this was reported to her by some shocked listeners who felt it a grave imprudence not to allow a single friar in that huge crowd of men to take thought for providing the necessities of life. But a miracle of unsolicited bounty soon filled the valley.

"It soon happened that [God] inspired the people of Perugia, Spoleto, Foligno, Spello, Assisi, and all the surrounding country to bring food and drink to that holy assembly. And all of a sudden men came from those places with many donkeys, mules, and wagons loaded with bread and wine, beans and cheese, and all other good things to eat which they thought those blessed poor men of Christ would need and could use. Moreover they brought large and small pitchers and glasses and tablecloths and other things which such a crowd would need. And you could see the knights and noblemen who came to the meeting gladly and humbly . . . serving. You could see members of the clergy faithfully and eagerly running around everywhere like servants. You could see young men serving with so much reverence that it seemed as if they served, not the poor friars, but the apostles of our Lord Jesus Christ."[12]

Most likely Clare kept in close touch with all that was happening at the Chapter. This year Francis recognizes that the huge number of brothers requires that some elements of organization be introduced. Accordingly, he divides the Order into geographical provinces. After much prayer Francis has decided that to help preserve the brotherly equality which he prizes so highly, he will give the various superiors titles which will indicate clearly that they are to be at the service of the brothers, not in power over them. Thus he names them ministers, custodians, and guardians.

We may believe that Clare's habitual reference to herself as "handmaid" and "servant" of the Poor Sisters is another example of her adaptation of Francis' ideals to the Poor Ladies.

The most exciting development at this Chapter, however, is Francis' announcement that he desires to send friars to preach outside of Italy. These are to be the first organized missions beyond the Alps. However, Francis refuses to appoint men for this new venture, for he prefers only volunteers who will go freely to lands where the customs, language, and dress are wholly strange to them. They are to go without provisions, without written authorizations, without any protection, to people who have not asked for them or even heard of them. Francis himself is the first to volunteer, choosing to go to his cherished France.

Eagerly other brothers volunteer for various countries, many hoping perhaps for that ultimate glory which the medieval world so highly prizes, martyrdom. Martyrdom they would not attain, but in its stead they would encounter suspicion, insults, scourgings, and near starvation.

Cardinal Hugolino, whom Francis joyfully met in Florence, sharply rebuked him for sending his brothers out in such a manner that they were certain to be taken for heretics. This, it seemed to Hugolino, was not gospel foolishness but outright stupidity in an age when anyone who did not carry credentials from the Church would be automatically seized and imprisoned.

Hugolino forbade Francis to leave Italy at a time when his Order was still in danger of being suppressed if certain factions in the Curia chose to take advantage of his absence.

The Cardinal proved correct when he foresaw that the brothers would have a very poor reception among strange people if they could not prove by written attestations from Rome that they were truly Catholic. Some bishops did not allow them to preach in their dioceses. And the ordinary people who were very distrustful of these strangely dressed men often mistook them for heretics. They refused to give them food and drove them from their towns.

Back in Italy Cardinal Hugolino had to exercise all of his considerable influence in the Curia to prevent the Friars Minor from being disbanded or, at least, censured. This handsome, robust, and articulate prelate had become a close collaborator of Honorius III after his election in 1216. He owed his early career to Innocent III whose nephew he was and whose ideas he wholeheartedly endorsed. He most probably had become acquainted with Francis through Innocent and he soon came to share the Pontiff's belief that the true reform of the Church rested more on men like Francis than on either crusades or ecclesiastical thunderbolts.

Hugolino had been named Cardinal-Bishop of Ostia in 1206, but spent most of his time at the Papal Court. He was a man of energy and a skilled politician but also a man of deep piety who led a personally austere life. His soul was attuned to mystic inspiration, and his heart was warm and loyal. Hugolino was a man who could fully appreciate Francis and his ideals. But he could also see what Francis could not. That if his great dream was to endure, it required support born of prudent planning and a carefully clarified rule.

Francis instinctively trusted that Hugolino had the true interests of his Order at heart and asked him to be a Father-Protector for the friars. This delicate task Hugolino fulfilled to the best of his considerable ability. If at times he scolded Francis or tried to check and control the wild-fire growth of the Order, it was only because he felt this necessary to preserve the genuine spirit of Francis' vision.

He venerated the divinely inspired dream that burned in Francis and esteemed Francis' fidelity to his call but this did not blind Hugolino to Francis' shortcomings as an administrator and legislator. Thus when he was appointed in 1218 to be the Cardinal-Protector of the Poor Ladies, he was not greatly surprised to find that their rule of life was as inadequate (to his mind) as that of the friars.

Hugolino's first act on behalf of the sisters at San Damiano was to obtain for them exemption from episcopal jurisdiction. This meant that the Poor Ladies would be directly subject to the Holy See rather than to a local bishop. It also made it possible for foundations of Poor Ladies to be made anywhere in the Catholic world. When Clare first learned of Hugolino's appointment, quite probably made at Francis' personal request, she was both gladdened and saddened. She was glad that her young community should have such a good and understanding friend who could help and protect them. But she was saddened because she foresaw that now Francis would withdraw even more from directing the affairs of the sisters. He would always be her own personal guide and his words would still be the leading inspiration for her way of life, but he was stepping aside from exercising authority over her community. Soon he would do the same with the friars, handing over to other men the role of highest superior. But first his heart would be torn by the dissensions and disunity which were breaking out among his own brothers.

The brotherhood had expanded so rapidly that very soon a large percentage of the new recruits had never met Francis personally and had never come into the orbit of his magnetic fervor. Francis was not a man who could exercise authority through others. When his brothers became too numerous for him to form personally, he would step aside, even as he was now doing with the Poor Ladies who were also on the verge of a remarkable expansion.

About this time, a Benedictine monastery at San Severino in the Marches of Ancona asked to adopt the way of life of the Poor Sisters at San Damiano. They thus would become the first community of Poor Ladies outside of Assisi. It was to this house that Francis would one day entrust the little lamb which he had rescued from among a flock of goats. The sisters tended it lovingly and from its fleece made a warm capuche for Francis.

Although Francis withdrew from any official position with regard to the Poor Ladies, he still recognized his "mandate (over them) in the spiritual order" and his very particular responsibility for his firstborn daughter, Clare.[13] There is a legend which delicately illustrates this concern.

One time while on a preaching tour far from Assisi, Francis found that his heart was oppressed with forebodings about his "Christian Sister" as he sometimes referred to Clare. He was worried, wondering if she were suffering or under some temptation. Perhaps the pressure which he knew was being brought to bear on her would be more than her gentle sex could withstand? Perhaps she was being forced to break her pact with Lady Poverty?

These thoughts tormented Francis, as he and Brother Leo walked through a wooded grove on a moonlit night. He did not speak of the cause of his sadness, but Brother Leo perceived that his father was suffering some great anguish. At length they came, weary and dusty, to an open well. Francis went up to it and stood for a long time gazing down into the depths as if fascinated by something in the water below. When he finally left the parapet of the well, he seemed transported with joy and began to walk on swiftly, singing and praising the Lord.

After a while, sensing the unvoiced perplexity of Brother Leo, he turned and asked him: "Brother Leo, what do you think I saw reflected in the water down in the well?"

"Did you not see the face of our sister, the moon, that is shining overhead?" responded Leo.

"No," replied Francis with a tender smile, "I saw there the face of our Sister Clare who I feared was suffering or was sorely oppressed. Instead, she was all peace and brightness. Because of this my heart is now at peace in her regard and I sing for joy in God our Savior."[14] Brother Leo, walking on behind Francis, saw him raise his hand toward the radiant moon surrounded by stars in the night sky as if to salute them.

At this time, 1218, Francis may indeed have had cause for concern about how Clare would be able to deal with a very difficult situation. Cardinal Hugolino began to interest himself very directly in the life of the Poor Sisters at San Damiano. There is no doubt that he esteemed them highly for their simple and austere life, so poor and yet so joyous. A letter, written to Clare after he had celebrated the Easter mysteries with them, bears eloquent testimony to this as well as to his fatherly and affectionate heart.

> To the beloved Sister in Christ and Mother of his salvation, the Lady Clare, Handmaid of Christ, Ugolino, miserable and sinful man and Bishop of Ostia, commends himself, all that he is and all that he can be.
>
> Dearest Sister in Christ! From that hour when the necessity of returning separated me from your holy conversation and tore me away from that joy of heavenly treasures, such bitterness of soul has overcome me, such abundance of tears and cruelty of sorrow, that unless at the feet of Jesus I had found the solace of His unchanging compassion, I fear I should have fallen into such straits that my spirit would perhaps have fainted away and my soul have melted within me. And with good reason, for, as the sorrow of the disciples was exceeding great when the Lord was taken from them and nailed to the gibbet of the

Cross, so I, being deprived of that glorious joy with which I discoursed with you on the Body of Christ when I was celebrating Easter with you and the other handmaids of Christ, am now rendered desolate by absence from you. And although hitherto I have known I was a sinner and always considered myself one, now that I have experienced the great worth of your merits and beheld the rigors of your Religion, I realize beyond all doubt that I am weighted down by the burden of so many sins and have offended the Lord of the whole universe in so many ways that I am not worthy to be admitted to the company of His elect and be freed from all earthly ties, unless your tears and prayers obtain me pardon for my sins. Therefore to you I entrust my soul and commend my spirit, as Jesus on the Cross commended His spirit to His Father, that on the day of judgment you may answer for me if you have not been zealous and concerned for my salvation. For I certainly believe that you will obtain from the Most High Judge whatever the insistence of your devotion and the flood of your tears demand.

The Lord Pope is not now coming to Assisi but I wish to seize the first opportunity of seeing you and your sisters. Greet the virgin Agnes, my sister, and all your sisters in Christ. Amen.[15]

Even when we take into account the high-flown style that was common to letter writing in the thirteenth century, this is an astonishing epistle from a high-ranking prelate to a young abbess of a scarcely established community. The warmth of affection, as well as the profound respect and trust in the power of Clare's prayers, is expressive of genuine love. One gains the impression that Hugolino's spiritual "Hearth" is the gray-stone convent clinging to the hillside below Assisi. His joy and refreshment, as well as his confidence of future mercy, were centered there.

Hugolino's almost filial trust in Clare, however, only rendered her position more delicate when she learned that he had personally written a Rule for her community. Obviously, Hugolino had decided that something must be done about the simple and naive "Way of Life" that Francis had given Clare as a basis for her community. Hugolino was a canonist and an experienced prelate who had seen many religious groups come to grief when they were not sufficiently strengthened by specific and clear rules. He loved and admired the Poor Ladies too much to allow this to happen to them. Furthermore he may have already been asked by the Benedictine nuns at Monticelli near Florence to be allowed to change their Rule for that followed by the sisters at San Damiano. "What Rule?" Hugolino may have wondered.

During his talks with Sister Clare, Hugolino had gained what he thought was a good picture of the customary manner of living of the young community. He admired and fully approved of it. He decided it would not be difficult to draft a Rule for them containing all the practices he had observed at San Damiano plus a few clarifications he felt necessary. He based this document on the Benedictine Rule, written in a precise and very detailed manner. This he presented to Clare.

We have no record of her reaction except that she categorically refused to live according to any of its prescriptions which contradicted the spirit of the "Forma Vitae" and the Privilege of Poverty which were the basis of the life of the Poor Ladies. It was not so much what Cardinal Hugolino put into the new Rule that bothered Clare as what he had left out. No mention whatever was made of perfect poverty and the document plainly presupposed that the nuns would own their own property. This struck at the very heart of the Franciscan renewal. Furthermore no reference to dependence on the friars was made, either implicitly or explicitly. Clare could not, indeed would not, concede her right to have the friars for the spiritual guides of her sisters.

Clare was a woman of great tact and, moreover, she greatly

loved Cardinal Hugolino for his fatherly kindness. Somehow, and it would be extremely interesting to know just how, she managed to make her feelings known to Hugolino without offending him and also, make her attitude of reverent obedience coincide with her refusal to accept all that the new Rule prescribed. The Cardinal had made some arrangements which were a consolation to Clare, as for instance, when he had obtained the privilege of exemption from episcopal control for the Poor Ladies. This indirectly reinforced their practice of poverty since the exemption held good only so long as the sisters remained without possessions which would require episcopal supervision.

Another point which gratified Clare and clarified the status of the Poor Ladies somewhat was that Hugolino had obtained from the Holy See the right for the Poor Ladies to be known as the Second Order of Francis. Hugolino's Rule did state that the sisters had the right to own nothing except their house and chapel which, while not quite the total dependence on providence that Clare desired, was still a step forward. She knew that Cardinal Hugolino's efforts were aimed solely at "enabling them to fulfill their divine vocation," and Clare was grateful.[16]

History has not left us an absolutely clear idea of what sort of solution Clare worked out with Hugolino, but a few things are evident. The sisters at San Damiano were not obliged to observe any part of the new Rule which clashed with the life they were already living. This applied especially to the practice of perfect poverty and dependence on the friars but may also have touched on such matters as the relationship of the abbess and the sisters, observances and usages that were more properly Benedictine regarding the allotment of manual work and probably the form of the Divine Office to be prayed, as well as the form of enclosure observed.

The Privilege of Poverty applied only to San Damiano, and Hugolino seemed to have considered this true also of Francis' pledge that he would always be "solicitous in word and in deed to cherish and take care of . . . his little plant."[17] Therefore, although Hugolino allowed the community of San Damiano to continue according to its own way of living, he made it mandatory that his Rule was to be observed in all other houses of the Poor Ladies. And so it was . . . for thirty years.

Francis could not have been much help to Clare in her struggle for he himself was being pressured by Hugolino to recognize that a way of life that was adequate for twelve men was not sufficient for several thousand. However, Hugolino would not do for Francis what he had done for Clare. Francis would have to write his own Rule. He promised to think it over.

About this time an incident occurred which highlights Francis' deep respect for Clare's holiness and the power of her prayers. One of the friars, Brother Stephano, went completely insane. "Francis sent him to the monastery of San Damiano in order that . . . Clare might sign him with the Cross," testified Sister Benvenuta. Apparently, all the sisters in the house flocked to the chapel when the poor Brother was brought in. Clare quite simply did what obedience asked of her. Then "the Brother slept for a while in the place where she [Clare] usually prayed. When he awoke, the sisters gave him a little something to eat, and he departed cured."[18]

By this act Francis indicated that he recognized a special grace for healing in Clare. We will hear more of this healing gift as the years pass. Confidently, Clare will invoke the gracious mercy of God on behalf of sick persons, both lay people and her own sisters. Her favorite method was to pray silently while marking the Sign of the Cross on the sufferer. The sisters, most of whom benefited from her healing touch at one time or another, strove to hear the words she said while doing this. Sister Pacifica admitted ruefully that they "were never able to make them out because Clare spoke very softly."[19]

Indirectly this incident of Brother Stephano's healing illustrates the fact that the regulations of enclosure, even as expressed in Hugolino's Rule, were not as specific as the rigid formulation which came into effect forty years after Clare's death.

This helps to explain how so many seculars, particularly the sick, could have direct contact with the nuns. This care for the sick and outcasts demonstrates in one more way Clare's manner of modeling the sisters' lives on that of the friars, whose first apostolate had been caring for lepers.

One spring, perhaps in 1219, a blow fell on Clare and Agnes which neither of them had anticipated. It came to them through Francis himself. It may have been Cardinal Hugolino who asked Francis to select some sister from San Damiano to be sent to the Benedictine community at Monticelli to introduce the nuns there to the life of the Poor Ladies. Francis' choice fell upon Agnes. She was stunned with grief. Leave San Damiano? Leave Clare? And all the other sisters with whom she had shared feasts and fasts, depths of prayer and heights of hilarity, work and silence for so many years? "I used to believe," she moaned, "that those who shared in one life and converse in heaven would share alike in death and life on earth, and that one sepulcher would enclose those who are one and equal by nature. But I see I am deceived."[20]

The sacrifice of separation which God had not asked of Clare and Agnes in the beginning of their religious life he asked of them now. They made it generously but not without deep pain. Holiness, far from making these two sisters indifferent to each other, had instead forged links of love between them that reached to the very center of their souls. Their very love for the Lord and the way of life which they had worked out together formed a unique bond between them. Each, simply by her presence, had encouraged and sustained the other. Francis' charism that shines so luminously in Clare burned no less brightly in Agnes. That was why Francis could send her off to a strange convent, taking with her the awkward Rule of Hugolino, with the confidence that Agnes could successfully implant the true spirit of the Poor Ladies there. Francis' trust was not misplaced. Agnes would succeed so admirably that she would be sent to found or instruct several other monasteries of Poor Ladies in the years ahead.

We know little about the personality and natural gifts of this younger sister of Clare. But from what we do know we may infer that she possessed the same strength of character and totality of devotion as Clare. She, too, has been recognized by the Church as having possessed heroic sanctity. Agnes may even have been more amply endowed with administrative gifts than her sister. She, at any rate, seems to have possessed a bit more prudence in matters of asceticism.

What we know with greatest certainty about Agnes is her profound and loyal love for Clare. The letter which she wrote to Clare soon after her arrival in Florence bears evidence through the centuries of how deeply and tenderly saints can love each other.

To her venerable Mother and excellent Mistress in Christ, the dearly beloved Lady Clare, and to her whole convent: Agnes, the humble and least servant of Christ, kneeling in all submission and devotion at her feet and petitioning for her whatever sweet and precious gifts the power of the Most High King can give.

Since the fate of every creature is such that it can never continue in the same state, when anyone therefore thinks himself to be in good fortune then he is plunged into adversity. Know, then, Mother, that in my body and soul there is great distress and overwhelming sorrow, and I am oppressed above measure and tormented and almost unable to speak because I am separated in body from you and from my other sisters with whom I had thought to live and to die in this world. This distress has indeed a beginning but it knows no end; never does it know surcease, but always gains increase; it has risen upon me recently but gives no promise of decline; it is always near me and never desires to be apart from me. I used to believe that those who share in one life and converse in heaven would share alike in death and life on earth, and that one sepulchre would enclose those who are one and equal by nature. But I see I am deceived; I am straitened, I am forlorn; I am in tribulation on every side.

My dearest sisters, be with me in my grief, I implore you; mourn with me, lest at some time you suffer like things, and see that there is no sorrow like to my sorrow (Lam 1:12). This sorrow torments me always, this homesickness ever plagues me, this fire ever burns within me. Because of this I am straitened on every side, and I know not what to choose. Help me, I implore you, by your pious prayers, that this burden may be made light and bearable for me. O sweetest Mother and Lady, what shall I do, what shall I say, for I have no hope of seeing you and my sisters again in the body! Oh that I could express my thoughts as I would! Oh that I could convey to you by this letter the sorrow that stretches out before me which I must ever face. My soul burns within me, tormented by the fire of intense suffering. My heart groans within me, and my eyes cease not to pour forth rivers of tears. I am filled with grief, my spirit is gone, I waste away. I find no consolation no matter where I seek; I feel grief upon grief, when I think in my heart that I can never expect to see you and my sisters again; and so in my sorrow I have completely lost heart. There is none to comfort me among all that are dear to me.

But on the other hand, I am greatly consoled, and you will be able to rejoice with me in this, that I have here found great unity of mind without the least division, far beyond what I could believe. All have received me with great joy and gladness and promised obedience to me with the greatest devotion and reverence. All these sisters recommend themselves to God and to you and your convent; and I recommend them and myself to you in all things and through all, that you may have in your heart a solicitous care for me and for them as your sisters and daughters, in the knowledge that they and myself desire to keep inviolate for the whole of our life your admonitions and precepts. In reference to these, you should know that the Lord Pope has agreed with me, as I said, and with you, in all things in accordance with your desire and mine concerning the question of property as you fully know (i.e., the Privilege of Poverty). I pray that you beg Brother Elias to take it upon himself to visit me often, very often, and console me in the Lord."[21]

A woman who knew that she did not have to deny her heart the right to love deeply, Agnes found her path to holiness in this very capacity of her nature. Her sensitivity became the instrument God would use to purify and anneal her sanctity. Her profound homesickness for Clare and San Damiano would follow Agnes the rest of her life as she obediently went from one monastery to another. Cardinal Hugolino would transfer her first to Verona in 1226 and after that, send her on to Mantua, Padua, and Venice.

The many letters which Clare must have written to Agnes during these years are lost, but we can be sure that they were no less affectionate in tone and content. To console her sister with whom, Celano attests, she was of "one heart and soul," Clare sent Agnes various objects from San Damiano.[22] Among these was her own veil which Agnes may have requested and which has been preserved at Monticelli since as a precious relic.

Agnes' circumspect reference to the Pope's "agreeing" with her about the observance of poverty at Monticelli arouses some interesting speculations. Did Agnes also manage to get around Cardinal Hugolino's Rule by obtaining some special arrangement for Monticelli similar to that for San Damiano? We cannot say for certain but it is unlikely that Agnes would be satisfied to inculcate a Rule which neither she nor Clare believed in.

These two sisters, so alike in their love for poverty, probably also shared equally in the feminine charm that could make even a Cardinal of the Church agree that his own Rule need not be observed where it was contrary to the original inspiration of the Order. Many more communities of Poor Ladies would soon come into existence and each would strive to live the ideals of Francis and Clare as best they could. All were autonomous, and it seems that Hugolino's Rule was not universally enforced which explains why, by 1247, another Pope would attempt to impose a uniform observance on all the Poor Ladies but with even less success than Hugolino.

In May 1219, the valley of Umbria was again a witness to a host of friars gathering for the Pentecost Chapter. This time the Breath of the Spirit was to scatter the hot embers of the Franciscan charism beyond the confines of the Christian world. Volunteers for the missions to non-Christian territories, inspired by the hope of martyrdom, came forward in great numbers, and Francis found great consolation in this display of zeal and self-sacrifice. The scene solaced him somewhat for the sorrow and hurt he had experienced when many of the brothers had asked that he change their Rule of life to make it more like that of other orders.

When Cardinal Hugolino had urged Francis to consider their suggestions, Francis had made no reply. Instead, "he took the Cardinal by the hand and led him before the friars assembled in Chapter. And he spoke to the friars in the fervor and power of the Holy Spirit, saying, 'My brothers, my brothers! God has called me by the way of simplicity and humility and has in truth revealed this way for me and for all who are willing to trust and follow me. So I do not want you to quote any other Rule to me . . . . or to recommend any other form of life except this way which God in His mercy has revealed and given to me. The Lord told me that He wished me to be a new kind of fool in this world and he does not wish us to live by any other wisdom but this. As for you, may he confound you with your wisdom and learning and make the ministers of his wrath compel you to return to your vocation should you dare to leave it!' "[23] Cardinal Hugolino, as well as all the friars, were deeply shaken by Francis' vehement condemnation and no more was said at this time about changing the Rule.

The great decision to send the brothers off to pagan lands rallied the friars and temporarily restored a sense of unity within the Order. Francis let Clare know that his chosen field would be the Near East where he hoped to meet and preach to the Sultan and perhaps visit the Holy Land if he did not receive martyrdom first. Clare wished him Godspeed with a heavy heart. She knew just how much the dissatisfaction among his brothers had hurt Francis and hoped that the challenge of this new mission would salve some of that pain. Within certain groups in the Order, however, dissension still smoldered, and Clare worried about what would happen while Francis, the only one capable of inspiring unanimity among the brothers, was far away. Would he, perhaps, even achieve his dream of a martyr's crown and not return at all?

Francis set sail from the port of Ancona in June, probably on a crusader's vessel which eventually put in at Acre. After that no news except insubstantial rumors reached Clare for more than a year. She endured exquisite torments of uncertainty about whether he was dead or alive, and also sorrowed to see what havoc was being wrought among the brothers during his absence. Overzealous ministers and provincials were beginning to take the simple and inspired way of life by which Francis had guided the friars and refashion it into a mitigated observance foreign to the spirit and will of Francis.

The Poor Ladies at San Damiano were given Brother Philip the Tall as their Visitor in the absence of Francis and for this Clare was sincerely grateful. It was Brother Philip who had often been Francis' companion during those idyllic days when Clare had first sought him out for guidance on living the gospel life.

Celano says of Brother Philip: "The Lord had touched his lips with a purifying coal, that he might speak pleasing things of him and utter sweet things. [He also gave him] understanding and interpreting of Sacred Scriptures, though he had not studied."[24]

We know that Clare delighted in a well-turned sermon and was always eager to have friars with a talent for preaching visit San Damiano and preach to the sisters. Brother Philip was probably one of the more frequent callers at her monastery and became a fast personal friend.

Another friend of Clare, Christiana di Suppo, entered the community about this time. This was the young house guest of the Favarone family who had witnessed the consternation of the family when Clare had secretly fled her paternal home to join Francis in 1212. Apparently Christiana had been so impressed by this event that seven years later she rejoined her friends, Clare and Agnes, in their joyous poverty at San Damiano.

The despoliation of the noble ranks of the Offreduccio family did not stop with Rufino, Clare, and Agnes. Daughters of their cousins also joined them. Because they bore the same names and are designated as nieces according to the custom of the times, some confusion surrounds their precise relationship to Favarone's daughters. Agnes was probably a daughter of one of Clare's first cousins on her father's side; Clare, designated as a grand-niece, may have been a more distant relative.

As the year 1219 drew to its close, Clare knew that the "honeymoon" days of her tryst with Lady Poverty under Francis' personal guidance were over and gone. A time of struggle but also of fruitfulness had opened, one which would endure until her death. Her way of life which she regarded as a gift from God through Francis was a treasure which would require a struggle unto death on her part to ensure that it would be transmitted in all its purity.

Even with the support and friendship of Cardinal Hugolino, Brother Philip, and the personable Brother Elias, Clare felt lonely and bereft. Agnes was no longer at her side, and Francis was somewhere in the East, alive she fervently hoped, but far from her reach except through prayer. From her little niche of a terrace, she frequently scanned the roads for messengers coming from the crusaders who were still besieging the walls of Damietta. They might be bringing news of Francis or perhaps they had even seen him.

Fervently, she laid siege to the Heart of the Crucified. Long were the hours she spent before that Crucifix which had spoken to Francis, summoning him to repair the Church of God. Months later she would learn that while she prayed in dark trust as the days of 1219 shortened, Francis was walking serenely into the midst of the Moslem camp and preaching the message of Christian redemption to the Sultan. Though he failed to convert the Moorish leader, he won the Sultan's respect. As a token of this, the Sultan granted Francis a safe-conduct to Jerusalem where he spent unforgettable hours praying in the same places where his Lord had prayed and died.

When he would finally return to Italy his eyesight would be dimmed by a disease contracted in the Orient. Home at last, his heart would be overshadowed by the havoc being done to his beloved Order. The sunlit years were now only a memory. The Lord was answering his prayer for martyrdom.

Chapter X Endnotes

1. Cause of Canonization, Wit. 1, #7.
2. Ibid., Wit. 1, #8.
3. Legend of Celano, #6.

4. 1 Cor 6:19–20.
5. Cause of Canonization, Wit. 2, #8.
6. Ibid., Wit. 1, #8.
7. Ibid., Wit. 2, #8.
8. Legend of Celano, #18.
9. Fioretti, #18.
10. Ibid.
11. Ibid.
12. Ibid.
13. Legend of Perugia, #76.
14. Piero Bargellini, *The Little Flowers of Saint Clare*, trans. Fr. Edmund O'Gorman O.F.M. Conv. (Padua: Messagero Editions, 1972) pp. 85–86.
15. Letter of Hugolino to Clare.
16. Constitutions of Hugolino.
17. Testament of Clare, #14.
18. Cause of Canonization, Wit. 2, #15.
19. Ibid., Wit. 1, #18.
20. Letter of Agnes to Clare, #2.
21. Letter of Agnes to Clare.
22. Legend of Celano, #24.
23. Mirror of Perfection, #68.
24. 1 Celano, #25.

XI Spirit-Fire

Tenderly Clare trails her fingers over leafy bushes as she makes her way through the green wood. Sunlight filtering through the thick crowns of oak and juniper creates shifting patterns on her path. A coolness lingers in the areas of deeper shade, a pleasant relief from the late summer heat. The year is 1220.

Brush and brambles twine among themselves, some heavy with berries which promise a feast for birds and the scurrying little creatures Clare hears but cannot spy. Her heart feels in harmony with this serene season just preceding harvest. The rush, struggle, and anxieties of growing time are past. The fruits of vineyard and field are assured for another year, and the land rests golden in the sun.

As Clare and her companion thread their way along the path which leads from San Damiano to the Portiuncula, Clare's heart is grateful for the peace she now has. Francis had returned from the East as one returning from the dead last June. Only after the messenger who had carried the glad news that Francis had landed safely at Venice had gone on his way, did Clare allow the tears of her immense relief to roll down her cheeks. He was alive! He was already in Italy and was traveling slowly toward Umbria, visiting his brothers as he passed from friary to friary.

Only later Clare recalled that the messenger had also mentioned infirmities—an eye affliction, stomach trouble, so weak he had to ride a donkey. Clare's elation dimmed. She could also foresee that Francis was not going to be received with total joy by all the brothers, particularly not by those who had, in his absence, devised a rule of life according to their own tastes. Had anyone forewarned him? Yes, she learned that Brother Stephen had traveled to Syria in search of Francis and acquainted him with the violence being done to the Order by his so-called vicars. Many of Francis' dearest companions were actually in hiding because of their protests about the changes which they felt were contrary to the spirit of the brotherhood.

Francis had boarded the first sailing vessel of the spring season and had landed in Italy on fire with zeal for the honor of Lady Poverty. His physical debility weighed heavily on him, though, and he had been forced to travel in easy stages.

Before Francis reached Umbria, Clare had heard of how he had forced the brothers, ensconced in a large and comfortable building at Bologna, to vacate the place at once. In his pain and anger he then cursed it together with its minister, Peter Staccia. Clare winced to think of the sorrow which drove him to this, and she longed to comfort his ravaged spirit, but what could she do or say? She turned her eyes again to the serene but sorrowing countenance of the Crucified Lord hanging in the chapel.

Francis passed by Assisi without even going near his beloved Portiuncula for he had no wish to encounter any more rebellious brothers. Humbly and sadly he took his problem to the Holy Father in Rome and begged Honorius III to appoint an arbiter and advisor for this brotherhood which had grown too large for him to manage. To Francis' vast relief, the Pope turned the delicate task over to Cardinal Hugolino. Only then did Francis turn his steps to the sanctuary of St. Mary of the Angels.

Clare had striven to conceal her dismay at the change in Francis' appearance when at last he had climbed the hill to visit her and the other Poor Sisters. His gaunt frame alarmed her, and she noted with pain how he now shielded his eyes from the sun as if the light he had always rejoiced in had now grown intolerable to him. Yet his voice when he greeted her was as full of tenderness and joy as it ever had been and Clare marveled to see the serenity that shown in the depth of his ravaged eyes. She attended eagerly to his descriptions of all he had experienced during his long absence, drinking in every word he said. Perhaps, as he was comforted and calmed by her quiet but intense interest, he opened his heart more than usual to share some of the more intimate moments of his pilgrimage to the Holy Places.

If Clare had hoped that Francis would now resume his frequent visits to San Damiano, she was disappointed. Even the friars wondered at the way Francis held himself aloof from the sisters, and some questioned him openly. Francis gravely replied: "Do not believe, dearest brothers, that I do not love them perfectly. For it if were a fault to cherish them in Christ, would it not have been a greater fault to have united them to Christ? . . . But I give you an example, that as I have done, so you also should do."[1]

Francis was slowly and painfully coming to the conclusion that he must hand over the government of his brothers to other men. He perceived that his role in the Order was to be one of inspiration and example rather than of administration. He did not like and, in fact, almost could not bring himself to wield the severe disciplinary actions that the present chaos in the Order seemed to require.

"My duty, my mandate, as superior of the brothers is of a spiritual order because I must repress vices and correct them. But if through my exhortations and my example I can neither suppress nor correct them, I do not wish to become an executioner who punishes and flogs. . . . Nevertheless, until the day of my death, I will continue to teach my brothers by my example and my life how to walk the road that the Lord showed me and which I in turn showed them, so that they may have no excuse before the Lord and so that later I may not have to give an account before God for them or for myself."[2]

Clare shared his anguish and longed to do something to comfort him and let him know that she understood. But he seldom came to the little monastery on the hillside. Although Clare knew his reasons, she suffered nonetheless from his absence. When she heard that Francis had resigned his office and had appointed Peter Catani as Vicar, she may have wondered if she would ever see him again. Francis had pleaded his poor health as reason for the resignation he tendered to the Chapter, but Clare well knew he was more sick at heart than sick in body.

Perhaps Brother Leo told her what Francis had confided to him: "When I realized that neither my advice nor my example could make them abandon the road on which they had embarked, I put the Order back in the hands of God and of the ministers. I relinquished my post and resigned, excusing myself at the general chapter because my sickness would not allow me to care for the brothers. And yet, if the brothers had walked and were still walking according to my will, I would prefer that they have no other minister but myself until the day of my death."[3]

Maybe it was Clare's urgent desire to find some way of solacing him that caused her to ask the favor of Francis of sharing a meal with him. But he always refused to permit this. Some of the brothers, probably those who were closest to Francis and Clare in the early days, took Clare's part. The Fioretti preserves the story:

> So it happened that his companions, perceiving Clare's desire, said to Francis: "Father, it seems to us that this strictness is not according to divine charity— that you do not grant the request of Sister Clare, a virgin so holy and dear to God, in such a little thing as eating with you, especially considering that she gave up the riches and pomp of the world as a result of your preaching. So you should not only let her eat a meal with you once, but if she were to ask an even greater favor of you, you should grant it to your little spiritual plant."
>
> Francis answered: "So you think I should grant this

wish of hers?" And the companions said: "Yes, Father, for she deserves this favor and consolation.

Then Francis replied, "Since it seems so to you, I agree. But in order to give her greater pleasure, I want this meal to be at St. Mary of the Angels, for she has been cloistered at San Damiano for a long time and she will enjoy seeing once more for a while the place of St. Mary where she was shorn and made a spouse of the Lord Jesus Christ. So we will eat there together in the name of the Lord.[4]

Now Clare smiles happily as she walks lightly along the leafy path. Even if she could not see the berries on the bushes and smell how dry the grass is, her ears would have told her that autumn is drawing near. Every so often an acorn plops to the earth around. The wind causes a dry rustling sound as it plays among the leaves overhead, very different from the silky whispers of fresh green leaves in spring. The drone of busy insects nearly drowns out the occasional chirps of unseen birds. Only the crows seem full of energy circling and cawing over the fields of goldening grain.

Clare quickens her steps while mulling over the many things she hopes to discuss with Francis. One topic surely will bring a joyful response from him and that is the news about the five friars who were recently martyred in Morocco. She herself had been profoundly moved when the report of their death at the hand of the Miramolin himself finally reached Assisi. In her exaltation, Clare startled her community by proposing to set out for Morocco herself in search of the same glorious fate. Only the tears of Sister Cecilia made her pause and reconsider her intention.[5]

When the facts of the friars' martyrdom had been relayed to Francis, he had exclaimed, "Now I can truly say that I have five Friars Minor!"

Francis meets Clare near the edge of the clearing which now

surrounds the Portiuncula chapel. He watches her with shy pride as she marvels over the arrangements of wattle huts which bear witness that Lady Poverty is still cherished and honored in this cradle of their Order. It seems to Francis that he had never really seen them as he does today through the radiant eyes of Sister Clare. Her presence is like a benediction, and suddenly Francis knows why it seemed so necessary to him to invite Sister Clare to St. Mary's. More than ever she personifies Lady Poverty, happily walking about in her rough gray habit and bare feet, marveling over every little detail.

Francis then leads Clare to the altar of the Virgin where she had knelt that wondrous night so long ago and had surrendered herself to Jesus with touching trust in Francis' vision. She appears even more radiant today than on that breathless spring night. A subtle quality bespeaking depth and serenity has taken the place of the ardent but untried resolve of the young Clare di Favarone. Gently and humbly he kneels at her side, both embraced by the smile of the Mother of God whose sanctuary this is.

Clare's bubbling laughter brightens the atmosphere of the place immeasurably, and for the moment Francis can forget his fears and distress and drink in the joy that underlies the surface upheavals. Again he recognizes that joy is the enduring reality, sadness only a passing shadow. Into the Rule he is writing, Francis will insert his reflection so strongly that it resembles an imperative: The brothers "must beware not to appear outwardly sad and like gloomy hypocrites; but let them show that they are joyful in the Lord and cheerful and truly gracious."[6] Seeking to raise the level of joy in the world was to be a part of their vocation.

"Francis has a table spread on the bare ground, as was his custom. And when it is time to eat, Francis and Clare sit down together, and one of his companions with Clare's companion, and all his other companions group around that humble table.

But at the first course, Francis begins to speak about God in such a sweet and holy and profound and divine and marvelous way that he himself and Clare and her companion and all the others who are at that poor little table are rapt in God by the overabundance of divine grace that descend upon them.

"After a long while, when Francis and Clare and the others come back to themselves, they feel so refreshed by spiritual food that they pay little or no attention to the material food."[7]

Completing the story of this marvelous picnic, the author of the Fioretti pictures all the people of the surrounding region alarmed by the sight of an immense conflagration consuming the entire place where the friars live. All able-bodied men rush to the rescue of the Portiuncula only to discover that the brilliance emanates not from material fire but from the fire of joy which blazes up in the friars and sisters. This embellishment demonstrates the medieval perception that genuine holiness is a light to the whole world, a consuming flame that purifies but does not destroy fragile human vessels.

The Fioretti concludes that when Clare returns to San Damiano "the sisters are very glad to see her, for they had feared that Francis might send her to direct some other monastery, as he had already sent her holy sister, Agnes, to be abbess of the monastery of Monticelli in Florence. For at that time Francis was sending sisters out to rule other monasteries. And he had once said to Clare: 'Be prepared, in case I have to send you somewhere else.' And she had replied like a truly obedient daughter: 'Father, I am always ready to go wherever you send me.' And so the sisters rejoice greatly when they have her back. Henceforth Clare is much consoled in the Lord."[8]

This allusion to Francis' sending sisters out to other monasteries could be a reference to a foundation at Reims made in 1220 by Marie de Braye. Several sisters from Assisi had journeyed to France to form the nucleus of this first convent of Poor Ladies outside of Italy. The next few years would witness houses of Poor Ladies springing up in numerous places on the Italian peninsula as well as in France, Austria, Hungary, Poland, Spain, and Bavaria.

In his poetic style, Celano summarizes this prodigious growth: "Meanwhile that this rivulet of heavenly blessing which had sprung up in the valley of Spoleto might not be confined within such narrow boundaries, it was turned into a broad stream that 'the stream of the river might make joyful the whole city' of the Church. For the news of such things spread far and wide in the world and everywhere began to gain souls for Christ. Clare remained enclosed, yet she began to enlighten the whole world and became a shining example in the praise of all.... Cities without number were enriched with monasteries and even the open country and the mountain tops were graced with such heavenly buildings."[9]

Such an abundant outpouring of grace did not go unopposed by the powers of darkness. Clare, situated at the very center of this upsurge of spiritual vitality spent many a dark and painful hour oppressed, harrassed, and tempted by the evil one. Clare had to cling with desperate courage to her Lord in blind faith while a diabolical intelligence probed her spirit, searching for that weak point, that tiny spot of vanity or self-reliance which would afford him a foothold with which to scale her protecting walls of prayer and bring crashing down the edifice of her holiness. It seems that Clare's frequent tears of love and compassion were particularly irritating to him. He chose his hour carefully and approached the young abbess while she was praying and weeping alone in the chapel. Celano records: "Once in the dead of night, as she was weeping, the angel of darkness stood by her, saying: 'Weep not so much for you shall become blind.'"

Perhaps he conjured up the image of Francis with his painfully inflamed eyes, groping helplessly through the world. Clare refused to be frightened and replied succinctly: "He will not be blind who shall see God." The tempter departed in confusion but only for the moment.

The story continues: "The same night after Matins, as Clare was praying and bathed in tears as usual, the deceitful counselor came again. 'Weep not so much,' he said, 'for your brain will soften and flow out through your nose; for sure, you will have a twisted nose.' " One wonders if Clare was struggling with laughter at this ridiculous picture for when she spiritedly responded, "He suffers no injury who serves the Lord," the devil made off miffed.[10]

But the evil one did not consider this the end of the contest. Finding that he could not appeal to Clare's vanity, he employed more direct tactics. We read in the Legend: "Once when Clare was praying in her little cell at the hour of None (about 3:00 P.M.), the devil gave her a blow on the cheek that made her eyes bloodshot and her face covered with bruises."[11] He was unwittingly answering her prayer "that she might be immolated as a victim with her sacrificed Lord." Clare could prove that "for those who love God all things work for good."

There were many things which did not at all appear to be working for the good of the Franciscan family during this period. In his zeal to protect the Poor Ladies, Brother Philip had obtained a Bull of Excommunication against anyone attacking his protégés. This was so contrary to Francis' way of thinking that after his return from the East, he had Brother Philip removed from his office of Visitor for the Poor Ladies, and the Bull was annulled. Brother Philip learned his lesson and when, years later, he was reappointed as Visitor, he filled that role with humble and admirable devotion.

While Francis sets himself to the nearly impossible task of composing a Rule that upholds his ideals and is legally correct and is acceptable to his diverse family, Clare struggles to accommodate Hugolino's Rule and directives with the life of the Poor Ladies. Pope Honorius also is debating a thorny question. Should he proceed to crown Frederick II as Holy Roman Emperor? Frederick has accomplished the subjugation of Sicily and claimed its iron crown and has also consolidated his sovereignty over the various German states north of the Alps. This leaves the Papal States as a sort of buffer region between Frederick's lands to the south and his fiefdoms in the north. It is not a pleasant prospect to consider what Frederick might do next in his drive to unite his separate kingdoms.

If he were crowned Emperor, one of his primary obligations would be to protect the sovereignty of the Papal States and to safeguard the Holy Father's independence from foreign domination. Honorius finally opts to give Frederick the imperial dignity in exchange for solemn pledges on Frederick's part to uphold the prestige of the Holy See, to come to the aid of the Papal States whenever need would arise, and to make good on his oath to take the Crusader's Cross and recover the Holy Land.

After Frederick is crowned, the German princes grow bolder and once again move into northern Italy to reclaim fiefs that had been lost to them during the ascendency of Innocent III. However, many of the communes of this mettlesome section have tasted the heady wine of independence and are in no mood to allow their former overlords to simply move in and start bleeding their fair land as before. The countryside, as a result, becomes a scene of continual ferment and frequent military skirmishes.

Despite the "wars and rumors of wars" that rumble back and forth across the land, the silent, invincible work of the Holy Spirit proceeds in peace.

Chapter XI Endnotes

1. 2 Cel., 205.
2. Legend of Perugia, #76.
3. Ibid., #76.
4. Fioretti, #15.
5. Cause of Canonization, Wit. 6, #6.
6. Earlier Rule Ch. 7, #16.

7. Fioretti, #15.
8. Ibid., #15.
9. Legend of Celano, #11.
10. Ibid., #19.
11. Ibid., #30.

XII Banked Embers

Two men stride up through the vineyards and olive groves toward San Damiano. The taller, dressed in a white habit which contrasts sharply with his swarthy skin and dark eyes, bends his head to listen to the vivacious, gray-robed friar at his side. On this June day in 1221, Dominic and Francis are glad to leave the contentious atmosphere of the Chapter at St. Mary's and pay a call on Sister Clare.

Dominic is eager to meet this woman about whom he has heard much. He has noted a curious shyness tinged with reverence in Francis' voice whenever he speaks of Clare, and it intrigues him. Now Dominic notices that Francis seems to approach the small stone monastery as if it were the castle of his liege lord and Clare, the chatelaine whose honor and interests he is vowed to protect.

As the two men pass a small hut at the foot of the garden, Dominic feels his spirit enfolded by a marvelous tranquillity. A great serenity lies over the simple garden of vegetables which is accented here and there by poppies and what was later called Queen Anne's lace. The subtle fragrance of herbs, thyme, basil, and rosemary, which are growing in stone pots, cleanses the air and mingles with the silence which lies like a benediction over the small compound.

Approaching the chapel entrance, Dominic and Francis hear the soft cadences of chanted psalms. For a brief moment, Francis poises on the threshold as if drinking in great draughts of the heart-easing peace. The harmony of creation, lost since the primeval sin, seems wondrously restored here where everything sings in trustful praise to the Good Giver of all good gifts.

Francis and Dominic descend into the dim chapel where Francis sinks wearily to the floor. The sisters who are chanting in their small choir to the left of the sanctuary are not visible to the two friars. The tensions of recent days aroused by the friction over his Rule have rubbed Francis' spirit raw, but now he feels as if a soothing hand were laid upon his aching heart. Perhaps it is in this chapel of many graces that there occurred the incident preserved by Celano:

> "For once when Francis was disturbed . . . and thus distressed gave himself over to prayer, he brought back this rebuke from the Lord: 'Why are you disturbed, little man? Did I not place you over My Order as its shepherd, and now do you not know that I am its chief protector? . . . I have called, I will preserve and feed, and I will choose others to repair the falling away of some. . . . Do not be disturbed, therefore, but work out your salvation, for though the order were reduced to three in number, it will by my grace remain unshaken.'" This tender assurance assuages all of Francis' anxieties and from now on he can say with conviction born of experience "that the deepest darkness can be dispersed by even a single ray of light."[1]

Dominic, kneeling close to his friend, senses that serenity and joy have returned to him. Francis' face is alight as he smiles at the Crucifix with the delight of a child receiving his father's caress. Francis almost laughs aloud, marveling at his own foolishness in ever thinking the future of the friars rested on his own thin shoulders.

Dominic Guzman's arrival at St. Mary's had given Francis not only pleasure but much needed encouragement. Dominic himself has recently gone through the troubles involved in developing a Rule for his Friars Preacher that would be acceptable to his own men and also to the Church. Dominic had had to return to France after the Lateran Council with the scroll of his Rule still tucked under his arm. After more debate, thought, and prayer, he and his men had settled on the simple, flexible Rule of St. Augustine as the basis for their Constitutions. Returning to Rome the following year, Dominic had known the reward of his labors by seeing this new redaction receive the approval of the Holy See.

Some time after this, Dominic and Francis had met each other in the house of Cardinal Hugolino. Possibly at Hugolino's initiative, Dominic had affectionately taken Francis' hands into his own and proposed: "Brother Francis, I wish that your Order and mine might be made one and that we might live in the Church according to the same Rule."[2]

There was something to be said in favor of such a merger for the Friars Preacher and Friars Minor shared a similar inspiration. By living in strict poverty, traveling about lightly in order to preach the Good News to all people, begging when the need arose, the members of these two Orders formed a style of religious life that was essentially new in the Church.

Despite the administrative advantages which Hugolino saw in such a union, Francis courteously but firmly declined to consider such a step. His brothers strove to speak the Word of God to the poor and spiritually neglected people of the countryside and villages. Dominic's followers, on the other hand, were concentrating on combating heretical trends by upholding Truth through skillful and learned debates with the heretics. Although both groups taught more eloquently through their poor and humble ways of life than by their words, Francis may have perceived how conflicts would arise over matters such as study and preparation for their respective apostolic callings. Moreover, most of Dominic's men were priests, while at this time the majority of Francis' followers were laymen. Instinctively, Francis recognized that both Orders had something unique to offer the

Church which would be better preserved if each retained its own identity.

Already stresses and strains were arising among Francis' brethren over the need for study and a university education. Francis had a very high regard for learned men and gladly and courteously received such men into his brotherhood. But he also entertained a certain apprehension that a too one-sided pursuit of scholarship could lead to an intellectual elitism that was the very antithesis of his conception of a true Lesser Brother.

When a few years later he would receive a request from a particularly loved and esteemed brother to teach theology to some of the younger men, Francis would express his mature attitude regarding scholarship. He wrote: "Brother Francis [sends his] wishes of health to Brother Anthony, my bishop. It pleases me that you teach sacred theology to the brothers, as long as—in the words of the Rule—you 'do not extinguish the Spirit of prayer and devotion' with study of this kind."[3]

Francis was quite clear in his own mind about the priorities to be fostered among his men. When Cardinal Hugolino suggested naming bishops and prelates from among the more exemplary followers of Francis and Dominic, Francis responded with a quiet but emphatic description of the proper place and role of his friars.

> Lord, my brothers are called minors so that they will not presume to become greater. Their vocation teaches them to remain in a lowly station and to follow the footsteps of the humble Christ, so that in the end they may be exalted above the rest in the sight of the saints. If [he continued with the wisdom born of holiness] you want them to bear fruit for the church of God, hold them and preserve them in the station to which they have been called, and bring them back to a lowly station, even if they are unwilling. I pray you, therefore, Father, that you by no means permit them

to rise to any prelacy lest they become prouder rather
than poorer and grow arrogant toward the rest.[4]

Dominic had replied to Hugolino's proposal with the observation that the dignity of preaching the word of God as a Friar
Preacher was honor enough for his sons. The mendicant orders
were not founded to supply the Church with prelates but to
bring the glad tidings of the gospel to every person by living as
nearly like Jesus as they could.

Cardinal Hugolino could appreciate the supernatural wisdom
which inspired these answers and did not press the issue with the
two founders. As Dominic and Francis were about to leave, he
witnessed a display of the sincere affection and esteem that existed between them. It is recorded by Thomas of Celano in this
manner: "As they left . . . Dominic asked Francis to kindly give
him the cord he wore about his waist. Francis was reluctant to do
this, moved by the same humility to refuse as the other was
moved to ask. Finally, however, the blessed devotion of the peti-
tioner won out and Dominic very devoutly put the cord that was
given him about himself beneath his inner tunic. Then the two
joined hands and commended themselves to one another with
great kindliness. . . . When at last they left one another, Dominic
said to several who were there at the time: 'In truth I say to you,
all other religious ought to follow this holy man Francis, so great
is the perfection of his sanctity.'"[5]

This strong brotherly affection had drawn Dominic to attend
a Chapter at St. Mary's, perhaps the one of 1221. There he
observed much that caused him to rejoice, but he also discerned
that the simplicity of life of the friars which was the hallmark of
the brotherhood was also proving to be its weakness. Strong
leadership and stable organization were clearly needed for the
thousands who now called themselves sons of Francis.

Dominic was astounded to behold God coming visibly to vindi-
cate the childlike trust of the founder by sending all the provi-

sions needed by the huge gathering through the people of the small towns and villages of Umbria. He never forgot this experience and frequently spoke of it with admiration to others.

As soon as the chanting behind the choir grille dies away, Francis makes known to the portress that he has come with a friend to see Sister Clare. The visiting room is remarkable only for its cleanliness and simplicity for the few rough benches clearly proclaim the poverty of the community. Dominic has scarcely absorbed this when Clare arrives swiftly and softly on her bare feet.

Instantly, Francis is transformed into a courtier, formally introducing his lady to a beloved and esteemed friend. Dominic responds with the unforgotten manners of the Spanish grandee while Clare graciously accepts their courtesies. Lady Poverty's Sister Courtesy retains her place as the sanctified expression of "holy simplicity, the daughter of grace and the sister of wisdom."[6]

Dominic feels immediately at ease in the gentle but vibrant presence of this young woman whom prelates and popes have praised. The light and sparkle in Clare's eyes reveal the joy she is finding in her austere life. As Francis relates the happenings of the Chapter, Dominic notes the compassion that replaces her joy and realizes that Clare, perhaps even more than Francis himself, foresees the problems and pain of the future.

The Rule, into which Francis has poured all his heart and spirit, is not getting an enthusiastic reception among all the friars. Francis had not expected that it would, but he felt morally bound to write it as uncompromisingly as the gospel which he knew he and his brothers were called to live. He counted on the power of the Spirit to make clear to them what was transparently true to him.

That power was felt by all the friars at the Chapter, even by those who disagreed with Francis' radical conception of their life. Cardinal Hugolino was unable to be present at the Chapter of 1221 and had asked Cardinal Rainerio Capocci to preside in his place. The small opposition party sensed how the magnetism of Francis' conviction would rally the majority of the brothers present to an enthusiastic acceptance of the Rule. They, therefore, decided not to push matters to a vote at this time. By citing certain weaknesses in the form of the text; i.e., it was too long, too repetitious, not couched in appropriate legal language, they managed to bring about only a general agreement that the Rule should be seen and "corrected" by Cardinal Hugolino before a final vote was taken. Even Francis himself had to agree that this seemed a reasonable step.

Perhaps Dominic, older and more worldly-wise, saw in this maneuver a scarcely disguised attempt to reject the uncompromising stand Francis had maintained on matters of poverty, asceticism, and their apostolates. Dominic was hurt to see his friend's great dream being torn at, criticized, and rejected, while Francis stood by in his simple honesty, not quite willing to believe what he saw happening. It must have been a relief to Dominic when the final decision was deferred.

Francis was willing to concede that the style of the Rule might be revised, but he knew that his stand on essentials could not change. He trusted that Cardinal Hugolino would support him on these controversial points. The "reforming faction" also placed their hopes in Hugolino, knowing that he was the only person who might successfully influence Francis to accept a compromise.

Clare may have seen a copy of this Rule of 1221. Perhaps she even managed to keep one at San Damiano for the Rule she would later write for her sisters contains some elements taken directly from this draft.

Francis' Rule, as would Clare's, flowed out of the lived experience of their communities. They did not first write a rule and then set out to find people to live it. On the contrary, as men and women flocked to them, drawn by the irresistibility of the pure gospel life, they simply allowed the Spirit to guide the practical development of the community's life. Their norm was the gospel. Anything contrary to that evangelical spirit was rejected while whatever enhanced that spirit was regarded as compatible with their accustomed manner of living.

Out of this rich matrix, lived over a period of fifteen years, Francis had drawn the outline and governing principles he put into the Rule of 1221. He sought to capture and clarify the original inspiration, that large, pure vision which had so stirred him and his first companions at Rivo Torto.

Although Francis laid down his principles "simply and purely," the Rule is far from being a harsh document. It is rich with scriptural texts, evocative and challenging, inviting anyone who wishes to "come, follow the teaching and footsteps of Jesus Christ."[7] The emphasis is on the servanthood of Jesus with all the members intent on serving the Lord and each other.

Chapter 22 is a long and eloquent plea for the brothers to appreciate the beauty of their calling. The final chapter, like an epilogue, is a poetic exhortation to the friars, and through them to the whole world, to join in the praises of the "one true God, who is the fullness of good, all good, every good, the true and supreme good, who alone is good, merciful and gentle, delectable and sweet. . . ." Francis' lyricism leaps to greater and greater heights as he sees the vast panorama of people "wherever they are in every place, at every hour, at every time of day, . . . continually loving, honoring, adoring, serving, praising and blessing, glorifying and exalting, magnifying and giving thanks to the most high and supreme God, . . the Father, Son, and Holy Spirit. . . ."[8]

All of Francis' great vision that could be compressed into words flowed into this unique document. But his brothers did not want the dream. Clare fathomed, as few others could, the exquisite pain Francis experienced at this virtual rejection of his inspiration. She could do little more to console his wounded spirit except to beseech the Comforter to come himself and heal him. The balm that came to Francis eventually and which enabled him to rejoice even in these dark hours was surely won in part, at least, by his hidden and silent sister within the walls of San Damiano. More dark hours lay ahead, for Francis would have to mount many Calvaries before he climbed Mount Alverna.

Francis' life at this time was not all gloom and disappointment, however. From the very beginning of his preaching activity, Francis had stirred up a tremendous surge of enthusiasm among the lay folk of the villages and countryside. They flocked to hear him preach, begged him to stay with them and show them how they, too, could live the joyful evangelism he and his brothers lived. The dream of Innocent of poor simple men tending the confused and straying sheep of the fold became a reality as Celano describes it:

> Men ran, women too ran, clerics hurried, and religious hastened that they might see and hear the holy man of God who seemed to be a man of another world. . . . It seemed at that time . . . that a new light had been sent from heaven upon this earth, shattering the widespread darkness that had so filled almost the whole region that hardly anyone knew where to go. . . . Francis shone forth like a brilliant star in the obscurity of the night and like the morning spread upon the darkness. . . . To all he gave a norm of life and he showed in truth the way of salvation in every walk of life.[9]

Francis must have drawn up very early some sort of short Rule of Life for the enthusiastic people who could not leave their family commitments and yet longed to strive for gospel perfec-

tion as he did. This may have been written in the form of a
Letter to the Faithful, of which two versions have survived. A
later version, reflecting the concerns of the Lateran Council,
particularly in the area of sound Christology and frequent reception of the sacraments, may have been presented to Honorius III about this time by Cardinal Hugolino. It received the
wholehearted approval of the Pope.

The apostolic heart of Clare would also have been gladdened
when she learned of this latest effort of Cardinal Hugolino on
behalf of the Franciscan movement. She hoped it would bolster
Francis' confidence in himself and assure him that he had indeed heard the Lord's call to live the gospel life and teach it to
others.

Hugolino, despite his heavy curial duties, did not allow his
interest in the spread of the Poor Ladies to flag. In that year of
1221, he arranged for the establishment of three more Poor
Clare communities, at Camullia, Gataiola, and Monte Lucio in
Italy. About this time, Clare also sent some of her sisters to
Judenberg in Upper Styria (Austria) to found a house there
which quickly flourished.

As Dominic and Francis prepare to take leave of Sister Clare,
Clare inquires when she and her sisters might see Francis again.
His visits have been far too few to satisfy their longing for the
spiritual unction that only Francis could give them. Dominic
notices that Francis gives Clare only a vague promise. He is not
surprised for from the brothers he has heard that Francis visited
the Poor Ladies very seldom these days.

Celano attests this when he wrote: "Though their father
[Francis] gradually withdrew his bodily presence from them, he
nevertheless gave them his affection in the Holy Spirit by caring
for them."[10]

Francis' purpose, as we have seen, was intended to provide the
brothers with an example. He loved Clare deeply and purely,

and the love he knew she bore him was marked by the same purity and depth. But Francis was ever a realist when it came to the weaknesses of human nature. He had declared to the Poor Ladies that he and his brothers would always give them help and counsel but had added "I do not want anyone to offer himself of his own accord to visit them. I command that unwilling and most reluctant brothers be appointed to take care of them, provided they be spiritual men."[11]

Finally, Peter Catani stepped in, perhaps at Clare's request, for Celano records: "Repeatedly asked by his vicar to preach the word of God to his daughters when he stopped off for a short time at San Damiano, Francis was finally overcome by his insistence and consented. But when the nuns had come together as was their custom, to hear the word of God, though no less also to see their father, Francis raised his eyes to heaven where his heart always was and began to pray to Christ. He then commanded ashes to be brought to him and he made a circle with them around himself on the pavement and sprinkled the rest of them on his head. But when they waited for him to begin and the blessed father remained standing in the circle in silence, no small astonishment arose in their hearts. The saint then suddenly rose and to the amazement of the nuns recited the *Miserere mei Deus* in place of a sermon. When he had finished, he quickly left. The handmaids of God were so filled with contrition because of the power of this symbolic sermon that their tears flowed in abundance."[12]

This profound symbolism was not lost on Clare for she intuited that the message Francis was able to preach only by symbolic action was an expression of his own state of soul at this time. The fire within him seemed reduced to ashes, his sins weighing upon him so that he felt utterly unworthy to even speak of the Lord except to plead for mercy. Clare knew, however, that the purifying work of the Spirit was the main cause of his misery. She remembered that banked coals often give off the most intense heat and when kindling is brought near, the flames leap up again to even greater heights.

Chapter XII Endnotes

1. 2 Cel., #158.
2. 2 Cel., #150.
3. Letter to Brother Anthony.
4. 2 Cel., #148.
5. Ibid., #150.
6. 2 Cel., #189.
7. Earlier Rule, Ch. 1, #1.
8. Ibid., Ch. 23, #9, 11.
9. 1 Cel., #36–37.
10. 2 Cel., #204.
11. Ibid., #205.
12. Ibid., #207.

XIII   Leaping to New Heights

A pall of anxiety hangs over San Damiano. Sisters go about their daily tasks subdued and prayerful. In the refectory there are empty places and when the community gathers in choir, the chanting sounds thin and strained.

Clare joins them whenever she can but she is often occupied with caring for the needs of the five sisters who are suffering in the infirmary. Among them is her dear and faithful Pacifica. The name of the malady that had stricken them is not recorded but Pacifica said later "that it had caused her to cry aloud with great shivering and cold."[1]

While Clare busies herself trying to make the sisters as comfortable as possible, she is praying in her heart. Five sisters are down already and some of those still on their feet are looking very tired. She places her concern in the hands of her Father. As she re-enters the infirmary with more blankets, a strong but familiar assurance floods her spirit.

Celano, drawing upon Sister Pacifica's memories, relates: "Clare as usual enters the infirmary with her usual medicine and as she makes the sign of the Cross five times, five sisters are immediately healed of their infirmities."[2] We can imagine the astonishment and joy of the rest of the community when five healthy sisters emerge from the infirmary carrying their bedding back upstairs to the dormitory.

All of the sisters of the monastery benefit at one time or another from their Mother's healing touch for Pacifica has reported that "very often when any sister had pain in her head or in any other part of her body, the blessed Mother would cure her with the sign of the Cross."[3]

Pope Alexander IV, in the Bull of Canonization, introduces the topic of these miraculous cures with the words: "Now because a great and shining light cannot remain hidden but must diffuse the rays of its brightness, so in the lifetime of Clare the power of her holiness shone forth in many different miracles."[4]

Light became associated with Clare's person even in the minds and hearts of the sisters who lived with her in daily intimacy. Sister Benvenuta, who had been one of the first to join Clare and Agnes, mentioned "that in the place . . . where Clare was wont to pray she had seen so great a splendor of light that she thought it came from material fire. [When she was] asked who else had seen this light, she replied that on *that occasion* she was the only one to see it. . . . This had happened, she said, before . . . Clare fell ill (c. 1222–23)."[5]

Many of the sisters in that fervent community were privileged to witness supernatural favors regarding their Mother, and, when the time came to give their testimony before Clare's canonization, they eagerly recounted them. But along with their narrations of many miraculous events, the sisters made it clear that it was Clare's unfailing kindness and compassion that impressed them most profoundly.

Clare's childhood friend, Philippa de Gislerio, who had also joined Clare very early remarked: "Ever since the Lord called Clare into religion, He greatly increased all her virtues and graces. She was most humble and devout, most kind, a great lover of poverty and having deep compassion for the afflicted."[6]

The description of an ideal abbess which Clare would one day incorporate into her Rule is an unconscious portrait of herself. The abbess is to be one who is the eager servant of all. "She is strictly bound to inquire with all solicitude by herself and through other sisters what the sick sisters may need both by way of counsel and of food and other necessities and, according to the resources of the place, she is to provide for them charitably and kindly.

"This is to be done because all are obliged to serve and provide for their sisters who are ill just as they would wish to be served themselves if they were suffering from any infirmity. Each should make known her needs to the other with confidence. For if a mother loves and nourishes her daughter according to the flesh, how much more lovingly must a sister love and nourish her sister according to the Spirit!"[7] These sentiments are lifted directly from Francis' Rule but express Clare's thoughts exactly.

About this same time, 1223, Agnes, daughter of Messer Oportulo of Bernardo was received into the monastery. She was still a child (according to her own statement[8]) but San Damiano, like all other monasteries of the time, accepted young girls and trained them for a life of piety along with educating them. When the girl reached her mid-teens, she could either ask to be admitted to the community or else return to her home.

Clare made provision for these young aspirants in her Rule, describing how they should be trained under the supervision of a sister who "shall form them diligently in a holy manner of living and proper behavior according to the form of our profession."[9]

Little Agnes appears to have been an ingenuous child who delighted Clare with her straight-forward simplicity and enthusiasm for everything the sisters did. She is the one who, noticing Clare's "cilice of knotted horse hair," begged to be allowed to wear it. Clare, surprisingly, said, yes; but after three days, Agnes, humbled, brought it back confessing that she "found it so harsh she could in no way endure it."[10]

Clare was praying with particular intensity for Francis these days. He was dividing his time between preaching and working on a second draft of the Rule for the brothers. The rumors which reached Clare told her clearly how deeply he was being torn by the conflict between what he knew to be the will of the Lord for the Order and the demands of some of the brothers who said the earlier version he wrote was inhuman and impossible for ordinary, weak mortals to observe. Francis fluctuated between righteous wrath and profound discouragement, unable to find peace except for brief moments when he was preaching to the people who, more than ever, thronged to see him.

A contemporary description of Francis and the effect of his words is given to us by one Thomas, Archdeacon of Spoleto, who was present when Francis preached in Bologna on the feast of the Assumption in the year 1222.

> In that year, I was residing in the Studium of Bologna; on the feast of the Assumption, I saw Francis preach in the public square in front of the public palace. Almost the entire city had assembled there. The theme of his sermon was: angels, men, and demons. He spoke so well and with such sterling clarity on these three classes of spiritual and rational beings that the way in which this untutored man developed his subject aroused even among the scholars in the audience an admiration that knew no bounds. Yet, his discourses did not belong to the great genre of sacred eloquence; rather they were harangues [exhortations that sprang from the heart]. In reality, throughout his discourse he spoke of the duty of putting an end to hatreds and of arranging a new treaty of peace.
>
> He was wearing a ragged habit; his whole person seemed insignificant; he did not have an attractive face. But God conferred so much power on his words that they brought back peace in many a seignorial family torn apart until then by old, cruel, and furious hatreds even to the point of assassinations. The people showed him as much respect as they did devotion; men and women flocking to him; it was a question of who could at least touch the fringe of his clothing or who would tear off a piece of his poor habit."[11]

No wonder his habit was so ragged! Although Francis did all he could to dissuade the people from regarding him as a saint, his self-deprecations only increased their adulation. Finally, Francis would manage to escape from the crowds and find refuge in some solitary place. But once alone he would be face to face again with the agonizing question of the brothers and the Rule.

He was so torn by this inward turmoil that he seemed unable to find peace anywhere he turned. He who could bring peace so effectively to others could find none for himself. He often refused to see the brothers because he could not hide his sadness from them. Yet he loved them and longed for their love and understanding.

The faithful few who composed the inner circle about him did what they could to console Francis. Instinctively, though, Francis knew that this was a suffering he had to bear alone. Only God could succor him and he seemed to have turned his face away. Had he failed his Lord also, Francis anguished?

The only light that still gleamed in Francis' gloom dwelt in the first church he had rebuilt, San Damiano. For there dwelt Clare. Occasionally, Francis would go there to warm his frozen soul in the deep, quiet sympathy that shone in her eyes. But Francis scrupled to do this too frequently, even though Clare must have assured him that it was not displeasing to their Lord that they should help carry one another's burdens.

An incident which, although possibly legendary, illustrates this.

> From time to time Francis did visit Clare but his appearances at San Damiano were momentary. He knocked at the door and greeted them: "Peace and good will." He glanced inside and noted that the convent was as a "strong tower of sovereign poverty." Nothing useless or purposeless, nothing sumptuous or superflous. Neither was there anything squalid or

sad about the place; a clean and serene poverty with joy everywhere. All was clear where Clare was; all was gracious where was the grace of God.

One cold winter's day Francis stood ready to leave as he had come. He walked toward the door. Outside the wind whistled and blew through the branches of the olive trees and snow was settling in little droves and sleet was forming on the front pathway. Francis' bare feet stepped out into the snow and Clare followed after him a few paces away. She hoped to detain him a little. At least she hoped to get a promise from him of another visit very soon.

Francis pulled his hood up over his head, "Sister Clare," he said, "it is better that we go our own ways, because of what the world might think. I will leave you to manage on your own."

Clare, standing in the brightness of the ground, felt lost and astray. "What will I do without you? You are my guide and support."

Francis raised his eyes to the somber sky: "Our blessed Lord will guide you."

"And we will not see you again?"

Francis looked about. Considering the weather conditions and seeing a thorny rosebush covered with snow, he said to Clare: "We will meet again when the roses reflower."

It was the beginning of winter and the roses would not flower again until well into the spring. He wanted to place a complete season between himself and Clare.

"Let it be as you wish," answered Clare, "but also as Our Lord wishes." And she bowed her head.

Francis made to move away but almost immediately he involuntarily stopped. On the bush that was near him, suddenly and miraculously, groups of roses had flowered!

Clare under her double veil smiled to herself; and

when Francis had gone off toward Spello in the snow-
storm, she went back into San Damiano with a bunch
of roses in her hands which she placed at the foot of
the Crucifix."[12]

Clare continued her ceaseless intercession on Francis' behalf.
The Rule had still to be given acceptable form, and the labor of
revising it nearly broke Francis' great spirit. After the Chapter
of 1221, he had withdrawn to the wild solitude of Fonte Colombo near Rieti. His faithful Brothers Leo and Bonizzo accompanied him. Amid much prayer and fasting, Francis dictated as
Christ inspired him and Brother Bonizzo, a jurist, took pains to
see that it was in proper form.

This precious text, fruit of so much toil and pain, was entrusted to Brother Elias, Vicar of the brotherhood. No one ever
saw it after that. Elias lamely explained that it was lost.

Once more Francis and Leo retired to the caves near Fonte
Colombo to begin yet again. Whereas the first form of the Rule
had flowed forth in rich and warm enthusiasm from the depth
of Francis' soul, it seemed like every word now cost him dear.
Unable to write as his heart desired, Francis felt stifled and
bound by the restrictions that the varying demands of the brothers placed on him. It did not help him when a group of ministers, with Brother Elias speaking for them, came to the cave
where Francis was working, to tell him yet again that they would
not accept any rule from him that did not meet their demands.

As so often happened in Francis' life, consolation and strength
came to him through the mediation of a symbolic dream. "It
seemed to him that he had to gather the finest crumbs of bread
from the ground and to distribute them to the many hungry
brothers who were standing around him. But while he was
afraid to distribute such small crumbs lest such minute particles
of dust should fall from his hands, a voice spoke to him from
above: 'Francis, make one host out of all these crumbs and give it

to those who want to eat of it." When he did this, those who did
not receive devoutly or who despised the gift they had received,
were soon seen to be greatly infected with leprosy."[13]

Francis awoke puzzled. He talked over the vision-dream with
his companions but it was only later on, while at prayer, that
Francis received an explanation of the mystery. "Francis," a
voice said, "the crumbs of last night are the words of the gospel,
the host is the Rule, the leprosy is wickedness."[14]

St. Bonaventure remarks that this vision not only encouraged
Francis but also led him to see that he should shorten and con-
dense the Rule, putting into it only the most necessary directives.
Thus, this version differed markedly from the Rule of 1221,
being three times as short and containing only ten verses from
the Gospel. It is carefully worded (here we may detect the fine
hand of Hugolino) so as to give as little offense as possible to
either the moderates or the extremists of opposing convictions.

Some of the brothers who clung tenaciously to the way of life
of the first years of the Order felt betrayed. A closer look at this
Rule, however, proves it to be even more demanding than the
earlier version. The emphasis is on pilgrimage, a state of life
which requires total poverty. "The brothers shall not acquire
anything as their own, neither a house nor a place nor anything
at all. Instead, as pilgrims and strangers in this world who serve
the Lord in poverty and humility, let them go begging for alms
with full trust."[15] They are to show they are truly Lesser Brothers for "when they go about the world, they do not quarrel or
fight with words, or judge others; rather let them be meek,
peaceful and unassuming, gentle and humble, speaking courteously to everyone, as is becoming."[16]

The brothers' "place" and home is to be found in the strong,
brotherly affection that binds them together. Their only security
is their reliance on one another. "Wherever the brothers may be
together or meet [other] brothers, let them give witness that they
are members of one family."[17] Thus, the most eloquent and

fundamental "mark" of the early days of the brotherhood is not only retained but strengthened by greater emphasis.

For then "people saw how they really loved one another," and, continues The Legend of the Three Companions, "seeing all this, many became convinced that the brothers were true disciples of Jesus Christ. [For] each deeply loved the other and cared for him as a mother cares for a cherished child. Charity burned so ardently in their hearts that it was easy to risk life itself, not only for love of Jesus Christ but also for the soul and body of any one of the brothers."[18]

Clare desired this same warmth of family love to characterize the lives of her sisters also. Because they, too, were to be "strangers and pilgrims" and were "not to receive or hold onto any possessions or property," Clare wished them to build their temporal security on the love they found in each other.[19]

"Loving one another with the Charity of Christ, let the love you have in your hearts be shown outwardly in your deeds so that, compelled by such an example, the sisters may always grow in love of God and in charity for one another."[20] Clare conscientiously modeled the life of her sisterhood on what Francis proposed for his brothers. Therefore, she rejoiced as ardently as Francis when Hugolino transmitted to them the happy news that the Rule had received formal approbation on November 29, 1223.

Relieved but spiritually exhausted by the painful wrangles over the Rule, Francis turned to his beloved mountains with their deep, womblike caves where he could once more seek a rebirth of spirit. The feast of Christmas, a celebration that always aroused Francis' intense joy and gratitude, was drawing near. He approached a nobleman of Greccio whom "he loved with a special love" because of his great nobility of soul. "About fifteen days before the birth of the Lord, Francis said to him: 'If you want us to celebrate the present feast of our Lord at Greccio, go with haste and diligently prepare what I tell you. For I wish to do something that will recall to memory the little Child who was born in Bethlehem and set before our bodily eyes in some way the inconveniences of his infant needs, how he lay in a manger, how, with an ox and an ass standing by, he lay upon the hay where he had been placed.'"[21]

The noble John did as Francis requested and apparently spread the news of the plan throughout the neighborhood. Celano describes the event with such limpidity that the reservoirs of joy it tapped still overflow for us.

> The day of joy drew near, the time of great rejoicing came. The brothers were called from their various places. Men and women of that neighborhood prepared with glad hearts, according to their means, candles and torches to light up that night that has lighted up all the days and years with its gleaming star. . . . The woods rang with the voices of the crowd and the rocks made answer to their jubilation. The brothers sang, paying their debt of praise to the Lord, and the whole night resounded with their rejoicing. Francis stood before the manger, filled with a wonderful happiness. The solemnities of the Mass were celebrated over the manger and the priest experienced a new consolation.
>
> The saint of God was clothed with the vestments of the deacon [possibly he wore the exquisitely wrought alb which Clare had made for him and which carried with it all the love and reverence of her heart for the mystery of the altar and the mystery that was Francis]. He sang the holy Gospel in a sonorous voice, sweet and clear.
>
> Then he preached to the people standing about with charming words concerning the nativity of the poor King and the little town of Bethlehem. A certain virtuous man saw a little child lying in the manger lifeless, and he saw the holy man of God go up to it

and rouse the child as from a deep sleep. This vision was not unfitting, for the Child Jesus had been forgotten in the hearts of many; but, by the working of his grace, he was brought to life again through his servant Francis."[22]

Thomas of Celano had most probably returned to Italy from Germany shortly before Christmas of 1223. The vividness of detail which only an eye witness could have supplied arouses the speculation that Brother Thomas may himself have been the "priest [who] experienced new consolation." He acutely observes that Francis awakened the innocent child that slumbered in the deep dreamworld of humanity's unconscious. For Francis seems to have helped restore to the world the privilege of its first innocence where the sons and daughters of God could, hand in hand, play before their Father in the Garden of created beauty, now sanctified anew by the presence in the flesh of the Eternal Son.

The swiftness with which Francis' literal re-presentation of the Bethlehem scene swept through Europe testifies that Francis' response to what he thought was his own inspiration was, in truth, a response to a yearning which had been evolving in Christianity's unconscious for long years. It is probable that Clare and her sisters at San Damiano also delighted in the idea of literally depicting the Christmas scene and adopted it as enthusiastically as the peasants of Greccio.

Of Clare's personal devotion to the mystery of the God-child, Celano records that she frequently underscored her exhortations about poverty with the example of the Holy Family's destitution in Bethlehem. "She exhorted them [her sisters] to be conformed in their little nest of poverty to the Poor Christ whom his poor little mother had laid as a Babe in the narrow manger."[23] And in Clare's Rule we find: "For the love of the most holy and beloved Child who was wrapped in the poorest of swaddling clothes and laid in a manger, and of his most holy mother, I admonish, entreat and exhort my sisters that they always wear the poorest of garments."[24]

Clare is appealing to the natural love of a woman's heart and to the tenderness that a helpless child evokes to confirm her sisters in their fidelity to poverty. Poverty in clothing does not come easily to a woman; but if it can be seen as an expression of love, such poverty becomes not only acceptable but actually desirable.

Attraction to the Poor Ladies' manner of living was continuing to spread. Between 1220–23, three more monasteries were established in France, at Besancon, Cahors, and Montpellier. The friars who had gone to Spain sent word to San Damiano that some groups of women living in the semireligious status of "beatae" were eager to adopt the Rule of the Poor Ladies. Perhaps as early as 1224 (sources for dates are confusing) Clare sent a Sister Agnes, daughter of Penanda, to Barcelona together with a Sister Clare. Both of these sisters were related to Clare although the degree of kinship is uncertain.

While Clare's thoughts and most likely her facile pen were kept occupied with the expansion of the Poor Ladies, she continued to follow and feel the interior struggles of Francis. The approval of the Rule of 1223 had failed to bring unity to the brothers and there was much friction still within the First Order. Francis struggled with severe temptations to either angrily denounce these troublesome brothers or to despairingly refuse to have anything at all to do with them. Pray as he would, he could find no peace. He, whose very presence could reconcile whole cities, could not calm the tumult within his own soul.

Clare spent more and more time before the smoke-darkened Crucifix in the chapel at San Damiano. The little she saw of Francis during this period confirmed her intuition that he was being conformed to the image of the Crucified Lord whose knight he had set out to be. When, in the late of summer of 1224 she learned that Francis planned to make a special Lent from the feast of the Assumption of Our Lady to that of St. Michael, September 29th, she may have experienced a certain premonition. Francis was setting out for Monte La Verna.

In her mind Clare may have tried to picture the rugged height which must have been described to her at the time of its donation to the friars. Maybe Brother Leo had told her of how impressive it appeared when a sudden turn in the road brought it into view on the horizon. Its crest, outlined against the sky created the strong impression of an enormous ship of rock cutting through an immense sea, pointing toward regions yet to be explored.

According to the Fioretti, Francis grew so fatigued during his journey that he had to ride a mule through the mountainous terrain surrounding La Verna. On the way, Francis, his companions, and the mule's owner stopped to rest under an oak tree. While resting, Francis was seen "studying the location and the scenery."[25] He would have seen stands of beech and oak trees reaching part way up the slopes, then sparser stands of dwarfed fir trees which became majestic, dark, and dense in the higher regions. Outcroppings of rocks to which beech trees clung with mighty roots crowned the summits of these elevations.

At the foot of La Verna, Francis and his companions again halted before making the final ascent. While he was contemplating the rugged and forbidding height, "a great number of all kinds of birds came flying down to him with joyful songs, and twitterings and fluttering their wings . . . and surrounded Francis in such a way that some of them settled on his head and others on his shoulders and others on his knees, and still others on his arms and lap and on his hands and around his feet. Francis rejoiced in spirit and said to his companions, 'My dear brothers, I believe it is pleasing to our Lord Jesus Christ that . . . we live a while on this solitary mountain, since our little brothers and sisters the birds show such joy over our coming."[26]

After reaching the hermitage built near the top, Francis searched about until he found a very wild and secluded spot. Something deep within urged him to find a place for prayer where he could be utterly alone. On La Verna, enormous rocks are clustered in formidable columns, especially where a side of the mountain had apparently been sheared off and swallowed up in the valley below. Huge rocks are partially detached from the mass of the mountain and stand by a miracle of equilibrium.

Among some of these, beech trees have sprung up, their half bare roots entwining the rocks in strange, almost hideous contortions. Under an imposing mass of overhanging rock, Francis took refuge for prayer. But something drove him even further on until he found where a huge wall of rock stood out, completely separated from the rest of the mountain. Brothers Leo and Masseo laid some tree trunks across the chasm so that Francis could reach the little hut of mud and branches which had been built in the shade of a tall beech which clung to this rocky and desolate plateau.

Just as the sounds and troubles of the valley died away before the brothers reached La Verna's heights, so the distresses and pains of the past few years gradually receded from Francis' awareness as he was drawn gently into a communion with his Lord which surpassed anything he had previously experienced. Loving and suffering, giving of himself and receiving from the Lord became fused into a single awareness of such depth and intensity that Francis was overwhelmed. He obscurely knew he was being drawn toward an unspeakable experience, and he did not resist.

> By divine inspiration he learned that if he opened the Gospels, Christ would reveal to him what was God's will for him and what God wished to see realized in him. And so Francis prayed fervently and took the Gospel book from the altar, telling his companion, a

devout and holy friar, to open it in the name of the Blessed Trinity. He opened the Gospel three times, and each time it opened at the Passion, and so Francis understood that he must become like Christ in the distress and the agony of his Passion before he left the world, just as he had been like him in all that he did during his life. . . .

The fervor of his seraphic longing raised Francis up to God, and, in an ecstasy of compassion, made him like Christ who allowed himself to be crucified in the excess of his love. Then one morning about the feast of the Exaltation of the Holy Cross, while he was praying on the mountainside, Francis saw a Seraph with six fiery wings coming down from the highest point of the heavens. The vision descended swiftly and came to rest in the air near him. Then he saw the image of a Man crucified in the midst of the wings, with his hands and feet stretched out and nailed to a cross. Two of the wings were raised above his head and two were stretched out in flight, while the remaining two shielded his body. Francis was dumbfounded at the sight and his heart was flooded with a mixture of joy and sorrow.

Eventually he realized by divine inspiration that God had shown him this vision in his providence, in order to let him see that, as Christ's lover, he would resemble Christ crucified perfectly not by physical martyrdom but by the fervor of his spirit. As the vision disappeared, it left his heart ablaze with eagerness and impressed upon his body a miraculous likeness. There and then the marks of nails began to appear in his hands and feet, just as he had seen them in his vision of the man nailed to the Cross. His hands and feet appeared pierced through the center with nails, the heads of which were in the palms of his hands and on the instep of each foot, while the points stuck out on the opposite side. The heads were black and round, but the points were long and bent back, as if they had been struck with a hammer; they rose above the surrounding flesh and stood out from it. His right side seemed as if it had been pierced with a lance and was marked with a livid scar which often bled, so that his habit and trousers were stained."[27]

Dazed, Francis first tried to conceal what had happened to him, but his brothers suspected that something extraordinary had occurred. Brother Leo, for all his love for Francis and his fear of offending him, could not restrain his curiosity. Gradually, he eked out from him an account of some of the events which he had himself witnessed from a distance. When Brother Illuminato, in answer to Francis' question about what a certain person should do when such receives a special grace, replied that while it is, at times, good to keep the secret of the King, concluded: "Remember, Brother, that when God reveals his secrets to you, it is not for yourself alone; they are intended for others too."[28]

So Francis haltingly described what he had seen but added that certain secret things had been told him that could be communicated to no man. He strove to keep his wounds covered as much as possible but could not entirely dissemble the pain they caused him. Walking any distance now became impossible for him, so Francis descended La Verna on a donkey. He knew in his heart that he would never return to this height which had become his Calvary and his Tabor. Fiery, love-mingled pain was to be his the rest of his days and he would have it no other way. His inspired prayer had been fulfilled:

"My Lord Jesus Christ, I pray You to grant me two graces before I die; the first is that during my life I may feel in my soul and in my body, as much as possible, that pain which You, dear Jesus, sustained in the hour of Your most bitter Passion. The second is that I may feel in my heart, as much as possible, the excessive love with which You, O Son of God, were inflamed in willingly enduring such sufferings for us sinners."[29]

As Francis descended into the valley of men, his heart aglow with deep compassion and love for all the children of earth, a flickering red flame played over an Image of the Crucified in a small chapel near Assisi. On the steep hillside in distant Umbria, the shadows of San Damiano concealed one whose heart had ever beat in unison with his. Could Clare fail to experience the "excessive love" that now burned so fiercely in Francis' breast?

Chapter XIII Endnotes

1. Cause of Canonization Wit. 1, #16.
2. Legend of Celano, #35.
3. Cause of Canonization, Wit. 1, #16.
4. Bull of Canonization, #18.
5. Cause of Canonization, Wit. 2, #17.
6. Ibid., Wit. 3, #3.
7. Rule of Clare, Ch. VIII, 7–9.
8. Cause of Canonization, Wit. 10, #1.
9. Rule of Clare, Ch. II, 12–14.
10. Cause of Canonization, Wit. 10, #1.
11. Sermon of St. Francis at Bologna by Thomas, Archdeacon of Spoleto in *Omnibus*, pp. 1601–2.
12. Piero Bargellini, *Little Flowers of St. Clare*, pp. 66–68.
13. 2 Cel., #209.
14. Ibid., #209.
15. Later Rule Chapter 6, #1.
16. Ibid., Ch. 3, #10.
17. Ibid., Ch. 6, #7.
18. Legend of Three Companions, #41.
19. Rule of Clare Ch. VI, #5.
20. Testament of Clare, #18.

21. 1 Cel., #84.
22. Ibid., #85-86.
23. Legend of Celano, #13.
24. Rule of Clare Ch. II, #18.
25. Fioretti. Part Two, First Consideration.
26. Ibid.
27. Legenda Major, Ch. 13, #2-3.
28. Ibid. Ch. 13, #4.
29. Fioretti, Part Two, Third Consideration.

XIV   Song of the Sun

Restlessly Clare turns on her pallet in the corner of the dormitory. Her eyes pass over the low-slung rafters and she gazes past them toward the empty sky, visible through an open half-door. But she scarcely notices its deep October blue. Her troubled thoughts are elsewhere.

A sister who is sitting nearby looks anxiously at Clare, concerned that the gravely weakened abbess may tire herself even more if she commences to weep again. Suddenly Clare turns and whispers, "I think I hear someone coming up the path from St. Mary's. Go quickly and see what news he brings."

The sister hurries down just as one of the friars arrives at the entrance. "How is she?" he inquires with concern.

"She is still living but very weak. Have you brought news about . . . about Father Francis?" the sister asks anxiously.

The brother smiles sadly, "I have a letter from him. Perhaps it will comfort her."

According to Brother Leo, who had lived through these intense days of early October 1226, "Clare . . . was very sick and was fearful of dying before blessed Francis. She wept bitterly and could not console herself at the thought of not seeing him again before his death, her only father after God, her interior and external comfort, he who was the first one to establish her solidly in the grace of the Lord."[1]

Possibly it was the good Pacifica who had suggested that Clare send a message to Francis through one of the brothers. So Clare had entrusted one of the friars with the commission to tell Francis of her love and deep sorrow at being unable to see him again.

On hearing this, the Legend recounts, Francis was moved with compassion for he loved Clare and her sisters with a paternal affection for the saintly life they were leading and because it was he who with the grace of God had converted her by his advice. . . . Since Francis could not grant her desire to see him again, because both of them were sick, he sent her in writing, for her consolation, his blessing and absolution from all the infractions of his orders and desires, and of the orders and desires of the Son of God. Furthermore, to rid her of all sadness and console her in the Lord, he said to the brother she had sent: "Go and bring this letter to Lady Clare. You will tell her to banish the sorrow and sadness she experiences at the thought of never seeing me again. Let her know, in truth, that before she dies, she and all her sisters will see me again and will receive great consolation from me.[2]

With the reception of this tender message, Clare grows quiet and peace tempers the pain in her heart. She is deeply touched that Francis, overwhelmed by intense suffering himself and poised on the threshold of eternity, should so delicately show his concern for her peace and comfort.

Clare smiles softly as she recalls the many little messages, songs, and exhortations which Francis has sent her during the past year and a half. One day she would lovingly refer to these "many writings" in her Testament: "While he was living, he was not content to encourage us by many words and examples to love and observe holy poverty; [in addition] he also gave us many writings so that, after his death, we should in no way turn away from it."[3] We learn of these writings in the Legend of Perugia where Brother Leo wrote that Francis "was well aware of the fact that his sickness greatly grieved them [Clare and her sisters]. Since he could not go in person to visit and console them, he had his companions bring them what he had composed for them."[4]

Francis' experience on Mount La Verna had not only altered his appearance but had weakened his whole constitution. Debilitated by both the mystic wounds which bled and pained him, and his other infirmities, he was no longer able to travel about freely. The wandering troubadour of the Lord, now more than half-blind and suffering from a chronic stomach problem, had to submit to the plans of others. In need of constant assistance, dependent on others even for the care of his personal needs, Francis was called by the Spirit to another form of preaching.

Francis had chosen Brother Leo to be his nurse, and it was this humble brother's privilege to bathe the wound in Francis' side and to wash out his blood-stained tunic. According to legend, Brother Leo would have given his life to have possession of Francis' tunic after his death. Francis was aware of this and dictated an order that at his death, Brother Leo, his "little sheep of God" should be given his tunic.[5]

Toward the spring of 1225, Brother Elias, as Minister General, "seeing that his [Francis] case was serious, ordered him to accept help and care . . . for he was suffering greatly. But at that time it was very cold and the weather was not propitious to begin the treatment [which Brother Elias had in mind]."[6] Elias wished to have Francis taken to Rieti to see a famous doctor there about his painfully inflamed eyes. The pain was becoming so excruciating that Francis' life was almost unbearable. The past winter had been the most severe that the Umbrian Valley and the Marches had ever known, a fact which had added to Francis' discomfort by forcing him to remain within a smoky little hut at the Portiuncula.

As soon as it was possible to travel, Francis was to set out. Before he left Assisi, however, he desired to stop at San Damiano to say good-bye to Sister Clare. Accordingly, the brothers turned the little donkey's head toward the pearly-gray monastery, starkly visible among the leafless olive groves.

As soon as Clare laid eyes on Francis, her joy at his coming turned to alarm. Not only were his poor eyes swollen and bloodshot but he seemed dazed by the pain of a raging headache which the short journey in the bright Umbrian sunlight had provoked. Clare's quick eye also noted how Francis quivered with weakness while his unnaturally bright cheeks made her suspect a fever.

It was obvious that he could not continue his journey in such a condition and Clare must have said so in terms that brooked no argument. She told the brothers to prepare a pallet for him in the hut at the foot of the garden where the chaplain or questing brothers occasionally stayed. Aware of the extreme sensitivity of Francis' eyes, Clare gave the brothers mats woven of rushes to seal off a portion of the hut so that he would be protected from any direct light. Even so, the diseased eyes continued to cause Francis exquisite pain.

> During his stay in this friary, for fifty days and more, blessed Francis could not bear the light of the sun during the day or the light of the fire at night. He constantly remained in darkness inside the house in his cell. His eyes caused him so much pain that he could neither lie down nor sleep, so to speak, which was very bad for his eyes and for his health. A few times he was on the point of resting and sleeping, but in the house and in the cell made of mats . . . there were so many mice running here and there, around him and even on him, that they prevented him from taking a rest; they even hindered him greatly in his prayer. They annoyed him not only at night but also during the day. When he ate, they climbed up on the table. . . ."[7]

Evidently, Francis did not entertain any great sense of fraternity with these particular rodents, and the brothers' conviction that they were a diabolical infestation may well have been true.

These fifty days were, perhaps, among the longest in Francis' life. Exteriorly and interiorly, he was plunged in deep darkness. The nearness of Clare was the only light he knew as the temptations, depression, and infirmity of the past months grew toward a climax.

Clare could not come to tend him personally but she exercised all her skill concocting cooling poultices for his burning eyes and special dishes to tempt his lost appetite. She searched the sisters' garden for the tender herbs just coming into season, particularly the parsley for which Francis had a special taste.[8] It was early spring by now but Clare divined that winter still held the heart of her beloved father in its unrelenting grip.

Perhaps it was during this period that Clare had the opportunity to devise a pair of sandals for Francis' nail-pierced feet. Wearing them, Francis could walk with somewhat less pain. But Clare's greatest gift and solace to Francis was her compassionate nearness in spirit.

During the endless nights, Francis would hear the sweet chanting from the sisters' choir and be momentarily soothed. During the tormenting days, the little bell would ring out the Hours and Francis would know that Clare and her sisters were gathering again for the praises of the Lord. The gentle serenity pervading San Damiano caressed his spirit. Celano notes: "Since Francis was thus worn out in every part by sufferings, it is surprising that his strength was sufficient to bear them. But he looked upon these trials not under the name of sufferings but of sisters."[9]

Despite Francis' firm conviction that "in bearing sufferings there is a great reward,"[10] he was desperately assailed by discouragement. He fought manfully, but felt as if he were approaching the very limit of his endurance.

> For one night [says Celano] when he was exhausted
> more than usual because of the many severe pains of
> his infirmities, Francis began to pity himself in the
> depths of his heart. . . . At length as he prayed thus in
> agony, he was given a promise of eternal life by the
> Lord under this simile: "If the whole bulk of the
> earth and the whole universe were precious gold
> without price, and if there were given to you as a
> reward for these severe sufferings you are enduring,
> after all the pain had been removed, a treasure of
> such great glory, in comparison with which that
> aforementioned gold would be nothing or not even
> worthy of mention, would you not be happy and
> would you not willingly bear what you are bearing at
> this moment?" "I would indeed be happy," the saint
> said, "and I would rejoice beyond all measure." "Re-
> joice, therefore," the Lord said to him, "for your sick-
> ness is a pledge of my kingdom; await the inheritance
> of that kingdom, steadfast and assured, because of
> the merit of your patience."[11]

Francis suddenly felt himself flooded with light and joy so
intense that he was utterly beside himself. For he realized that he
had been told that his salvation was an absolute certainty. All his
inner darkness, temptations, and struggles vanished never to
return. Deep within, a great sun was shining.

During these weeks in which Francis had lain a virtual prisoner in the darkness, spring had come to the Umbrian countryside. Fresh growth carpeted the gently rolling plain, pale
green shimmered in the olive groves while vines put forth leaves
and tendrils. Once more the nightingales sang in the woodlands
while at dawn the larks spiraled upwards trailing melodies behind them.

When the brothers came in to tend Francis, they found their
patient ecstatic with joy. Only haltingly could Francis describe

what had occurred. Finally, he abandoned the effort and allowed the great hymn thrumming in his spirit to burst forth. Words of praise, through which Francis sought to inflame his brothers as much as he could, rose like a fountain from the pristine depths of his spirit. For him, all creation had now become the great treasure his vision had revealed it to be.

> Most High, all-powerful, good Lord,
> Yours are the praises, the glory, the honor and all
>   blessing.
> To you alone, Most High, do they belong,
> and no man is worthy to mention your name.
>
> Praised be you, my Lord, with all your creatures,
> especially Sir Brother Sun,
> who is the day and through whom you give us light.
> And he is beautiful and radiant with great
>   splendor;
> and bears a likeness of you, Most High One.
>
> Praised be you, my Lord, through Sister Moon and
>   the stars,
> in heaven you formed them clear and precious and
>   beautiful.
>
> Praised be you, my Lord, through Brother Wind
> and through the air, cloudy and serene, and every
>   kind
> of weather
> through which you give sustenance to your
>   creatures.
>
> Praised be you, my Lord, through Sister Water,
> which is very useful and humble and precious and
>   chaste.

Praise be you, my Lord, through Brother Fire,
through whom you light the night
and he is beautiful and playful and robust and
    strong.

Praised be you, my Lord, through our Sister
    Mother Earth,
who sustains and governs us,
and who produces varied fruits with colored flowers
    and herbs.[12]

As the song mingled and died with the morning breeze, the brothers stood wordless, stirred to their inmost depths by a participation in a mystery of unity and praise that surpassed description. Francis was before them like a man newly risen from the tomb; exuberant, transformed, almost translucent in the blinding radiance of the joy that shone in him.

Very gently he began to teach them to sing as he did, longing that they might participate in this wondrous peace that enveloped his soul. No more could fear, pain, or trouble penetrate his spirit. All, all were caught up in a mystic hymn of unity which he had become.

Perhaps Clare, as the sun was beginning to rise behind Monte Subasio, had stepped out into the dew-fresh garden. As she waited there, watching the rays of the invisible sun shoot up behind the wooded crest of the mountain, she suddenly felt, rather than heard, a new song upon the air. Francis was singing, singing in that strong, sweet voice which was like no other.

Transfixed she listened as the one who sang proclaimed that the sun was now his brother, the moon his sister, that all the cosmos was a sacred single word of praise. Clare heard and rejoiced with great joy. The sun broke over the mountain peak and the valley was flooded with light.

Francis' ravaged and weakened body began to improve now that the spirit within it had become so lightsome. Soon Br. Elias would be coming to take him to Rieti for treatment by the Pope's own physician. But before Francis could leave the environs of his own city, he had a service to render. Totally reconciled and at peace within himself, he wished to bestow a portion of this rare grace upon the faction-torn city of his birth.

Probably Clare had let him know how grieved was little Sister Agnes because her father, the Podestà Messer Oportulo di Bernardo, had been excommunicated by Bishop Guido. The Podestà, in retaliation, had forbidden all the citizens to transact any business whatever with Guido. According to Brother Leo "there was a savage hatred between them."[13] Francis felt sick at heart, knowing that every single person from serf to noble would soon be embroiled in a destructive civil strife. And for what gain?

> So he said to his companions: "It is a great shame for us, the servants of God, that at a time when the podestà and the bishop so hate each other no one can be found to reestablish peace and concord between them!" On this occasion he added the following strophe to his canticle:

> > Praised be you, my Lord, through those who give pardon for your love
> > and bear infirmity and tribulation.
> > Blessed are those who endure in peace
> > for by you, Most High, they shall be crowned.[14]

Francis then sent one of the brothers into the city with a message for the podestà. He requested the podestà to go to the square before the Bishop's palazzo together with the leading citizens and everyone else whom he could assemble. To other brothers, Francis confided the mission of singing to the assembly the Canticle of Brother Sun. "I have confidence," he said, "that the Lord will put humility and peace in their hearts and that they will return to their former friendship and affection."[15]

After the brothers had set off, Francis turned to the Lord in his darkened cell while Clare and her sisters joined their petitions to his before the Crucified One in their chapel. They pleaded that the great mystery of reconciliation with all creation that Francis' hymn celebrated would reach its logical crown when man would forgive and embrace his fellow man as his true brother.

"When everyone had gathered at the place of the cloister of the Bishop's palace, the two brothers stood up, and one of them was the spokesman: 'Despite his sufferings, blessed Francis,' he said, 'has composed the "Praises of the Lord" for all his creatures, to the praise of God and for the edification of his neighbor; he asks you to listen with great devotion."[16]

With that the brothers began to sing. A hush fell over the excited throng as the hidden power of the hymn of cosmic unity began to move over them, as once the Spirit of the Lord had brooded over the chaos. The podestà stood as if in a cathedral listening to the Gospel. The Bishop was absorbed as if hearing the Lord address him by name. As the song of the brothers swept to its climax, tears were coursing down the cheeks of many. Messer Oportulo "threw himself at the feet of the lord bishop and said to him: 'For the love of our Lord Jesus Christ and of blessed Francis, his servant, I am ready to make any atonement you wish.' The bishop stood up and said to him: 'My office demands humility of me, but by nature I am quick to anger; you must forgive me!' With much tenderness and affection, both locked arms and embraced each other. . . .These two men forgetting all past offensive words and after a very great scandal, returned to a very great concord." concluded Brother Leo.[17]

Only those who lived in Assisi and had had experience of how destructive such internecine strife could be could fully appreciate how great was the gift Francis had obtained for his beloved city. Clare and all her sisters rejoiced but perhaps none quite so much as the little sister whose carnal father and spiritual father were once more at peace.

Before Francis left San Damiano, he wished to express his gratitude to Clare and the other Poor Ladies for their compassionate hospitality. He would leave this dear place much as he had left Mount La Verna eight months before—a changed man, knowing he would never return to this sanctuary of many graces. Francis' tribute would take the form of a troubadour's. He composed a canticle to celebrate the chatelaine and ladies of the great castle of San Damiano.

His song was a hymn praising women who live in unity, reconciled to their sisters and bound into deep harmony within themselves. There is a striking parallel in the imagery and ideas expressed in the five stanzas Francis wrote for Clare and her sisters with the last five stanzas of the Canticle of Brother Sun. Were they meant to be sung as an alternate ending of the great Canticle?

In words of great gentleness Francis appeals to the sisters to always live together in the same harmony as the elements of the physical universe display. He touches on areas of greatest sensitivity for woman and offers motives most in harmony with feminine aspirations. By doing so, Francis reveals that now, only seventeen months before his death, his own feminine side has been fully accepted and reconciled with his strong masculinity.

> Listen, little poor ones called by the Lord,
>   who have come together from many parts and
>   provinces:
> Live always in truth,
>   that you may die in obedience.

Do not look at the life outside,
for that of the Spirit is better,

I beg you through great love,
to use with discretion
the alms which the Lord gives you.

Those who are weighed down by sickness
and the others who are wearied because of them,
all of you: bear it in peace.

For you will sell this fatigue at a very high price
and each one of you will be crowned queen
in heaven with the Virgin Mary.[18]

A point which Francis stressed in both of his canticles is the sanctification of illness. In his day, people were more often ill than fully robust. The average length of life was about thirty years. By this time, Francis had accepted infirmity as part of his daily life. For Clare, also, infirmity was to become a constant companion. Francis was approaching the end of his physical crucifixion; Clare was just beginning hers. From 1224 to her death in 1253, she would never again enjoy strength of body.

Francis was not insensitive to the toll on those who bear the burden of caring for the sick. Once he expressed his sympathy toward the faithful brothers who were so devotedly caring for his needs by saying:

My dearest brothers and my little children, bear with joy the pain and fatigue that my infirmity causes you. The Lord will take the place of his poor servant to recompense you both in this world and in the next; he will credit you with the good works that you have to neglect in order to take care of me. You will obtain an even greater recompense than those who serve the whole Order." The holy Father spoke in this fashion to encourage and sustain the weak and scrupulous who might have thought: "We can no longer pray, and this additional fatigue is beyond our strength."[19]

The four brothers to whom these words were addressed are described by Celano as those "upon whom the blessed father Francis leaned, like a house upon its four columns. . . . Modesty adorned all these brothers and made them lovable and kind to men . . . but a special virtue adorned each one. One was known for his outstanding discretion (Brother Angelo Tancredi), another for his extraordinary patience, (Brother Rufino), the third for his great simplicity (Brother Leo), and the last was robust of body and gentle of disposition (Brother Masseo)."[20]

Clare's excessive fasting during her first years at San Damiano is frequently cited as the reason why her health gave way and made her susceptible to a chronic and debilitating illness. We do not know just what this was, but it induced such weakness that for long periods of time, Clare was unable to leave her bed. She would ask the sisters to prop her up with a support behind her back so that she could work with her skilled needle. There were days when she could not take a single step unaided. At other times, however, she experienced a respite and would regain sufficient strength to join her sisters again in the choir and refectory. Twenty-eight years of progressive collapse were ahead of Clare as Francis lay dying.

Now Clare rests her hand lightly on the message sent to her by him. Though she has feared death for herself, and even more his, the reality of its imminence now removes all fear. Francis is yielding himself into the arms of Sister Death. Sister Death! He has even transformed that chill spectre into his sister. Rather, not transformed it but simply recognized death for what she

really is, the inseparable sister of every child born of woman.
The last strophe of Francis' great song was composed in Guido's
palace.

> Praised be you, my Lord, through our Sister Bodily
>   Death,
> from whom no living man can escape.
> Woe to those who die in mortal sin.
> Blessed are those whom death will find in your
>   most holy will,
> for the second death shall do them no harm.
> Praise and bless my Lord and give him thanks
> and serve him with great humility.[21]

Softly Clare repeats this new strophe which one of the brothers may have taught her: "Praise and bless my Lord, and give
him thanks, and serve him with great humility."

The brothers had told her that toward the end of September
Francis had extracted from the doctor—his life-long friend,
Bongiovanni, the admission that death was indeed very near.
"Then blessed Francis who was lying on his bed in an extremely
weakened condition, extended his arms and raised his hands
toward the Lord with great devotion and respect, crying out, his
body and soul permeated with joy: 'Welcome, Sister Death!' "[22]

When Francis had left San Damiano in early summer of 1225,
Clare had wondered if she would ever see him again. He had
had to ride on a donkey guided by others and wearing a large
hood pulled well forward which one of the brothers had made
for him. In addition "since he could not bear daylight, he wore a
woolen and linen band over his eyes sewn to his hood."[23] Possibly it was Clare's last gift to him, devised with the hope of sparing him some little pain.

Wherever Francis was taken during these months of vain
search for a remedy for his many ills, Clare followed him with
her prayers and concern. She was deeply happy when she

learned he had finally returned to Assisi even though she knew it was because Francis wished to die in his own city.

Clare's health was deteriorating during all this, but she felt grateful that she might share in some small way in his pain and may have hoped that by her willingness to bear it, Francis' pain might be somewhat alleviated. Quite possibly, God blessed her generous love and allowed this to be so. Still "there was scarcely a single part of his (Francis') body which did not suffer some pain. The prolonged agony he endured eventually reduced him to a state where he had no flesh left and his skin clung to his bones. He was hemmed in with agonizing pain, but he continued to call his trials his sisters, not his pains. The vigor of his mind increased as his body became weaker."[24] Joy emanated from him and touched all who came near. The singing at his bedside even aroused a mild scandal among some of the brothers who were concerned the people might be shocked at such light-heartedness displayed by their "saint" at such a solemn moment. Clare understood.

Quietly Clare listens to the evening breeze and to the subdued chirping of the swallows sheltering under the eaves. Her mother, Ortolana, approaches softly. Sometime earlier this same year, Ortolana had felt herself free to follow the desire of her heart and had joined Clare at San Damiano. Little Beatrice, now in her late teens, had found a home with some of their many relatives. Possibly one of the other families of the Offreduccio clan had moved into the huge palazzo on the square of San Rufino. Gladly and simply, Ortolana traded the life of a great feudal lady, surrounded by luxury and accustomed to ordering a large household staff, for that of a poor sister within the walls of stark San Damiano.

Perhaps it falls to her to tell Clare the latest news from the Portiuncula. As she steps into the darkening room, Clare makes a sign to her to listen. Larks are singing! singing as they do only when morning is cresting the mountain peaks! Clare has only to look into her mother's sad and compassionate face to guess the message she is bringing—and of which the larks are singing.

At the Portiuncula, Brother Leo remains at Francis' side. Of this hour he would later write: "After his [Francis'] death, his flesh became white and soft, and he seemed to smile. He appeared to be more handsome than in life, and those who looked at him found more pleasure in looking at him dead than they did when he was alive; for he seemed to them to be a saint with a smiling face."[25]

Even in death, Francis did not forget his "Little Plant" and the promise he had made to her.

> In the morning, the people of Assisi, men and women and all the clergy, came in search of his body at the friary. To the chant of hymns and canticles, holding green palms in their hands, they bore him by the will of God to San Damiano, so that the word the Lord had spoken by the mouth of his saint might be fulfilled and that his daughters and servants might be consoled. The iron grill of the window through which the sisters received holy communion and heard the word of God was pulled back; the brothers lifted up the body of blessed Francis from the stretcher and held him in their arms before the opening for at least a minute. Lady Clare and her sisters experienced a very great consolation from this.[26]

Celano tells us that "divided between sorrow and joy, they kissed his most radiant hands, adorned with the most precious gems and shining pearls; and when he had been taken away, the door was closed to them which will hardly again be opened for such great sorrow."[27] As Clare withdraws into her cloister, she feels more bereft and defenseless than on the night she had fled her father's house to follow Francis into an unknown future.

Now he is gone. But the words and deeds he has done live in

her heart together with a fear. She would one day write of this hour: "Our most blessed Father Francis, following the footsteps of Christ, never while he lived departed in example or in teaching from His holy poverty, which he had chosen for himself and for his friars. And I, Clare, the unworthy handmaid of Christ . . . and the little plant of the holy Father, considered with my sisters our most high calling and the command of so great a Father, and the frailty of the other sisters, which we feared in ourselves after the death of our holy Father Francis, who was our pillar of strength, and after God our one consolation and support . . . bound ourselves again and again to our Lady most holy Poverty."[28]

Francis' last admonition to his brothers now rings in Clare's heart: "I have done what was mine to do. May Christ teach you what is yours."[29] Though tears still dampen her cheeks, she gazes steadily at the Crucifix from which Francis had received his commission from his Lord. Her chin is firm and her head is held high. She feels as if half of her soul has been riven from her—but what remains of her on this earth has work to do.

Chapter XIV Endnotes

1. Legend of Perugia, #109.
2. Ibid., #109.
3. Testament of Clare, #10.
4. Legend of Perugia, #45.
5. 2 Celano, #50.
6. Legend of Perugia, #42.
7. Ibid., #43.
8. 2 Celano, #51.
9. Ibid., #212.
10. Ibid.
11. Ibid., #213.
12. *Omnibus of Sources*, p. 130.
13. Legend of Perugia, #44.

14. Ibid., #44.
15. Ibid.
16. Ibid.
17. Ibid.
18. Cajetan Esser O.F.M.: *Rule and Testament of St. Francis* (Chicago: Franciscan Herald Press, 1977), pp. 217–18.
19. Legend of Perugia, #47.
20. 1 Celano, #102.
21. *Omnibus*, p. 131.
22. Legend of Perugia, #65.
23. Ibid., #45.
24. Legenda Major XIV, 2.
25. Legend of Perugia, #108.
26. Ibid., #109.
27. 1 Celano, #117.
28. Testament of Clare, #10-11.
29. Legenda Major XIV, 3.

XV   Smoldering Flames

The city and the world in which Francis Bernardone, herald of the Prince of Peace had strewn seeds of brotherhood still smoldered and seethed with class resentment, power politics, and brutal revenge. Although the seeds of peace were potent, the ground was ill-prepared to receive them. But here and there they fell upon a fertile patch where "they sprang up and began to yield a rich harvest."

When Francis had died in 1226, the aging Honorius III, the "Interim Pope" elected in haste at Perugia in 1216, still had his hand firmly on the tiller of Peter's bark. The Crusade which he had launched in 1217 had ended in failure and disgrace. Although John of Brienne had declared himself King of Jerusalem and had conquered Damietta in 1219, he had later been forced to hand the Egyptian settlement back to the Moslems. In 1221, surrounded and besieged, he had had to surrender to humiliating terms just to escape with his life.

Undaunted, Honorius called for another Crusade, the Sixth, in 1223. The key to the success of his appeal lay with Frederick II whom Honorius had crowned as Holy Roman Emperor in 1220. One condition demanded of Frederick at the time was that he would take the Cross and lead the European armies on a conquest of the Holy Land whenever the Pope deemed a Crusade to be necessary.

Wily Frederick knew it would not be expedient for him to publicly recant his oath, but he had no desire to leave Europe just as he was in the process of consolidating his political position. With the German states behind him, Frederick had again sought the crown of Sicily which he claimed was rightfully his through his mother, Constance. The Sicilian nobility chose to contend that claim to their sorrow. By 1225 Sicily lay prostrate under Frederick's control.

Seeking to appease Honorius, who was opposed to having German dominance to the south as well as to the north of the Papal States, Frederick solemnly "took the Cross." He insisted, however, that he would need time to raise his army, arrange for ships, provisions, and so forth. Honorius reluctantly agreed.

Frederick then proceeded about his wars in Europe and, despite Honorius' pointed reminders, delayed taking any positive steps toward preparing for the Crusade. The feisty old Pope died March 18, 1227, and to no one's surprise, Cardinal Hugolino was elected the next day as his successor. As Pope Gregory IX, he inherited Honorius' formidable task of trying to curb Frederick's colossal will to power.

Gregory was a vigorous fifty-seven, a nephew of Innocent III, and he shared that great prelate's political finesse and moral courage. Frederick quickly learned that Gregory was not a man to be put off so easily as Honorius. For when he made no move to follow through on his crusader's vow, Gregory excommunicated him. Although this meant little to Frederick personally, as he appears to have been one of the few genuine atheists of his age, it meant a great deal to the rulers and princes who would all risk canonical censure by allying themselves with him. Their vassals, as well as the people of the land, were automatically absolved of their oaths of fealty to an overlord who was excommunicated.

Thus pressured, Frederick finally assembled his army and fleet, setting out for the Holy Places in 1228. But rather than get involved in protracted sieges or warfare on terrain unfamiliar to him, he negotiated a settlement in 1229 which allowed Christians to visit the Holy Places though the land itself remained under Moslem control. Reluctantly, Gregory had to accept this unsatisfactory arrangement and lifted the ban of excommunication from the Emperor.

Frederick had early discovered that an alliance with a country through a political marriage worked to his advantage. He made several such alliances, his wives unfortunately dying after only a few years of marriage to the "Stupor Mundi"! Thus when Elizabeth of Thuringia, sister to the king of Hungary, was widowed in 1227, Frederick sought her hand in marriage.

Although Elizabeth had been dispossessed by her jealous in-laws and her children deprived of their rightful inheritance, she refused the offer to become Empress. Her marriage to Ludwig had been a profoundly happy one and she was nearly devastated with grief when he died at the age of twenty-five while on crusade. After that, Elizabeth turned her thoughts wholly to the things of God and to the service of her beloved poor. She managed to reclaim her dowry and personal patrimony. Most of it she set aside for her three children's future. Then she placed them in either a noble household or a convent where they could be educated and brought up as befit their rank.

Elizabeth took the vows of a Franciscan tertiary, and with what remained of her money built a hospital at Marburg where she tended the sick poor. Her strength was soon exhausted and on November 7, 1231, Elizabeth died at the age of twenty-four.

Her body, exhumed for her canonization in 1235, was found to be incorrupt. Frederick attended this elaborate ceremony and in front of the vast crowd, which included her own children, he removed the crown from his own head and placed it on the brow of the still-lovely princess. "I could not crown her in life as my empress," he is quoted as saying, "so I will crown her in death as a queen in heaven."

Around 1231, Frederick desired to cement relations with Bohemia, and asked for the hand of Agnes, the daughter of the King of Bohemia. Much pressure was brought to bear on Agnes because of the political advantages to be had by such a match, but Agnes refused to consider his suit for she had other plans in mind for her future.

In the same year a Portuguese friar who was teaching and preaching with remarkable success in Northern Italy, died in Padua at the age of thirty-six. Although Anthony was probably only known to Clare by reputation, she mourned his loss to the Order. She must have heard of Francis' great affection and esteem for this brother whom he had jokingly referred to as "my bishop."

When Francis had died amid the singing larks at Assisi, the citizens of the city were standing around the death place of their saint with weapons in their hands. Only their extreme reverence for the wishes of the dying Francis had prevailed over their fear of the Perugians when they permitted him to be carried outside the city walls to St. Mary of the Angels.

They suspected, with good reason, that their perennial foe would be only too eager to possess the body of the greatest saint of Umbria and would not shrink from armed robbery if they felt they could succeed. Therefore, even while Francis remained in the Bishop's palace within the city, knights and members of the civil militia maintained a twenty-four-hour guard about him.

These guards were doubled when Francis was taken to the Portiuncula. They replaced one another in watches as regularly as the men who guarded the ramparts of the city. As soon as the news of his death was abroad, the citizens of Assisi poured out of its gates in the evening twilight. From the villages, the fields, the outlying castles, everyone who could walk converged on the little chapel in the woods.

Many were nervously watching the roads to the west, fearing that a band of armed men might appear at any moment. The man who had preached and prayed for the peace of God to enter the lives of all people nearly became the cause of yet another civil strife. As soon as it was daylight, the body was hastened up the hillside into the safety of the city walls. There in the church of San Giorgio, where he had studied under the canons as a boy, Francis' body was laid in a temporary tomb.

Implacable rivalry between Perugia and Assisi had kept the Umbrian valley in a constant state of strife since the dawn of communal life in the area. Assisi, often defeated, never remained down for long. Whenever circumstances permitted, Assisi organized raids on Perugia's border lands, razed lookout towers, captured and tortured any hapless Perugian they could lay hands on. Perugia repaid them in kind.

Within the community of the Poor Ladies which harbored women and girls from both Perugia and Assisi, from feudal families as well as from the rising merchant class, from daughters of serfs on the land and of tradesmen in the city, the seeds of peace which Francis had implanted were being carefully nurtured. Like fragile seedlings which require hothouse tending until they attain a certain maturity, the ideals and vision of the pure gospel life which Francis had revived in the Church were being kept alive. They flourished within the silent walls of San Damiano, blooming and then scattering like seeds on the wind.

Storms and feuds were raging in the First Order, however. Clare could only stand quietly by like a lighthouse beacon for the boats being tossed about on the waves. Perhaps Brother Leo besought Clare's prayers for himself before he went into hiding as a fugitive from Brother Elias' wrath. For Elias, with Pope Gregory's blessing, had set about raising funds to erect a magnificent basilica to the honor of the most revered saint in Christendom. Leo violently opposed this idea, considering it totally contrary to Francis' desires and to the way of life of the Lesser Brothers. According to one account, Leo kicked over the large stone urn which Elias had set up in the piazza to collect the donations of the faithful. Elias ordered Leo expelled from the Order. So Leo chose to flee into exile as did many other brothers who, for one reason or another, had aroused Brother Elias' displeasure.

Despite this opposition within the Order, Elias went ahead with the plans for his two-level cathedral which he hoped would rival even the most magnificent of churches rising in great urban centers all over the European continent. The work, spearheaded by Elias' insatiable energy, proceeded so swiftly that by 1230 the lower church was ready to be dedicated. The ceremony took place May 25, 1230.

A huge procession formed at the church of San Giorgio to accompany the transferral of Francis' body to the new crypt made ready for it. All the nobility of Assisi were present with the wealthy merchants and craftsmen, rivaling them in richness of robe and gown. Mounted knights wearing the blue and red municipal colors trotted along beside the throng of people and clergy walking behind the casket.

Trumpeters raised their slender, flag-draped instruments to sound the "Call to Arms" of the city of Assisi. The procession wound through flower-bedecked streets and past brilliant tapestries hung over balconies of the palazzos. As the procession neared the new church, an unexpected disturbance erupted. Without warning a closed phalanx of mounted men bore down on the coffin, swept it up from the shoulders of the bearers and disappeared with it into the gloom of the lower church.

People were thrown into an uproar fearing that the Perugians had boldly snatched their most precious treasure from their very midst. Actually, this body snatching episode appears to have been a plan of Brother Elias to make sure that no such loss could ever occur. Before the crowds had reached the church door, the coffin was lowered into a secret chamber far below the floor and a huge block of granite, weighing over two hundred pounds placed upon it. Over this, a one-hundred-ninety-pound iron grill was fastened. After the ceremonies, Elias had the entire hidden sarcophagus bound with twelve strips of metal welded in place and yet another block of stone laid over this. Finally, the marble floor of the lower church concealed the location so well that its exact site was lost to memory. Six hundred years would pass before the tomb would be found again.

One wonders if Clare, learning some of these details, winced inwardly. The man she loved and revered, who so often seemed to her like a spirit of living flame, now lay beneath a crushing weight of stone. In her faith, however, Clare knew well that Francis' spirit now winged more free than the larks he had loved.

How great must have been her exultation when on July 16 of 1228, she heard all the bells of Assisi pealing in wild joy as Gregory IX solemnly pronounced Francis to be a saint of God and deserving of the honors of the altar. Is it a mere coincidence that this date marked her thirty-fourth birthday? The little bell in the campanile of San Damiano rang as vigorously as the deep-throated bells of San Rufino. An eye-witness of this glorious event described what he had observed during this great moment of Assisi's history!

> The Pope came to Assisi where in the second year of his pontificate, surrounded by cardinals and prelates, vested in precious ornaments amidst a profusion of palms and candles, in the presence of a crowd that had come from all parts of the world, he delivered a sermon which began with these words: "Like the morning star among the clouds, like the sun shining on the Temple of the Most High, this is how this man shone in the house of the Lord." This was followed by a public reading of the miracles and their explanation. Then the pontiff, his eyes bathed in tears, decreed that blessed Francis, the servant of the Crucified One whose stigmata adorned his soul and body, was to be inscribed in the catalogue of saints.[1]

One of the principal orators at this grand celebration was Cardinal Rainerio Capocci, O. Cist. He had been Hugolino's delegate at the Chapter of 1221 when Francis had first presented his rule to the friars. Rainerio spoke so feelingly of "my friend Francis" that according to Celano who was probably an eyewitness, the Pope and all present were moved to tears.

When enumerating the various classes of people present at this glittering ceremony, Thomas mentions that "the most bashful habit of the sacred veil was seen there, too."[2] Could this be a reference to Clare and the other Poor Ladies from San Damiano? Since all women religious were cloistered in that era, no nuns could have attended the canonization without special permission. To whom would Gregory have granted this privilege more readily than to his beloved Poor Ladies?

Hugolino was profoundly moved by the privilege of canonizing his old friend and former protégé. This same Pontiff would later preside at the Canonization of St. Dominic in 1234 and of Elizabeth of Hungary in 1235.

The thirteenth century teemed with extremes. In the year 1225, a boy was born in the castle-fortress of Roccasecca, the last son of the Count of Aquino. Baptized Thomas, he was entrusted to the care of the monks of Monte Cassino at the age of five. This may have been done as an act of reparation by his father, for some years earlier, the Count leading imperial troops, had sacked the monastery. Quite probably he included in this "gift" of his son to the monks, the stipulation that in due time Thomas would become abbot of this influential monastic center.

The year 1231 also witnessed Frederick II's invasion of the Italian peninsula from the north. At one time most of Lombardy, Tuscany, Umbria, and the submontane provinces had been fiefdoms of German overlords. Frederick planned to restore this arrangement and he found allies among many of the feudal families of the region.

These lords had lost much of their prestige and power as the serfs and vassals they had controlled began their determined push to attain the status of freedom. Many serfs moved from the countryside into the cities where they became craftsmen. As members of the various guilds, so influential in that century, they attained a limited amount of autonomy. Then, too, the rising middle class of merchants had, along with their wealth, begun to enjoy a state of near-equality with the older aristocracy in matters of city government.

If the former imperial order could be re-established, these feudal families could expect special consideration and, hopefully, the restoration of their ancient privileges. Therefore many allied themselves with the emperor's forces. The communes, however, were absolutely unwilling to surrender their hard won freedoms and return to their former situation in which heavy taxation, together with the necessity of supplying food and soldiers for the endless wars of the empire, drained their cities' resources and reduced them to the state of mere tributaries to the emperor's good pleasure.

The only bastion powerful enough to oppose Emperor Frederick's schemes for expansion of his influence was the Roman Church. Many cities, therefore, sought to put themselves under her protection by pledging to come to the assistance of the Holy Father and the Papal States as need arose.

Perugia was proud to be called a Papal city, situated as it was on the very edge of the Papal States. Assisi (naturally) supported the emperor. Yet each was mainly interested in preserving and increasing its own autonomy and power. Within the cities themselves, there was frequent and bitter division. Blood feuds or vendettas raged among the feudal families; merchants clashed with the nobility over civil liberties and equal rights; serfs and persons bound to the land made desperate bids for emancipation.

Francis' secular Order members were forbidden to take oaths of fealty or to carry arms. This leveled the final blow at the already tottering feudal structure, for if men could not be bound in vassalage to overlords and could not be forced into military service, the main support enabling the supremacy of the noble classes drained away.

In addition to the general unrest in Italy due to invading armies and conflicting allegiances, we must add the ferment caused by various heretical religious sects. In and around Assisi the Cathari were to be found in great numbers. In fact the entire region was a hotbed of fanatical dissenters.

In the midst of all this turmoil, the small, unprotected monastery of San Damiano stood on the hillside below Assisi's walls. It appeared as rooted and silent as the olive groves which surrounded it. And like those groves which produced their rich olives in due season, San Damiano would produce its fruits of holiness by which the warring world, unknown to itself, would be nourished, soothed, and enlightened. This hidden gift, like the olive oil itself, would flow most abundantly from between the heavy stones of a press.

Chapter XV Endnotes

1. Thirteenth-Century Testimony #3 in *Omnibus*, p. 1603.
2. 1 Celano #124.

XVI   Steadfast Radiance

A papal courier in travel-stained attire trots his weary horse toward an insignificant complex of buildings which is nearly hidden among the cypress and olive trees surrounding it. He seems uncertain that these rude buildings of undressed stone are the place to which he had been sent. But as there is nothing else suitable in sight, he spurs his horse up the hillside and reins in before a heavy wooden door which, he notes, can be opened only from within.

When, in response to his vigorous tug on the bell rope, a sister dressed in a rough gray habit opens the door, the messenger decides that he has found the right place. He is somewhat dismayed for when Pope Gregory IX had personally entrusted a sealed letter to him with instructions to deliver it as quickly as possible, the courier had assumed that it must be a vitally needed document for some large and influential monastery. Many times he has been sent in haste to deliver papal decisions upholding a monastery's jurisdiction over a disputed piece of land or empowering a community to accept new endowments. At times he had delivered briefs appointing some influential person whom the Pope wished to reward, as abbot of a community of which he is not even a member. Such an "abbot" enjoyed the right to collect revenues from the monastery without even being in residence there. A prior would govern the community in his name. Occasionally, such benefices were granted even to lay persons.

The nature of the missive he now delivered piques the courier's imagination. Why would the newly elected Pontiff, who was occupied with the many thorny situations bequeathed to him by his predecessor, be so concerned about this extremely poor, almost makeshift little convent?

Yet when Gregory IX had handed the letter to the courier, he seemed more concerned about its safe and rapid delivery than he was with the dozens of rescripts, bulls, briefs, and privileges that passed daily across his desk for his signature and seal.

The young sister who opens the door takes the letter, glances at the handwriting and the seal of the Fisherman's ring, and flushes with excitement. In her eagerness to take it to Clare, she almost forgets the messenger standing expectantly on the doorstep. She remembers her duties sufficiently to direct him around to the back where he can tether his weary horse in the shade and receive some refreshment from the sister in the kitchen.

When he reaches the open kitchen door and glances in, he sees the same sister waving the letter eagerly before another sister clad in a similar lazzo tunic. She, engaged in washing out some large pots, has her arms buried to her elbows in greasy water. Laughingly, she bids the younger sister to please hold the letter still so she can at least read the address.

"Didn't I tell you, Mother," crows Sister Agnes, "that 'our' Cardinal would not forget us after he was elected Pope? What do you think he has to say?"

Clare smiles gently and replies that the best way to find out would be to open and read it. Hastily she dries her hands and arms while Sister Agnes summons everyone she can find to come to the cloister court. Clare waits in the sun-filled yard until all the sisters have gathered and then shows them the letter, impressively sealed with the new Pope's insignia but bearing the familiar, strong handwriting of their beloved Cardinal-Protector, Hugolino.

Impatiently the younger aspirants urge Clare to open it instead of just admiring it. But Clare, knowing how precious each little joy can be in a life of outward sameness, will not deny her sisters the pleasure of seeing and handling such an impressive letter. Only after everyone has had her chance to see the great seal and admire the rich vellum does she break the seal and open the letter.

Most likely Clare, after hearing the news of Hugolino's election in March, 1227, had sent him a note of heartfelt congratulations together with an expression of her gratitude for all he had done for them since his appointment as their special guardian nine years earlier.

As she begins to read the letter aloud to the sisters, she notices immediately the difference in its tone from his previous letters to her. No longer does Hugolino address her with the warm familiarity of a brother and spiritual confidante. Now it is the voice of the Vicar of Christ on earth that speaks through the words of paternal encouragement and exhortation. Perhaps he has been too busy to write it with his own hand and so had to dictate it, she muses. Still his genuine care for her and all the Poor Ladies is evident in every line and Clare is grateful.

> To His beloved Daughter, the Abbess Clare, and the Convent of Cloistered Nuns of San Damiano of Assisi:
>
> God, the Father, to whom you have offered yourselves as handmaids, has in his mercy adopted you as his daughters, and through the quickening grace of the Holy Spirit, has espoused you to his only-begotten Son, our Lord Jesus Christ, to be crowned with this heavenly Bridegroom in happiness in the kingdom of heaven. Since you are bound then to love your Spouse above all things who in his love of those who love him makes them his co-heirs, so you must delight in him alone with all your heart and will, that nothing may separate you from his love. For this end indeed through God's inspiration, you have sought seclusion in your cloister, that, having abandoned unto your salvation the world and the things that are in the

world, you may embrace your Spouse in untainted love and run to the odor of his ointments, until he introduce you into the chamber of her who bore him to be refreshed forever by the sweetness of his love. These things We are confident and certain, you thus attentively and diligently consider. Now they seem to you bitter, but they are becoming wholesomely sweet, and what seems harsh grows mild, and what is rough, softened, so that you will glory if you merit to suffer anything for Christ, Who for us endured the passion of an ignominious death.

But, because you are Our consolation amidst the innumerable trials and boundless difficulties that beset Us without end, We ask of you each and all, We exhort you in the Lord Jesus Christ, and more, We command you through these Apostolic letters that even as you have received from Us, you should walk in the Spirit and in the Spirit also live, forgetting what is behind and straining forward with the Apostle to what is before, zealous for the better gifts; so that as you walk more and more in virtues, you cause God to be glorified in you and fill up Our joy who cherish you with a deep love as Our closest daughters (nay, if the word is not out of place, as Our Ladies, for you are the brides of our Lord).

Now, because We are convinced that you have become one spirit with Christ, we beg you to make a remembrance of Us in your prayers always and lift up your pious hands to God in unceasing supplication, that he who knows that in Our human weakness We are not equal to the dangers that surround Us will strengthen Us and grant that We may so worthily fulfill the ministry entrusted to Us by him that it will redound to his glory and bring joy to the angels and salvation to Us and those committed to Our care. Amen.[1]

Despite the formality in tone, Gregory's letter attests to his profound esteem for the Poor Ladies as well as his high appreciation of their role in the Church. One is tempted to conjecture that this letter of encouragement and exhortation was intended for circulation among all the convents of Poor Ladies. By this time, 1228, there were at least twenty-four monasteries of Poor Ladies on the Italian peninsula and possibly thirty, some cities having two communities of Poor Sisters.

Clare's thoughts might have turned to Agnes who, in 1226, had been sent by Hugolino from Monticelli to Verona where he had purchased land on which a monastery was to be built. Agnes, together with some other sisters from Monticelli, established a new community there which soon flourished. The desire to enter upon this novel way of life, a life outwardly so poor but overflowing with the richness of interior vitality, stirred young girls and women everywhere. The joy and holiness radiating from these enclosed oases was contagious, and houses of Poor Ladies were rapidly coming into existence.

Some houses were already established communities which chose to change over to the way of life of the Poor Sisters, such as the Benedictine community at Monticelli to which Francis had sent Agnes. Others sprang into being where a group of pious women, who had been living together under a loose rule of some sort, desired to become more firmly united under the Rule followed by Clare and her sisters.

Occasionally, a flourishing monastery of Poor Ladies trying to "ease the squeeze" caused by the steady influx of new vocations, would send a group of sisters to form the nucleus of a new community near a city or town which offered them a suitable location. Many municipalities recognized the hidden grace and influence that flowed from these silently eloquent preachers of gospel life.

Each of these houses was an autonomous foundation depending directly on the local bishop or the Holy See. The monastery at Assisi served as prototype of what each new foundation strove to be, but Clare did not exercise any authoritative control over them. When asked, she sent sisters from San Damiano to help initiate the new community into the spirit and ideals lived by those who were first instructed by Francis himself. For instance, she would send Sister Pacifica to instruct the sisters at Valle Gloria near Spello for a year around 1248. Agnes would go in 1229 to Padua where Blessed Helena Enselmini, under the direction of St. Anthony, had gathered a group of ladies who wished to embrace the Franciscan ideal. Later Agnes would be sent to houses of Poor Ladies at Mantua and Venice.

Possibly as early as 1218 some women from Spain had traveled to Assisi and spent several months with Clare and her sisters. They then returned to Spain with the necessary documents to establish houses of Poor Ladies at Burgos and Salamanca. The exact dates are uncertain, and the first documented recognition of these communities is found in a Bull dated 1234. It presupposes that these monasteries had been in existence for some time previous to this date.

Numerous houses were thriving in France by 1228 as well as in Germany, Moravia, Switzerland, Croatia, Silesia, Sweden, and Denmark. Clare was no doubt in touch by letter with many of these, although, as noted already, she did not exercise any jurisdiction over them.

Regarding this marvelous spread of the Poor Ladies, Celano has written: "The fame of her (Clare's) virtues filled the dwellings of illustrious ladies, it reached the palaces of duchesses and penetrated even the inner chambers of queens. The highest nobility stooped to follow in her footsteps and though proud in lineage was brought low by holy humility. Not a few who were worthy of the marriage of dukes and kings undertook severe penance after the example of Clare, and some who had married a ruler followed Clare in their own way. . . . By these blessed flowers which Clare has brought forth, the whole Church has been decked with springtime beauty."[2]

Thomas was not simply being carried away with poetic enthusiasm when he spoke of ladies of illustrious rank and lineage who were so attracted by Clare's way of life that they left their palaces and spurned royal alliances to follow in her footsteps. Several of these noble women were known to him by name. Among them were two royal princesses, Blessed Agnes of Prague and Blessed Salome of Cracow. Possibly, too, by the time he composed his biography of Clare (c. 1255), Blessed Isabelle, sister of St. Louis IX, King of France, had founded the Poor Clare community at Longchamps which she and a number of ladies from the court then entered.

Pope Gregory, in his letter to Clare, and through her to all the Poor Ladies, highlights the particular role they are expected to. fulfill in the Church of God. Their function is defined by the unique and total love-relationship they have with Christ. It is what they are in reference to the Lord that gives them a valuable and irreplaceable position in the Church.

They have, first of all, offered themselves as "handmaids" to God and have been "adopted as his daughters." Through the "quickening grace of the Holy Spirit," they are made brides of Jesus. Their whole lives are to be spent "delighting in him alone" in the seclusion of their cloister. Pope Gregory expects them to walk and live in the Spirit and by so doing fill up the joy, not only of Christ's Vicar but of the entire Church.

Because they have become "one spirit with Christ," their power of supplication is immense. Clare understood this most keenly. Seldom does she speak of the joys of intimate contemplation of the Lord without expressly linking it with its effects on all the people of God. Once she wrote to Agnes of Prague: "In this contemplation, may you remember [me] your poor little mother."[5] This was Clare's last letter to Agnes, written only a few months before her death.

Elsewhere she urges her daughters to live truly holy lives so that they may diffuse the "fragrance of a good name, both among those who are afar off and those who are near."[4] If they live according to the form (of life) given them, they shall, by very little effort, leave others a noble example.[5] Mist clear of all her written words are those to Agnes in which she first praises Agnes for having left all to lay hold of "that incomparable treasure" which is union with Jesus through total poverty and then adds: "I consider you a co-worker of God himself and a support of the weak members of his ineffable Body."[6]

That Clare herself fulfilled this high mission is beautifully summed up in the Bull for her Canonization: "She was the new woman of the Valley of Spoleto, who poured forth a new fountain of the water of life to refresh and benefit souls, a fountain which has since flowed in many streams through the whole of Christendom."[7]

Gregory, in the closing lines of his letter to Clare begs her to lift up her "hands to God in unceasing supplication," because he feels he is not equal to the many dangers that surround him. Gregory was referring not only to the dangers to which power and prestige expose a person but also to the immediate threats to his life posed by the citizens of his own See city, Rome.

Apparently Frederick II had taken advantage of the rebellious factions in Rome and had fomented an uprising. Thomas of Celano spares no words in his harsh description of the leading families of Rome. "The Romans, a rebellious and ferocious race of men, raged against their neighbors, as was their custom, and being rash, they stretched forth their hands against the holy places. The distinguished Pope Gregory tried to curb their growing wickedness, to repress their savagery, to temper their violence and, like a tower of great strength, he protected the Church of Christ."[8]

Gregory shrewdly assessed the situation and finally decided that circumstances had reached such a pass that a bloody civil war within the city was imminent. On March 27, 1228, the party of citizens won over to Frederick's side openly rebelled against the Pope. To prevent a civic disaster, Gregory left Rome around April 20, scarcely a year after his election.

With the members of the Curia, he took up a wandering existence, spending a few weeks in Rieti, a couple more in Spoleto, then two weeks in Assisi. Most likely one of the reasons for this frequent change of residence was the economic burden placed on the city that harbored him. The honor of having the Supreme Pontiff in their midst included the additional honor of providing food and suitable lodging for the Cardinals and their suites, as well as for the Curial officials. To be able to entertain the Vicar of Christ in as sumptuous a manner as was customary placed a huge strain on a municipal budget.

Thomas of Celano records that Pope Gregory and the Cardinals visited the community of Poor Ladies at their monastery of St. Paul near Spoleto. He probably had also called upon the Poor Ladies established near Rieti. This convent had been founded by the noble lady, Philippa Mareri. She and some companions had, in their zeal to imitate St. Francis, retired to a cave in the nearby mountains. Later, her brother Thomas gave them an abandoned monastery named after St. Peter. There they had adopted the Rule of San Damiano. Francis himself had appointed one of his friars, Roger of Todi (later blessed), to be their spiritual guide. When Philippa died in 1236, Innocent IV very soon approved the veneration paid to her. She thus became the first Poor Clare to be beatified.

The description of the Holy Father's visit to the Poor Ladies is embellished by Thomas of Celano in his desire to highlight the marvel that the great of this world would go out of their way to visit the obscure and lowly servants of God. The Pope, "after the affairs of the Church had been provided for, kindly visited, in the company of the venerable Cardinals, the Poor Ladies of Christ, who were dead and buried to the world. The holy life of these Poor Ladies, their highest poverty, and their glorious way of life moved him and the others to tears, stirred them to contempt of the world, and kindled in them a desire for the life of retirement."9

From Spoleto, Pope Gregory moved on to Assisi. While there he convened a consistory of Cardinals to consider the cause for Francis' canonization. In short order it was unanimously approved and the ceremony set for July. Most of June the Pope spent in Perugia, perhaps trying to keep the jealousy of the two cities somewhat placated.

After the canonization, he remained in the Umbrian valley. Later that year Gregory was sitting in his papal residence at Perugia with a look of mild wonderment on his face. Before him lay a document which he just signed and dated: "Given at Perugia, the 17th of September, in the second year of our Pontificate." "How did she do it?" he may have mused, "how did she persuade me to confirm what I had definitely decided to revoke?"

Pope Gregory thought back to his most recent visit to San Damiano. The knowledge of the poverty of the little monastery had distressed him and he had determined to alleviate the situation. In the presence of the sisters, garbed in their rough lazzo and barefoot, he and the members of his retinue had felt acutely self-conscious of their ample garments of fine cloth, their glistening jewels, and heavy gold chains.

The overwhelming joyousness of these gentlewomen, most of whom were young, made them seem as radiant as brides. Gregory never failed to be impressed by the almost unearthly peace which seemed to permeate the atmosphere of Clare's home as if some mysterious incense was wafting heavenward from unseen censers. Thomas of Celano records: "The Lord Pope Gregory . . . loved the Saint dearly with a fatherly affection. But when he sought to persuade her, because of the conditions of the times and the dangers of the age, to consent to some possessions he himself generously offered, she wholeheartedly resisted and refused to agree. Then the Pontiff answered, 'If you fear for your vow (the Privilege of Poverty), we release you from it.'"[10]

Such a suggestion from the Vicar of Christ must have struck near terror in Clare's heart for suddenly she was on her knees with a desperate plea: "Holy Father, never do I wish to be released in any way from the following of Christ.'"[11] Among the sisters who witnessed the scene and added their pleas to hers were Sisters Pacifica, Benvenuta, and Philippa, all of whom had joined Clare very early and had participated in her struggle to live in highest poverty.

Sister Philippa, daughter of the noble house of Gislerio and a life-long friend of Clare, later testified concerning this incident that Clare "held the Privilege of Poverty that had been granted to her in great honor and reverence, guarding it with much care, fearful lest she should lose it."[12]

Sister Pacifica later noted that "Clare was as anxious concerning the observance of her order and the government of her sisters as any man might be regarding the custody of his worldly treasure."[13] And she continued, "The blessed Mother's love of poverty was so great that she could never be induced to own anything of her own, and she never wished for any possession either for herself or for her monastery."[14]

Sister Benvenuta added that Pope Gregory was not the only prelate who had tried to offer Clare security in possessions and had been refused. Cardinal Rainaldo dei Conti de Segni, when he was named Protector of the Poor Ladies, also tried and had met with the same humble but implacable refusal by Clare. It would be his supreme joy when later, as Pope Alexander IV, he presided at the canonization of his indomitable protégé.

Celano, echoing phrases from the Bull for Clare's canonization relates: "So strict was the pact she thus entered with holy poverty and so great the love she had for it, that she would have naught else but the Lord Jesus nor wished her daughters to possess aught else. The most precious pearl of heavenly desire, which she had bought by selling all, could not be possessed, she would say, together with a gnawing worry over temporal things. In frequent words she impressed on the sisters that only then would the community be pleasing to God when it was rich in poverty, and that it would have permanence only if it were always fortified by the watchtower of holy poverty."[15]

To this supernatural prudence Gregory was forced to bow and thus as he contemplated his personal confirmation of the Privilege of Poverty, first issued by Pope Innocent in 1216, his smile was rueful.

The text of this Confirmation is simply a repetition of the original Bull but omitted the prescription that allowed any sister among them who did not wish to follow the way of strict poverty to go to another monastery. For Gregory had seen with his own eyes that it was obviously a superfluous permission. The simple joy and extraordinary serenity that had shone from the faces of all the sisters whenever Gregory visited them spoke as eloquently as Clare's impassioned plea to be allowed to follow Jesus and to have only him as her security and treasure.

Whether it was during this visit or at another time, Gregory managed to get his own way for once, though causing Clare a mild discomfiture. Warned beforehand that the Papal entourage planned to visit the monastery, Clare and her sisters did all they could to prepare for this honor. They cleaned the little convent from the dormitory above the chapel to the steps at the kitchen door. The rough stone floor was scrubbed with stiff brushes until it fairly shone. The long refectory tables, the crude benches, the wooden choir stalls were all lovingly polished with oil.

Great armfuls of flowers and greens from garden and field were gathered to decorate the chapel. What was later called Queen Anne's lace, bright buttercups, and scarlet poppies were arranged in earthenware pots with leafy vines. Palm branches and olive leaves were scattered along the roadway just outside the convent. In the refectory Clare set out loaves of bread on one of the tables.

When Pope Gregory arrived with his retinue, he may have secretly enjoyed their dismay at discovering that not only they, but the Holy Father himself, were offered only rough wooden benches to sit on in the sisters' simple visiting room. But this was quickly forgotten as Gregory relished the renewed joy of sharing spiritual converse with Clare, an experience that never failed to kindle his own heart. According to the Fioretti, he considered Clare "a shrine of the Holy Spirit."[16] When he reluctantly announced his intention of leaving, Clare begged of him the favor of blessing the loaves of bread she had set out.

Once in the refectory, Pope Gregory said sternly, "Very faithful Sister Clare, I want you to bless those loaves of bread and to make over them the Sign of the Cross of Christ to whom you have offered yourself completely as a spotless sacrifice."[17] Taken aback by such a suggestion, Clare responded that it would be a most unseemly thing for her to do, especially in the presence of the Vicar of Christ.

Not to be outmaneuvered yet again, Gregory replied firmly: "So that it should not be attributed to presumption, but that you may also earn merit by doing it, I command you under holy obedience to make the Sign of the Cross over these loaves of bread and to bless them in the name of our Lord Jesus Christ."[18]

Meekly Clare submitted and did as she had been commanded and "all of a sudden a very beautiful and clearly marked cross appeared on all the loaves!"[19] When Gregory departed with several loaves tucked under his arm, can he be blamed for the little gleam of triumph in his eye?

To Clare's great joy, Brother Philip was again appointed, in 1229, as Visitor for the Poor Ladies, a service he fulfilled with wise and zealous love until 1246. In the preceding years, from 1221 to 1229, the Visitor of the Poor Ladies had been a Cistercian. Although the exact duties of a Visitor in those days are not known, one of them was surely the imparting of spiritual instruction to the community. As Clare's letters reveal, she absorbed much of the monastic and mystical wisdom of the great Cistercian tradition which she deftly combined with the spiritual principles which Francis had inculcated in her so successfully.

Clare was open to all the genuine sources of spirituality so that she might nourish her own soul and instruct her sisters. It is obvious to anyone who reads her writings that she drew daily enrichment from the celebration of the liturgy and most particularly from the Divine Office for she understood the Latin texts and wrote in that language with great fluency.

Scripture, too, fed her contemplative spirit from its limitless springs of life. Quotations from both, obviously written from memory, abound in her writings. In addition, many subtle allusions to these sources creep into her works. It was as if her very manner of thought was formed on the word of God. She seems to have truly "put on the mind of Christ" as mediated to her through the inspired texts.

The words of Francis, so beloved and so full of fire, were another privileged source of spiritual insight for Clare. To this unfailing source of light, preserved in part on paper but even more so on the tablets of her heart, Clare would ceaselessly turn. From this storehouse she would bring out the new as well as the old as she sought to preserve the precious trust Francis had given her and to pass it on to future generations of Poor Ladies.

At the very time when many of the friars seemed intent on dissolving all that was distinctive about the First Order founded by Francis "through divine inspiration," Clare was clinging with tenacity to his will in its most radical and life-giving form.

Thus when Pope Gregory was issuing bull after bull to the friars who were asking for mitigations and privileges which would ensure that they would have everything but poverty, Clare had calmly requested and received a new confirmation of her Privilege of Poverty. In the eye of the storm which was raging in such divisive fury throughout the First Order, Clare was a torch, flaming and bright, which no wind of worldly prudence, power, or prestige could extinguish.

Holding out with clear and calm conviction in her lonely struggle, Clare made of San Damiano a true citadel of gospel observance and became, in the words of Pope Alexander IV "a lofty candlestick of holiness that burned brightly in the tabernacle of the Lord."[20]

Chapter XVI Endnotes

1. Letter of Gregory IX to Saint Clare, in Brady, pp. 112–13.
2. Legend of Celano, #11.
3. Fourth Letter to Agnes of Prague, #33.
4. Testament of Clare, #17.
5. Ibid. #6.
6. Third Letter to Agnes of Prague, #8.
7. Bull of Canonization, #10.
8. 2 Cel., #122.
9. Ibid., #122.
10. Legend of Celano, #14.
11. Ibid., #14.
12. Cause of Canonization, Wit. 3, #14.
13. Ibid., Wit. 1, #14.
14. Ibid., Wit. 1, #13.
15. Legend of Celano, #13.
16. Fioretti, #33.
17. Ibid.
18. Ibid.
19. Ibid.
20. Bull of Canonization, #12.

XVII   A Guiding Light

Brother Thomas' quill flies swiftly across sheets of crackling parchment as he tries to keep pace with the flow of eager words from the sisters gathered about him. He is sitting in the visitor's room at San Damiano where he has come to collect additional information about their Father Francis. Pope Gregory IX has commissioned him to write an official biography of the newly canonized saint, and Thomas is trying to collect all the first-hand accounts he can.

It pleases him to see Sister Clare's pallid features flushed with joy as she shares her happiest memories with him. All the sisters have a word to add about what Francis had meant to them and all he had done to encourage and sustain them. Lovingly, Clare recounts the story of how Francis, while engaged in restoring the ruined little chapel of San Damiano, had been inspired to predict the coming of Ladies to praise God continually in this place. It seemed all the more remarkable to her because, at that time, Francis had not even acquired any brothers.

As Clare and her companions enthusiastically respond to Thomas of Celano's queries, he is savoring the serenity that fills the poor monastery. A peaceful joy, a deep harmony of will, seems to unite all the sisters. He marvels, for despite the fact that they are all clad in similar tunics of undyed lazzo, with their feet bare and faded black veils covering their heads, he can see the great variety of ages, temperaments, and backgrounds among them.

Here is Sister Ortolana, once the mistress of a great house in Assisi, sitting quietly among the sisters, her work-roughened hands unconsciously folded in her lap in the manner of the well-bred lady she is. In the group of newcomers is Beatrice, Clare's youngest sister who, upon reaching the age of eighteen, chose to follow her mother and two older sisters on the way of most high poverty.

Perhaps Thomas also recognizes Amata de Martino, daughter of Clare's cousin, who has but recently been the talk of the countryside. According to legend, the date for the marriage of this eligible young beauty of the Offreduccio family had been set when she paid a call at San Damiano. Her sister, Balvina, was already a member of the community, having entered eight years earlier.

According to Amata's own statement, Clare had exhorted her to enter religion "saying that she had asked this grace of God . . . that Amata might not be deceived by the world into remaining in secular life."[1] Clare's prayers won for Amata the light to perceive the beauty of the divine Bridegroom and the girl had broken her alliance with the fiancé of her family's choice, to enter into a marriage whose inner splendor outshone all the passing glories of which she could ever dream.

Thomas observes women from noble feudal families mingling easily with the daughters of serfs and small land owners. Great family names from Perugia, Spoleto, and as far away as Rome are represented among the sisters as well as names of the merchant families who are beginning to rival the aristocracy in splendor and power. As Thomas collects anecdotes about Francis from the sisters, some of whom had been personally recruited by the saint, his admiration for the community and for Clare's fidelity to Francis' ideals deepens.

Thus, in the first life of Francis which he composed during the months between July 1228 and February 1229, Celano inserted a glowing panegyric of Clare and her growing community. It is a valuable appraisal of the life pursued at San Damiano which has the additional merit of having been composed during Clare's own lifetime. Wrote Thomas:

> [San Damiano] "is the blessed and holy place where the glorious religion and most excellent order of Poor Ladies and holy virgins had its blessed origin about six years after the conversion of St. Francis and through that same blessed man. Of it, the Lady Clare, a native of the city of Assisi, the most precious and firmest stone of the whole structure, was the foundation. For when after the beginning of the Order of Brothers the said lady was converted to God through the counsel of the holy man, she lived unto the advantage of many and as an example to a countless multitude. She was of noble parentage, but she was more noble by grace; she was a virgin in body, most chaste in mind; a youth in age, but mature in spirit, steadfast in purpose and most ardent in her desire for divine love, endowed with wisdom and excelling in humility, Clare by name, brighter in life and brightest in character.
>
> Over her rose a noble structure of most precious pearls. . . . For above everything else there flourishes among them that excelling virtue of mutual and continual charity, which so binds their wills into one that, though forty or fifty of them dwell together in one place, agreement in likes and dislikes molds one spirit out of many.[2]

Thomas goes on to detail the virtues which impressed him most. He marvels to see "glowing there the gem of humility, the lily of virginity or chastity and the highest poverty in food and clothing." The grace of abstinence and silence fills him with admiration as well as the patience that quietly endures tribulations and vexations.

He concludes his paean of praise by mentioning that "they have so merited the height of contemplation that in it they learn everything they should do or avoid . . . persevering night and day in praising him and in praying to him. May the eternal God deign by his holy grace to bring so holy a beginning to an even more holy end."[3]

The fame of the hidden life that Clare followed so quietly day by day at San Damiano kept spreading, for wherever the friars went, they had only to mention the feminine branch of the Order to stir women with the desire to enter it. It would one day be written of Clare: "Though Clare was hidden, her life was known to all; though Clare was silent, her fame cried out; though Clare was enclosed in her cell, she was preached to men in all the cities. . . . She planted and cultivated in the field of faith a vineyard of poverty, from which are gathered rich full fruits of salvation. In the lands of the Church she prepared a garden of humility, planting there a great lack of many things; yet it yields a great harvest of virtues."[4]

When Cardinal Rainaldo was appointed Protector of the Poor Ladies around 1228, he sent a circular letter to all the communities in Italy. Outside of Italy, Spain seems to have had the next largest number of houses of Poor Sisters, possibly as many as ten by this time. The monastery of St. Mary the Virgin at Pamplona and the Monastery of Reparation at Zamora are documented as having been founded at this time.

As the numbers of Poor Ladies increased, their natural desire to have the friars as confessors and spiritual guides began to cause problems within the already troubled First Order. Some of the friars began to complain that looking after the Poor Sisters was too great a burden for them. These men made their dissatisfaction known to the Minister General, John Parenti. He, in turn, appealed to Pope Gregory.

Only a year earlier, Pope Gregory had written to the newly elected Minister General: "Seeing that the Order of the Friars

Minor is most pleasing to Almighty God, I commit the charge of these women to you and to your successors for ever. Take heed that you bestow on them such solicitude and care as a good shepherd does on the lambs of his flock, and We place you under strict obedience to carry out this command to the letter."[5]

Why was such strong language necessary? Obviously, Gregory must have been aware that the Poor Ladies were being neglected; for as their official Protector until his election as Pope, he would have known their problems. But now Gregory seems to contradict his own written command for he issues a Bull "Quo elongati" on September 28, 1230, which exempts the friars from any responsibilities toward the Poor Ladies. It also establishes a form of trusteeship through which lay persons can hold property in the name of the sisters and friars.

When Clare learned of this Bull, she must have been pierced to the heart for with one stroke of his pen, Pope Gregory had revoked the two dearest privileges Clare held from Francis. How could she submit to a ruling that was so totally contrary to all she had been struggling to establish and maintain for these past eighteen years?

As always, Clare took her problem to the Lord and there received the inspiration to be absolutely obedient to the Bull. Thomas of Celano tells the story: "When at one time the Lord Pope Gregory had forbidden any friar to go to the monasteries of the Ladies without his permission, the loving Mother lamented that her daughters would receive less often the food of sound doctrine, and said with a sigh: 'Let him take away all the friars from us now that he has taken away those who furnished us the food of life.' And forthwith she sent all the friars back to the Minister, since she was unwilling to keep the questers who provided only material bread if the sisters could not have those who provided spiritual bread. When Pope Gregory heard this, he immediately mitigated his prohibition, leaving the matter in the hands of the Minister General."[6]

Once again Clare had prevailed in her desire to preserve intact the trust given to her by Francis. But it was only a temporary victory. Six years later, when Brother Elias was Minister General, another decree from the Holy See, dated November 22, 1236, would release the First Order from any obligation to minister to the Clares.

This decree did not actually forbid the friars from acting as spiritual guides and questers for the Poor Ladies and in some cases, they obviously continued to do so. This seems to be true of San Damiano in particular.

Through the reluctance of the friars to assist them, houses of the Poor Ladies were being forced to endure great hardship. Gregory did what he could by issuing an appeal in 1235 to all Christians to "assist these women, who are so weighed down by the burden of penury that it is impossible for them to live unless charitable folk stretch out their hands to relieve their necessities."[7]

Clare never feared poverty for in her eyes Lady Poverty was a gracious and single-minded Lady who led those who loved her to live with the trust that literally opens the granaries of heaven, those same inexhaustable sources that have ever supplied the birds of the air and dressed the grass of the field with beauty.

Even the idea of trusteeship, which was a way of exercising ownership through an intermediary, was not acceptable to Clare either. She had not embraced a poverty that would constantly be looking for legal loopholes in the regulations defining it. She chose poverty so that she could be poor in fact, as well as in canonical definition.

In her testament, Clare would command those sisters who would come after her that "they are bound to observe that form of poverty which we have promised God and our most blessed Father Francis."[8] She defined the vocation of the Poor Ladies as a little flock "which our Lord and Father has begotten in his holy Church by the word and example of our blessed Father Francis, who followed the poverty and humility of his beloved Son."[9]

Clare was at pains to spell out in specifics precisely what she meant by professing the "way of Most High Poverty." In her Rule she states: "they [the abbesses and sisters] are not to receive or hold onto any possessions or property acquired through an intermediary, or even anything that might reasonably be called property, except as much land as necessity requires for the integrity and the proper seclusion of the monastery; and this land is not to be cultivated except as a garden for the needs of the sisters."[10] Legal fictions were not for Clare!

One of the main reasons why Clare had been distressed by the Pope's restrictions on the friars acting as spiritual guides for the Poor Ladies was her high esteem for solid doctrine and good spiritual theology. Her writings reveal that, although she had not attended any schools of theology, her quick mind had attended to and retained all she heard in sermons and spiritual exhortations. "Though Clare was not versed in letters, she delighted to hear sermons of learned men, believing that the kernel of doctrine lies within the shell of words, and this she would discerningly attain and enjoy with relish. She knew how to derive what was of benefit to the soul from the sermon of any preacher; for she knew it was no less prudent to pluck flowers from a wild thorn than to eat the fruit of a noble tree."[11]

There is preserved for us an anecdote about one of these sermons given in the chapel at San Damiano. Brother Giles one day brought an English friar, a master in theology, to visit Clare and her sisters. Clare asked him to preach to them which he obligingly began to do. The sisters were in their places behind the iron grille to the left of the sanctuary.

The English friar had spoken for some time when suddenly Brother Giles jumped up from the corner where he had been seated, apparently absorbed in prayer. "Stop, Master," he cried out, "for I wish to preach." Quietly the theologian stepped aside while Giles poured out fervent phrases from his heart. When Brother Giles finished his impromptu exhortation, the English friar took up the thread of his interrupted discourse.[12]

Clare was delighted by both sermons but she was even more impressed by the humility of a Master from the Schools who would yield his pulpit to a simple lay brother of the land. This was the true spirit of brotherly esteem which she knew Francis had so yearned to see among his friars.

Clare had been well educated according to the standards of her day, standards which were high for women of the upper classes. Her letters reveal not only her fluency in Latin but also how retentive was her memory and how sharp her intellect. She knew how to present a logical argument and follow through from a basic premise to its full development. She seems to have digested and assimilated what she heard and read so well that she could bring it forth again quite spontaneously and endowed with an original freshness.

Nor was Clare the only educated woman in the monastery. Her many girlhood friends who had joined her at San Damiano came from the same social strata as she and had, no doubt, received much the same education. Although pride of rank and social prestige found no place within the walls of San Damiano, the gifts of mind and character with which these women were amply dowered imparted a stamp of quality to the life of the community.

There was no artifical opposition between learning and living a genuine contemplative life in Clare's mind. The description of how she instructed her community given by Celano bears testimony to the marvelous balance and synthesis that came to be a hallmark of Clare's matured thought.

"Now, as she was the teacher of the unlearned and, as it were, the directress of the maidens in the palace of the Great King, she molded them with the best of training and enkindled them to such a love of piety that no words can describe it."[13]

Probably Celano based this observation on the testimony that the sisters had given under oath as part of the Process for Clare's canonization. For there, Sister Christiana had related that Clare "had ever inculcated the manners and virtues which are required from consecrated women."[14]

Clare well knew that the "manners and virtues" appropriate to consecrated women did not include the pride of rank and class distinctions which dominated the social mores of her time. To assist the girls of noble lineage to overcome such a mind-set "she first taught them to shut out all tumult of this earth from their minds, that they might heed only the hidden things of God. Then she would teach them not to be influenced by love of kinsfolk, and to forget their father's house if they would please Christ."[15]

Wisely Clare kept gossip out of her monastery. Although she and all the sisters were aware of the turbulent state of affairs outside the monastery, Sister Benvenuta attested that "Clare always spoke of the things of God and would not speak of secular matters, neither did she wish the sisters to remember them. But when any [public] person in the world was known to have committed some action against God, she grieved with many tears."[16]

By word and example, Clare showed her sisters how to hate the sin but love and pray for the sinner. Sister Lucia of Rome who had come under Clare's guidance while still a child, reported that "in every way within her power . . . Clare studied how to please God and instructed the sisters in His love."[17]

Thomas of Celano noted that Clare "exhorted them to contemn the demands of the body and to subject the conceits of the flesh to the control of reason."[18] Another witness, Sister Benvenuta, supplied the reason and the goal for this salutary asceticism when she recounted the personal teaching Clare had given her. "First," she said, "Clare taught me to love God above all things; then second, she taught me to confess my sins thoroughly and often, and third, she taught me always to have in mind the Passion of Our Lord."[19]

Clare was becoming a skilled spiritual guide through experience, observation, and divine enlightenment. In her Legend it is stated that Clare "showed them [the sisters] how the cunning enemy lays hidden snares for pure souls, and tempts holy persons in one way and worldlings in another."[20]

The source of this wisdom? Clare "was assiduous in prayer." Pacifica tells us, "and when she came from prayer she admonished and comforted the sisters, and always spoke with the words of God which were indeed always on her lips for of vanities she would neither hear nor speak. When she came from prayer, the sisters rejoiced as though she had come from heaven." When Pacifica was asked how she knew this, she said simply, "because I was with her."[21]

Clare had early recognized the wisdom of the Benedictine motto "Ora et labora." (pray and work) and had combined it with Francis' mandate to his friars that those "to whom the Lord has given the grace of working should do their work faithfully and devotedly so that . . . they do not extinguish the Spirit of holy prayer and devotion to which all other things of our earthly existence must contribute."[22]

The insight that work is a grace impressed Clare profoundly and she incorporated the very same phrases in her own Rule. Celano expanded on this when he concluded his account of how Clare instructed her sisters. "Finally, she desired them to work with their hands at definite hours that thereafter through the exercise of prayer they might be rekindled with longing for the Creator and that thus, while they avoided torpor and negligence, they would drive out the coldness of indevotion by the warmth of holy love."[23]

How well Clare knew and respected the composite nature of the human person! An angelic spirit could spend itself always in uninterrupted praise and adoration but a human being is not designed to engage solely in "spiritual" activities. Being an embodied spirit, the physical side of the person must be allowed its proper activites or it will fail to be the helpmate of the soul and become, instead, its tormentor and tyrant.

The manual labor and creative crafts in which the sisters tranquilly engaged were themselves praise of the Creator as they furthered his plan of perfecting creation. Strong arms, gentle hands, skillful fingers were all gifts from the Lord and to be able to employ them in the service of others is indeed a grace.

No one was exempted from contributing whatever she was able to give for the well-being of the community. According to legend, Lady Ortolana (whose name means gardener) spent her final years tending the vegetable garden of the sisters. Clare herself set a clear example of her intentions in this matter. When she was well enough to be about, she found countless little ways to serve and assist the sisters, from lighting the troublesome oil lamps for the Night Office to washing up in the kitchen. She would wait up in the evening to open the heavy wooden door when the begging sisters were late in returning and then she would relieve them of their laden baskets and wash their tired feet.

She loved to provide touches of beauty to uplift the hearts of the sisters and would plant flowers in the sunny courtyard where the sisters spent much of their time. She even had a planter on the tiny terrace outside the dormitory. Most probably she assisted the sacristans in adorning the altar and chapel for feast days as well as helping with the never-ending round of cutting and peeling in the kitchen.

Nor did Clare allow the grace of work to be lost to her during her long illnesses. Sister Pacifica told "how Clare was very often so ill that she could not get up, but then she caused herself to be raised in bed with a support behind her back so that she could spin and then with the linen she made corporals which she sent to nearly all the churches of the valley and hills around Assisi. The corporals were given to the priests who came to the monastery for them to distribute to the different churches."[24]

Sister Cecilia added the information that these "corporals were made with silken cases to protect them and these were sent to the Bishop of Assisi to be blessed."[25] This was a much needed service in those times when numerous small churches and chapels dotted the countryside. All too often the linens for use in these little oratories were in a sorry state of disrepair and even filth.

It may have been Francis himself who first requested this service of Clare and her sisters. He frequently swept out abandoned little chapels, driving out not only insects and rodents but also birds and bats who quite literally laid their young on the altar of the Lord. He adjured priests to "consider the sad state of the chalices, the corporals, and the altar-linens upon which the Body and Blood of our Lord are sacrificed."[26]

Although San Damiano quickly became a full house, Celano notes that: "Nowhere was silence better observed; nowhere greater the pursuance of all that was beautiful and good. Nor did constant chatter reveal instability of soul nor thoughtless words betray levity of character. For the mistress herself was sparing in words and would aptly express her wishes in brevity of speech."[27]

It is interesting that Celano links silence with the "pursuance of all that was beautiful and good." All great creative work requires silence and solitude for its execution. This is eminently true of the supremely creative work of contemplation. The purpose of silence was to create an atmosphere conducive to prayer and to the fuller development of the sisters' inner life. Therefore it did not exist as an end in itself nor was it ever to be an obstacle to genuine love among the sisters.

Clare designated certain times and places in the monastery where silence was to be especially observed but exempted the infirmary where "they may speak discreetly at all times for the recreation and service of those who are sick."[28] Her delicate sense of charity led her to appreciate that a sister who was ill needed more than just competent care. She also needed refreshment of spirit which came through cheerful recreation with her sisters.

Perhaps Clare had noticed during her brief stay with the Benedictines, that the use of sign language meant to preserve silence often proved more distracting than a simple spoken word. She incorporated into her Rule a flexible and extremely practical directive on speech: "They may briefly and quietly communicate what is really necessary always and everywhere."[29] This is an enduring norm which, where it is understood and faithfully observed, results in a genuinely prayerful but also relaxed atmosphere of silence.

Sister Cecilia, who had joined the San Damiano community while it was still in its springtime, was convinced that "God had elected the Lady Clare to be the Mother and principal Abbess of the Order in order that her example should confirm the other sisters of all the monasteries of the Order in their observance of this holy religion and that she should watch over the flock; and certainly she was most diligent in her exhortations to the sisters, as in her care for them."[30]

When one takes a careful look at the manner in which Clare strove to fulfill the responsibility which the Lord, through Francis, had laid upon her, it is evident that she saw her duty toward the entire Order in terms of witness, rather than as an exercise of authority. Giving witness to the love of the Lord who had called and cherished her took the form of loving service.

She knew herself as one beloved of God, and it was all her joy to pass the overwhelming love on to others. She knew that the surest way to experience the reality of divine love was through total surrender expressed concretely by total dependence, total poverty. "Love Him in complete surrender who gave himself totally for your love,"[31] she would counsel her sisters.

She felt quite certain that if she simply permitted divine love to light up her own life, others would be drawn by that radiance. All of her service, her exhortations, occasional reprimands and her instructions were directed to assisting her sisters to see and appreciate this same light of love.

Her example, far more than her verbal teaching, was the foundation of the Order of Poor Ladies. In the Bull of her Canonization we read: "Her very life was for others a school of instruction and doctrine. In this book of life, the others learned the rule of life; in this mirror of life the others beheld the path of their own life."[32]

Thomas of Celano makes this poetic description quite precise: Clare's sisters "cherished the tender affection of their Mother; they revered in this teacher the dignity of her spiritual office; they followed in their guide the path of perfection she set before them; and in the spouse of God they admired her prerogatives of highest holiness."[33]

Occasionally, the sisters at San Damiano were even privileged to share in the special marks of love that the Lord granted to their mother and guide. A delightful incident of this nature occurred around 1232 during Paschaltide. Sister Agnes related the event twenty-one years later with vividness of detail which demonstrates the profound impression it had made upon her.

"Once when Brother Philip of Atri of the Friars Minor was preaching, I saw a most beautiful Child of about three years near to the Lady Clare. Then I prayed fervently in my heart that I might not be deceived in this matter, and in my heart I heard the words: 'I am in the midst of them.' Thus I understood that the Child was Jesus Christ, who is ever present among those who preach and those who listen as is their duty. The Child remained in that position for the greater part of the sermon. It appeared to me as though the Lady Clare was in the midst of a wonderful radiance and was no longer like a material being but had the splendor of the stars. I myself was filled with an inexplicable sweetness when I saw this apparition."[34]

Sister Agnes was questioned about who was present when this occurred and whether any of the other sisters had seen the Child. She replied that as they were leaving one of the sisters had said to her, "I know you have seen something." But apparently Agnes never divulged this sweet grace to anyone other than the canonical commission.

The light, the beauty, and the joy of that experience epitomized for Sister Agnes all that she had come to believe of the holiness of the simple, eager, servant-mother of San Damiano. In Clare holiness was a kindness, an inexpressible gentleness, a sweet joyousness, and a steadfast radiance that seemed to all who met her to be the essence of a Christ-fulfilled human being.

Chapter XVII Endnotes

1. Cause of Canonization, Wit. 4, #1.
2. 1 Celano, #18, 19.
3. Ibid., #20.
4. Bull of Canonization, #4, 12.
5. Quoted by Nesta de Robeck, *St. Clare of Assisi* (Chicago: Franciscan Herald Press, 1980), pp. 81-82.
6. Legend of Celano #37.
7. Quoted by de Robeck, op. cit., p. 87.
8. Testament of Clare, #15.
9. Ibid., #13.
10. Rule of Clare, VI, #5, 6.
11. Legend of Celano, #37.
12. Piero Bargellini, *Little Flowers of St. Clare*, trans. Edmund O'Gorman O.F.M. Conv. (Padua: Messaggero Editions, 1972), pp. 93–98.
13. Legend by Celano, #36.
14. Cause of Canonization, Wit. 13, #2.
15. Legend of Celano, #36.
16. Cause of Canonization, Wit. 2, #10.
17. Ibid., Wit. 8, #3.
18. Legend of Celano, #36.
19. Cause of Canonization, Wit. 11, #2.
20. Legend of Celano, #36.
21. Cause of Canonization Wit. 1, #9.
22. Later Rule, Ch. 5, #1, 2.

23. Legend of Celano, #36.
24. Cause of Canonization, Wit. 1, #11.
25. Ibid., Wit. 6, #14.
26. Letter to the Clergy, #4.
27. Legend of Celano, #36.
28. Rule of Clare, Ch. V, #3.
29. Ibid., Ch. V, #4.
30. Cause of Canonization, Wit. 6, #2.
31. Third Letter to Agnes, #15.
32. Bull of Canonization, #14.
33. Legend of Celano, #38.
34. Cause of Canonization, Wit. 10, #8.

XVIII   Radiant Kindness

Assumption in the year 1232! The entire countryside is in a festive mood as the people prepare to celebrate one of the greatest feasts of the year. On the eve, huge bonfires are lit in honor of the Virgin. Eagerly Clare and her sisters gather to watch for them from the vantage point of their hillside cloister. As twilight deepens, glowing pyres dot the plain, the peaks of low hills, and the mountain slopes. Each little hamlet and village vies with the others to build the biggest and brightest bonfire for the honor of their heavenly Queen.

This day has both religious and secular importance for this is one of the designated days on which the serfs present their overlords with certain gifts, thus acknowledging their authority over them. For the Assumption, bread and chickens constitute the required offering. Such tokens are also presented to abbots by tenants on the monastic domains and to bishops by the men and women who work on the usually large ecclesiastical holdings.

This custom is likely the origin of Francis' practice of giving the monastery of San Benedetto a yearly tribute of a basket of fish from the stream near the Portiuncula. By this he acknowledged the monastery's ownership of the little chapel and its portion of land. Though evidence is lacking, Clare probably did the same, tendering Bishop Guido a yearly tribute indicating his proprietorship of San Damiano. For she, no more than Francis, had any wish to be a landholder on this earth.

On the morning of the Assumption the sisters may have been wakened while the sky was still gray by the chatter of peasants passing by on their way up to Assisi with baskets of bread and trussed, but still squawking, chickens. Anticipation enlivens their voices as these simple men and women, whose lives are tied to endless drudgery on the land, look forward to one of their few holidays. In addition to the magnificent religious rites, purposely designed to offer the people a foretaste of the heavenly glory promised them, there will also be a chance to feast their eyes on some earthly glories as well. For all the nobility and wealthier citizens will be decked out in their finest and most lavish apparel.

After the solemn celebration in the cathedral, the people will turn to the fair which has sprung up in the Piazza del Commune. Here they will frequent the bright stalls of the sellers of sweet meats, fruits, and wine. These can be savored while watching the antics of a dancing bear, the skill of a juggler of golden balls, or an acrobatic team's performance. Strolling troubadours and minstrels will offer both song and news to the milling crowds. For a few brief hours, the back-breaking toil and heart-breaking conditions of serfdom can be forgotten for the sake of the joy set before them in the person of Mary, daughter of earth and now Queen in heaven.

On this particular Assumption day, however, Clare's thoughts are not on the festivities in the cathedral or piazza. And, though it is Mary's greatest feast, she may have felt some twinge of exasperation with her. Sister Benvenuta is standing before Clare, eyes alight with hope. Sister Pacifica and several other sisters are also hovering about expectantly.

Two years ago, Sister Benvenuta had lost her voice "so," as she later said, "I could hardly speak."[1] Was this such a trial in a community vowed to almost perpetual silence? Clare knew that it was, and her compassion had often been stirred. She had seen tears glistening in Benvenuta's eyes as she stood in choir day after day, unable to add her voice to the psalms her sisters were praying. And when the rest of the sisters sang out their joy on feast days, she could only listen in mute silence. Recreations, where conversations would fly back and forth in swift repartee, also tried the young sister's heart for she could not express the remarks and ideas leaping to her lips. Perhaps, as so easily can happen, the sisters almost seemed to ignore her for why address a question to someone who cannot answer?

Now Clare frowns slightly for Sister Benvenuta has just whispered that "I was told by the Blessed Virgin in a vision that I will be cured by you today through the sign of the cross."[2] Does Clare wonder why, if the Blessed Mother has shown herself to Benvenuta, she didn't cure the girl herself? Nevertheless, Clare knows that her only duty is to obey, so she signs Benvenuta with cross. Immediately, her voice is restored—and she never tired thereafter using it to proclaim this great grace, as several sisters testified twenty years later!

Many of the sisters who are living in San Damiano experience the power of Clare's prayer, even when they do not specifically ask for it. Sister Cecilia had for several years suffered from a spastic condition in her throat so that she had frequent attacks of coughing and choking. According to Sister Amata, "as soon as Sister Cecilia began to eat, it seemed as though she would suffocate. One Friday Clare gave her a small piece of cake which she took trembling, eating it for obedience since so she was commanded. She never suffered again from that cough."[3]

Sister Amata herself experienced a remarkable cure through the hands of Clare. For thirteen months she had grown progressively worse with dropsy until she was so swollen she could hardly bow her head. A fever, cough, and severe pain accompanied the condition. She testified that Clare "having laid her hands on me, prayed to God that if it were to the profit of my soul, I might be freed from my infirmity."[4]

Sister Philippa added: "I was present when she made the sign of the cross and touched Sister Amata and. . . the following morning she was fully cured, her body reduced to the normal size of a healthy person."[5]

Balvina, Amata's blood sister, was also healed by Clare of a recurring fever and an abscess in her right breast which was so acute the sisters thought she would die of it.[6]

Thomas of Celano offers the reflection: "The beloved Crucified repaid the love of His lover, so that she who was inflamed with such great love toward the Mystery of the Cross was glorified in signs and miracles by the power of the Cross. For when she signed the sick with the life-giving sign of the Cross, she marvelously caused their maladies to disappear."[7]

Clare's natural compassion blossomed into a power-filled love which could not help but respond when a suffering person claimed her concern. Yet, physical problems among the sisters were not all cured as soon as they appeared. Clare seems to have acted in this manner only when she felt the prompting of the Spirit. She knew from whence the power came and which, like the wind, would blow wheresoever it pleased and whenever it pleased.

Clare herself suffered from a chronic and progressive illness which she simply accepted as part of God's design for her life. She respected his sovereign right to treat his other daughters as he knew best. Yet she was far from indifferent to sufferings, even if they did come from the Lord and employed all her skill in trying to alleviate them as far as she was able. She would procure whatever the poverty of the monastery would permit in the way of medicinal herbs and compounds, as well as skilled advice. The strict rule of fasting was set aside for the sick and she would try to tempt the appetite of a sick sister by preparing special dishes for her, remembering how Francis had done the same.

Yet Clare could not prevent Sister Death from visiting her

community from time to time. It is remarkable how frequently the sisters who gave their depositions to the bishop's committee after Clare's death would answer that, of the witnesses of a certain event, two or more were already dead.

Clare experienced both the sadness of death and departure and the joy of new vocations and new monasteries springing up. Frequently, she sent sisters from San Damiano to assist these fledgling communities to learn the spirit and customs of the Poor Ladies. She sent Sister Balvina, her cousin Martino's daughter, with another sister to Arezzo to instruct a new community there for about a year.

Around this same time, 1234, Pope Gregory invited Clare to send four of her sisters to Rome where he gave them a former Benedictine house, St. Cosmas in Trastevere. It was a consolation to him to have these sisters of Clare close by as he wrestled with the endless troubles besetting the Church and Europe during this turbulent period. And one must admire the courage of the sisters who were willing to go to a city where violence and riots were everyday occurrences. Even the Holy Father himself lived in the constant threat of sudden death.

Clare also knew fear only one but it was great one. She feared to betray Francis' vision through her own weakness and frailty. As her body began to weaken, this dread seemed to weigh more heavily upon her. A vivid dream or a waking vision came to her during this period, making a deep impression and consoling her greatly. Sister Philippa, one of Clare's closest friends since girlhood, recounted it in detail after Clare's death.

Clare "told me that once she had seen St. Francis in a vision. She was bringing him a jug of hot water and a towel for wiping the hands. With this she was ascending a long stairway but so easily that it was though she walked on level earth. When she reached St. Francis, he bared his breast, saying: 'Come, take and drink.' And as she did so. . . the substance was so sweet and delightful that she could not describe it. . . . and what was in her mouth seemed to be such pure shining gold that she saw her own reflection in it, as in a mirror."[8]

The unusual imagery of this vision/dream reveals a great deal about how Clare conceived her relationship to Francis after his death. Although he is high above her (in heaven), symbolized by the long stairway, Clare approaches him with ease, carrying in her hands the items customarily used as a gesture of hospitality. It was a service she often performed for her own sisters for, according to Sister Benvenuta's testimony, "Clare [often] brought the sisters water to wash their hands" before or after meals.[9]

Clare's intention of ministering to Francis, indicated by the basin and towel, would seem strange since Francis, already in glory, would not need personal service. But his ideal, his charism, which he had been called to live and to transmit, definitely stood in need of all possible assistance. Clare surely knew this and was doing all she could to maintain the integrity of that original vision as far as the Poor Ladies were concerned.

But when she reached Francis' side after her easy and light-footed ascent, it was he who ministered to her. In a surprising image, he offered her his breast from which to drink—as if assuring her that she was still drawing her life-inspiration from its genuine source. As she accepted his offer of refreshment, the sweetness and delight which filled her expressed the profound harmony of her whole being with that which Francis had first given her.

When she saw her own image reflected perfectly in this shining substance, she was given the assurance that she was indeed as perfect a witness to Francis' vision as an image in a clear mirror.

The brightness of Clare's witness was spreading far and about the year 1232, a princess in Bohemia heard of the Poor Ladies of San Damiano. Agnes was still living in her father, King Ottokar's palace in Prague. Betrothed at the age of three to Boleslaus, son of Henry, duke of Silesia, Agnes was six when the alliance ended, due to Boleslaus' death. Frederick II then sought her for his young son and heir, Henry VII. However, Henry "jilted" her to marry Margaret, daughter of Duke Leopold of Austria.

When it became know that Agnes was "available" again, Henry III of England sought her in marriage as also did Frederick II, this time for himself since his second wife, Yolanda of Jerusalem, had just died. By this time Agnes had "had" it as far as the game of political marriage was concerned.

Furthermore, her heart had been set afire with desire for another and greater Lover. Pope Gregory IX upheld her right to refuse the marriage to Frederick which her brother was intending to force upon her. In 1232, when Agnes was twenty-seven, the first Friars Minor came to Prague. Immediately, she took them under her personal protection and had a church and friary built for them. The following year she erected a hospital for the sickpoor in Prague in honor of St. Francis.

Although Agnes often personally cared for the patients there, as her distant cousin Elizabeth of Hungary had done, she was not wholly satisfied. She yearned to give herself to God even more fully. Rather than minister to Christ in the poor, she now dreamed of becoming one with him in his poverty. She decided to build a monastery next to the friars' hospital with the hope that she could establish a community of Poor Ladies there.

Perhaps it was one of the brothers returning to Assisi from Prague who carried her letter to Clare. Although the letter is lost, we can surmise its contents by Clare's response. Early in the spring of 1234, as soon as the roads were passable after the winter snows, five sisters left San Damiano and set out for Bohemia to form the nucleus of a new community of Poor Ladies in the monastery which Agnes had erected.

Clare sent a letter with them to Agnes in which she expressed her joy and admiration of Agnes who was choosing to forego the most brilliant match in Europe to become a poor and humble spouse of God. This letter reveals Clare as an astute advisor, one who knows how to encourage a budding vocation with delicacy and wisdom. She dwells on the freedom, as well as the supernatural inspiration, of Agnes' choice.

The courtesy, in which both she and Francis had always delighted, permeates the letter. Clare, though she is considered by Assisian standards to be of noble lineage, is well aware of the gulf which separates the royal house of Bohemia from the mere knightly family of the Offreduccio's. She recognizes Agnes' superior rank and pays graceful homage to it while at the same time retaining her own dignity as a daughter of God.

In the four extant letters of Clare to Agnes, we have the most fruitful revelation of Clare's personality and her values. The limpid style in flawless Latin displays the quality of the education Clare had received, as well as the clarity of her thought and her gift of expression. Her absolute dedication and the unification of her life with her ideals stands out. The letters are a mirror of her soul.

When Clare wrote this first letter, she knew very little about Agnes personally so she could offer only rather general advice and warm encouragment. She drew upon the motives which had brought her into religious life and offered them to Agnes for her inspiration.

This letter reached Agnes sometime before the feast of Pentecost, June 11, 1234, for on that date, she, together with seven companions of noble birth, entered the monastery of the Most Holy Redeemer where the five sisters from Assisi were living. For the next forty-eight years, Agnes would cling to and fight for holy poverty as tenaciously as Clare herself.

Clare's letter opens with a graceful salutation:

> To the esteemed and most holy virgin, the Lady Agnes, daughter of the most excellent and illustrious King of Bohemia, Clare, an unworthy servant of

Jesus Christ and useless handmaid of the cloistered Ladies of the Monastery of San Damiano, her subject and servant in all things, wholly presents herself with a special, reverent [prayer] that she may attain the glory of everlasting happiness.

As I hear of the fame of your holy conduct and irreproachable life which is known not only to me but to the entire world as well, I greatly rejoice and exult in the Lord. I am not alone in rejoicing at such great news but [I am joined by] all who serve and seek to serve Jesus Christ. For, though you, more than others, could have enjoyed the magnificence and honor and dignity of the world, and could have been married to the illustrious Emperor with splendor befitting you and His Excellency, you have rejected all these things and have chosen with your whole heart and soul a life of holy poverty and destitution. Thus you took a spouse of a more noble lineage, Who will keep your virginity ever unspotted and unsullied, the Lord Jesus Christ."[10]

This paragraph shows how Clare, with graceful competence, meets Agnes where she is at this time—still a royal princess with all the options of a woman of her rank. Clare seems to take a special delight in emphasizing Agnes' noble station and the splendors which accompany it. She sees how it will benefit the life of the entire Church that a woman of Agnes' nobility would willingly renounce all her privileges to follow Jesus as a poor and humble virgin.

Clare is a daughter of her time and culture. The royal families of Europe were regarded by their subjects almost as their possession, for they regarded them as representative of the best and greatest possible to their nation. These royal personages were a symbol of what the nation as a whole was capable of. Despite the hardships these rulers often inflicted on them, their subjects still held them in esteem with a certain gratitude and pride.

So for Clare, Agnes, the royal princess, symbolized the epitome of womanly greatness so extolled by the troubadours in their epic songs. To this high human condition, Clare beholds Agnes adding the perfection of spiritual nobility by preferring Jesus Christ to any earthly lord, even to the Holy Roman Emperor himself. So, as her point of departure, Clare speaks not of the poor and humble Christ but of this glorious Spouse of "even more noble lineage."

With tactful artistry, Clare then turns to describing Him in poetic phrases taken from the liturgical office for the feast of another Agnes, the young Roman martyr:

> When you have loved Him, you remain chaste;
> when you have touched Him, you are made purer;
> when you have taken Him to yourself, you remain a
>   virgin.
>
> Whose power is stronger,
> Whose generosity is more abundant,
> Whose countenance is more beautiful,
>
> Whose love more tender,
> Whose courtesy more gracious.
>
> In Whose embrace you are already caught up,
> Who has adorned your breast with precious stones
> and has placed priceless pearls in your ears
> and surrounded you with sparkling gems
> as though with blossoms of springtime
> and placed on your head a golden crown
> as a sign [to all] of your holiness.[11]

From this lyrical height where Clare praises and encourages Agnes to embrace this noble and dazzling Lover, she makes a stunning switch of perspective and suddenly describes him as the Poor and Crucified One.

Therefore, most beloved sister, or should I say, Lady worthy of great respect: because you are the Spouse and the Mother and the Sister of our Lord Jesus Christ and have been resplendently adorned with sign of inviolable virginity and most holy poverty; be strengthened in the holy service you have undertaken out of an ardent desire for the Poor Crucified, Who for the sake of all of us took upon Himself the passion of the Cross and delivered us from the power of the Prince of Darkness to whom we were enslaved because of the disobedience of our first parents, and so reconciled us to God the Father.[12]

Here we find an example of Clare's realistic appreciation of our human condition and also of her solidly scriptural understanding of the need for and meaning of Jesus' redeeming act. From this clearsighted recognition of our radical neediness and the sheer gratuity of our deliverance, Clare's thought flows naturally to a consideration of poverty.

O blessed poverty,
who bestows eternal riches on those who love and
    embrace her!
O holy poverty,
    to those who possess and desire you
    God promises the kingdom of heaven,
    and offers indeed eternal glory and blessed life!
O God-centered poverty
    whom the Lord Jesus Christ,
    who ruled and now rules heaven and earth,
    who spoke and things were made
    condescended to embrace before all else!

The foxes have dens, He says, and the birds of the
    air have
nests, but the Son of Man, Christ, has nowhere to
    lay his head
but bowing His head, gave up His spirit.[13]

Here we enter the throbbing heart of why Clare so cherished poverty. She saw that Jesus united in himself outward destitution with profound inner emptiness. Only such total surrender could receive the fullness of eternal life and demonstrate the only way for peace and unity upon earth. Clare goes on to compare Agnes' proposed act of renunciation with that of Jesus' himself and assures her that the result will be joy, here and hereafter.

> If so great and good a Lord then, on coming into the Virgin's womb chose to appear despised, needy, and poor in this world, so that men who were in utter poverty and want and in absolute need of heavenly nourishment might become rich in Him by possessing the kingdom of heaven, then rejoice and be glad, be filled with joy without bounds and happiness of spirit! Contempt of the world has pleased you more than its honors, poverty more than earthly riches, and you have sought to store up greater treasures in heaven rather than on earth, where rust does not consume nor moth destroy nor thieves break in and steal. Your reward then, is very great in heaven! And you have truly merited to be called sister, spouse, and mother of the Son of the Father of the Most High and of the glorious Virgin.[14]

How naturally Clare opens and closes this consideration with a reference to Mary! Jesus was able to embrace poverty only through her—and thus by analogy—Agnes may expect that only through Mary will she be able to fully embrace this evangelical poverty. From here Clare moves into some considerations whose logic and conclusions are inescapable —if one accepts the gospel.

> You know, I am sure, that the kingdom of heaven is promised and given by the Lord only to the poor; for

he who loves temporal things loses the fruit of love. Such a person cannot serve God and Mammon, for either the one is loved and the other hated, or the one is served and the other despised.

You also know that one who is clothed cannot fight with another who is naked, because he is more quickly thrown who gives his adversary a chance to get hold of him; and that one who lives in the glory of earth cannot rule with Christ in heaven. Again [you know] that it is easier for a camel to pass through the eye of a needle than for a rich man to enter the kingdom of heaven. Therefore, you have cast aside your garments, that is, earthly riches, so that you might not be overcome by the one fighting against you, [and] that you might enter the kingdom of heaven through the straight path and the narrow gate.[15]

Clare here deftly weaves scriptural metaphors with a passage from the writings of St. Gregory the Great which she most probably had encountered in the patristic readings assigned for Matins in the breviary. Because books were rare and expensive, Clare quite likely quoted these passages from memory. Her ease in using them to bring out her thought attests to how thoroughly she had pondered them, and what is more, had built her life upon them.

This manner of quoting Scripture and the Fathers to support a thesis was the common methodology in the Schools. Apparently, Clare had been exposed to this style of teaching, probably through the many learned preachers in whose sermons she had always found so much delight and nourishment.

But logic, however cogent, never moves anyone half so deeply as a few words of personal conviction uttered with passionate sincerity. So Clare briefly lifts the veil which guards the treasures in her heart to reveal the life-spring of her joy. Is it surprising that she uses words of lyrical poetry?

What a great and laudable exchange:
> to leave the things of time for those of eternity,
> to choose the things of heaven for the goods of earth,
> to receive the hundred-fold in place of one,
> and to possess a blessed and eternal life.

Because of this I have resolved, as best I can, to beg your excellency and your holiness by my humble prayers in the mercy of Christ to be strengthened in his holy service,
> and to progress from good to better,
> from virtue to virtue

so that He whom you serve with the whole desire of your soul may bestow on you the reward for which you long.[16]

For Clare, as for most of her contemporaries, *desire* is the characteristic mark of the spiritual person. The more one loved, the more one desired to love; one's desire was quickened with each new perception of the Beloved. In the Cistercian tradition with which Clare must have been quite familiar, desire was a prime element in the development of the mystical life. It became the hallmark of the Franciscan school of mystical theology as it was being developed at this time by Alexander of Hales. His student, Bonaventure, would erect his marvelous synthesis of spiritual development upon the evolution of desire.

But all that these scholars really did was to write out in scholastic formulae the charism that the early Franciscans had spontaneously lived. Clare took over the spiritual ideals which Francis had taught and lived and brought them into even clearer expression. For her, the contemplative aspect was predominant—as it was also meant to be among the brothers. Even their apostolic works, even their poverty, flowed from the abundance of the heart inflamed by the Spirit in prayer.

Yet contemplation was not to exist solely as a support to the apostolate. Humankind exists for the glory of God first and foremost—and that glory is man's exaltation. This was the "message" that Clare and the Poor Ladies were to epitomize. It is through contemplation and mystical exchange that the glory of God is made most fully manifest and integrated into the human condition.

For Clare mystical communion with the Lord was never an achieved state but a living, ever dynamic process, growing "from good to better, from virtue to virtue." She urges Agnes never to be satisfied but to constantly endeavor to serve the Lord with her "whole desire," a desire that increased from day to day.

Clare closes this first letter to Agnes, who is just on the threshold of the life which she has been living and fighting for, for twenty-two years, with a sincere plea for her prayers and spir-. itual support.

> I also beg you in the Lord, as much as I can, to include in your holy prayers me, your servant, though unworthy, and the other sisters with me in the monastery, who are all devoted to you, so that by their help we may merit the mercy of Jesus Christ, and together with you, may merit to enjoy the everlasting vision. Farewell in the Lord. And pray for me.[17]

Chapter XVIII Endnotes

1. Cause of Canonization, Wit. 2, #13.
2. Ibid.
3. Ibid., Wit 4, #9.
4. Ibid., Wit 4, #7.
5. Ibid., Wit. 3, #11
6. Ibid., Wit. 7, #13.
7. Legend of Celano, #32.
8. Cause of Canonization, Wit. 3, #29.

9. Ibid., Wit. 2, #3.
10. First Letter of Agnes of Prague, #1–7.
11. Ibid., #8–11.
12. Ibid., #12–14.
13. Ibid., #15–18.
14. Ibid., #19–24.
15. Ibid., #15–29.
16. Ibid., #30–32.
17. Ibid., #33–35.

XIX   The Light Diffuses

Compassionately, Clare looks upon the little boy who has buried his face in the folds of his mother's shawl. At the sound of
her soft voice, he turns to look at her but winces as the light
strikes his eye which is not an eye, for a festering growth has
completely covered it. Gently Clare touches the child's cheek,
then signs him on the brow with the cross.

The youngster whimpers and tucks his face again into the
protective folds of the shawl. Clare suggests to his mother:
"Take him to my mother, Ortolana, and let her sign him with
the cross."[1] By the time she finds Sister Ortolana, who is cutting
some greens in the garden, the boy is wailing loudly, and the
distraught mother is near tears herself. However, one glance
into the wise, patient eyes of the older nun is like balm to her
afflicted heart.

This Perugian mother, who has risked the danger of walking
openly through Assisian territory, drawn only by a desperate
hope that her little boy might be healed, suddenly experiences
great peace. Whatever happens now, she feels she can accept it.
She senses that Ortolana, a mother like herself, understands the
anguish tearing at her heart.

Without hesitation she places her son in Ortolana's waiting
arms and the child grows still. Ortolana traces the sign of the
cross on his forehead while cradling the little body against her
heart. The child's frame, taut with pain, relaxes in her arms.
Laughing softly, she kisses him, and suddenly he wiggles free
from her embrace and slips to the ground, looking about him
with the two bright eyes of a curious little boy.

As his mother tries to express her joy and gratitude, Ortolana disclaims any credit, saying that it was her daughter who is responsible for the healing. And, as Celano records, "Clare asserted that the child had been healed by the merits of her mother."[2] Sister Amata, who witnessed this exchange between her kinswomen, never learned the names of this mother and child.

Sister Francesca, however, does supply us with the identity of another little boy who benefited from Clare's healing touch. Messer Johanni of Assisi, who may have been the son of the procurator for the sisters, knocked in desperation upon the convent door one day. In his arms he carried his five-year-old son, afflicted with scrofula and burning with fever.[3]

Sister Philippa was present when the they came in and even her untrained eye could discern how feverish the child was. She watched as the "Mother touched him and made the sign of the cross. Afterward, the child left the monastery and she did not see him again."[4] But Sister Francesca later said that "the child's father has said in the parlor that he had been cured instantly and she herself has seen him come back afterward to the monastery quite well."[5]

It is interesting to note the two actions which Clare performed in nearly every instance of a miraculous cure. She touched the suffering one and she made the sign of the cross either over or on them. We know from Sister Pacifica's statement that while doing this, Clare prayed softly to herself though what she said could never be ascertained. Sister Amata did hear Clare's words when she cured her of dropsy. Clare had simply asked her Father that if it would be for the profit of her soul, may Sister Amata be healed.

Clare's gift for healing does not seem to be a power she exercised purely on her own initiative. Her action and her prayer seem to have been motivated by some inner prompting of the Spirit. Clare respected the designs of God for each person and would not interfere unless, through some mysterious intuition, she knew that the pain or illness had done its work or that it had reached a pitch where the sister could no longer bear it in peace.

Sister Benvenuta and Sister Philippa both related an unusual episode of healing in regard to Sister Andrea of Ferrara. "She was suffering from scrofula of the throat," Sister Philippa said. "Blessed Clare knew by means of the Spirit that this sister was grievously tempted by the desire to recover. One night Sister Andrea was below in the dormitory [of the infirmary] and she pressed on her throat so hard with her own hands that she lost her voice. This was revealed to Clare, and she instantly called Sister Benvenuta, who was sleeping near her and said: 'Go down quickly to the dormitory where Sister Andrea is grievously ill: Warm an egg and give it to her to swallow and when she is able to speak, bring her to me.' This was done, but when Clare wished to know from Sister Andrea what had happened she did not wish to tell it. Then the blessed Mother told her exactly all that had befallen and," added Sister Philippa, "this was recounted [with awe] among the sisters."[6]

Apparently, it was not the cure which caused the sisters to marvel so but rather the awareness that their Mother could know their thoughts and dangers from afar, a thought which must have been both consoling and sobering. Clare did not consider it wrong for someone to wish to be healed except when this desire included the intention to be cured independently of God's will and by some desperate act of one's own. This was the "grievous temptation" which had assaulted Sister Andrea.

Clare was not insensible to the fact that there is a limit to what the human psyche can bear, no matter how generous the love of the sufferer. Such was the case with Sister Benvenuta of Madonna Diambra. She herself related: "I had suffered from sores under my arm and in my breast, sores commonly called fistulas. Five fingers could be put into this fistula, it having five heads. I had endured this for twelve years, but one evening I went to the blessed Mother Clare in tears asking to be healed. Then the kind Mother, moved by her usual pity, got up from her bed and prayed on her knees to the Lord. When she had finished praying she turned to me, and having first signed herself with the cross, she then made the sign of the cross over me, and touched the sores with her naked hand, saying the Our Father. Thus I was healed of those sores which had seemed incurable. I never again felt any pain from them."[7]

This healing occurred less than two years before Clare's death so the bed she rose from was one to which she was more or less totally confined by that time. The experience of her own continual infirmities added a quality of deep empathy to Clare's natural compassion for the sick, a sentiment she had had since girlhood.

Suffering in any form stirred Clare profoundly. In this instance, it was not simply the physical distress which Sister Benvenuta had borne for twelve long years but her overwrought spirit which had reached the limits of its endurance that moved Clare.

All the sisters could see that while Clare's own physical strength was ebbing, she seemed to draw renewed vitality from the springs of prayer, a joyous strength which she shared with all of them. Thomas of Celano summarized their feelings thus:

> When Clare returned with joy from holy prayer, she brought with her burning words from the fire of the altar of the Lord, which enkindled the hearts of the sisters. They marveled indeed that such sweetness came from her lips while her face shone more radiantly than usual. For "God in his kindness provided for the poor one" and let her soul, which had been filled with his true light in prayer, be reflected outwardly in her body. Thus in this changing world Clare was joined unchangingly to her noble Spouse and found her constant delight in the things that are above. Thus in the turning wheel of time she stood

fast in solid virtue and, though hiding the treasure of glory in a vessel of clay, and remaining here below in body, in mind she dwelt on high.[8]

This radiance of holiness continued to inspire women in all parts of the world to follow her example. In 1236 the Magdalen Nuns at Regensberg, Bavaria, officially adopted the Rule of the Poor Ladies. In 1237 Clare sent sisters to the Tyrol where they opened two houses, one at Brixen and another in the vale of Trent. That same year other Poor Ladies from San Damiano established a "poor little convent" at Ulm in Switzerland.

Clare's dearest daughter-house abroad was the monastery of the Most Holy Redeemer in Prague. From there Clare received a letter which rejoiced her heart. Agnes had been appointed abbess of the new community by Gregory IX on August 31, 1234, less than three months after she and her companions had entered the monastery. Such appointments were not unusual in those times, particularly where a person of royal lineage was concerned.

Agnes proved most worthy of the charge demanded of her and, to Clare's deep joy, also showed herself to be as zealous for Lady Poverty as was Clare herself. What may have prompted Agnes to contact Clare at this time was her confusion over some recent Papal decisions which modified the practice of poverty for the Poor Ladies, as well as those directives which released the friars from caring for the sisters.

Clare's response, written sometime between 1235 and 1238, contains some practical advice but is mainly devoted to enkindling a still greater fervor and love in Agnes' heart. From Agnes' letter, Clare must have judged her ready to respond to the inspiring words she addresses to her. Agnes was hungering for the "something more" which haunts every aspiring contemplative.

To the daughter of the King of kings, the handmaid

of the Lord of hosts, the most worthy bride of Jesus
Christ and, therefore, the most noble Queen, Lady
Agnes; Clare, the useless and unworthy servant of the
Poor Ladies: greetings and [a wish for your] perse-
verance in a life of highest poverty.[9]

In Clare's first letter to Agnes, she is addressed as the
"daughter of the most excellent and illustrious King of
Bohemia," but here she is called the "daughter of the King of
kings." In the earlier letter, she was praised for passing up an
earthly throne as a consort to "the illustrious Emperor"; here
she is named a "most noble Queen" because she has become the
bride of Jesus Christ. Earthly royalty has been exchanged for a
heavenly nobility. What is more striking is that Clare declares
that Agnes is a queen *now*. Many times do we find this theme
that through a voluntary embrace of most high poverty, the gifts
of the world to come are already enjoyed. Did not Jesus say:
"Blessed *are* the poor in spirit, the kingdom of heaven is theirs
[now]?"
   In the next paragraph Clare highlights a theme which runs
like a golden thread through all of her writings and was a hallmark of her spirituality, namely, gratitude.

I give thanks to the Giver of grace from whom, we
believe, every good and perfect gift proceeds, because
he has adorned you with such splendors of virtue and
signed you with such marks of perfection, that, since
you have become such a diligent imitator of the Father of all perfection, his eyes do not see any imper-
fection in you.[10]

Clare obviously has no fear that sincere praise of another's
virtue might harm humility. Quite the contrary! She is at pains
to help Agnes see what great things God is doing in her. Clare
well knows that any woman who feels that she is beautiful in the
eyes of her beloved will be most effectively moved to rise above

any form of personal vanity, realizing that she is called to be as worthy of his gifts as she can possibly become. Such an attitude also preserves one from discouragement. Adorned with the gifts of her lover, Agnes can walk with wings on her feet, knowing that all her beauty comes from him and for him alone she will jealously guard it.

> This is the perfection which will prompt the King himself to take you to himself in the heavenly bridal chamber where he is seated in glory on a starry throne because you have despised the splendors of an earthly kingdom and considered of little value the offers of an imperial marriage. Instead, as someone zealous for the holiest poverty, in the spirit of great humility and the most ardent charity, you have held fast to the footprints of him to whom you have merited to be joined as a Spouse.[11]

Here Clare plays on a theme that is very dear to her heart, the bridal relationship of the consecrated soul with the Lord. We do not find this theme expicitly treated in any other Franciscan writings of the early thirteenth century. It is probable that Clare drew her appreciation of this symbolism from current monastic literature. Celano drew from these same sources when he interpreted Clare's first spiritual direction from Francis in these terms: "Francis, impressed by the fair fame of so gracious a maiden, desired to see and speak with her, for ... he would fain somehow deliver this noble prey from the wickedness of the world and restore her to his Lord. .... He manifested to her the sweetness of the nuptials of Christ and persuaded her to keep the pearl of her virginal purity for that blessed Bridegroom whom love made man."[12]

Francis willingly played "the role of a loyal bridesman."[13] When he was questioned regarding his reticence to visit Clare and her sisters, he defended himself by saying that he acted thus for the sake of example to the other brothers. For himself he "cherished them in Christ to whom he had sought to unite them."[14] All consecrated virgins were, in his eyes, "brides of Christ."[15]

Clare must also have been familiar with the mystical tradition of the Cistercians who through their flourishing monasteries created the spiritual literature popular at this period. Whatever books or spiritual treatises the San Damiano community had probably had come to them through the bounty of the several Benedictine houses in the vicinity. St. Bernard's lyrical writings, epitomized in his commentaries on the Song of Songs were almost certainly among the works known to Clare and her sisters.

However, Clare imbued even this traditional mysticism with an original freshness by combining it with the ideals of "holiest poverty." This is the virtue which conforms one so closely to Jesus that one walks in his footprints (vestigia), i.e., vested in his attitudes of humility and loving service.

> But since I know that you are adorned with many virtues, I will spare my words and not weary you with needless speech, even though nothing seems superfluous to you if you can draw from it some consolation. But because one thing alone is necessary, I bear witness to that one thing and encourage you, for love of him to whom you have offered yourself as a holy and pleasing sacrifice, that, like another Rachel, you always remember your resolution and be conscious of how you began.
>
> What you hold, may you [always] hold.
>
> What you do, may you [always] do and never abandon.
>
> But with swift pace, light step
>   [and] unswerving feet,
>   so that even your steps stir up no dust,
>   go forward
>   securely, joyfully and swiftly,
>   on the path of prudent happiness.[16]

These passionate pleas reveal the very heart of Clare, a woman whose whole reason for being is "to bear witness to this one thing." That "one thing" is that God exists and we exist solely to respond to his love like another Rachel.

By the thirteenth century, the figure of Rachel had come to represent the ideal contemplative. Rachel, the seemingly barren woman clung to her husband beseeching: "Give me children or I shall die."[17] From her were born the favored sons, Joseph who became a type of the Messiah and Benjamin from whose descendents, mingled with the tribe of Juda, would come the Christ.

This paragraph reveals Clare's familiarity with the mystical writers who influended contemplative spirituality most strongly in her times. In the Dialogues of Gregory the Great is found the metaphor that the active life stirs up dust so that one's spiritual vision becomes clouded. Spontaneously, Clare lays hold of this imagery and reiterates it in delicately balanced phrases alive with burning conviction.

Reading these lines, one cannot doubt that Clare's choice of a contemplative way of life was not something simply forced upon her by the customs of her times. Actually, because of the great religious ferment of that period, there were groups of women experimenting with styles of living outside of the strict monastic mold. If Clare had felt called to something of that nature, she was courageous enough to have tried it.

However, it seems clear that from the very beginning, she conceived of her place in the Franciscan family as one of prayer and penance within the seclusion of a small monastery. Firm in her convictions, Clare counsels Agnes to be likewise so that

> believing nothing,
> agreeing with nothing
> which would dissuade you from this resolution
> or which would place a stumbling block for you on
>   the way,

you may offer your vows to the Most High
in the pursuit of that perfection
to which the Spirit of the Lord has called you.[18]

A stronger injunction can hardly be expressed! Clare will not permit Agnes to entertain any thought that now that she has made the decisive break with the world, all the rest will just fall easily and naturally into place. Struggle will be the mode of life until the end. When Clare warns Agnes to trust nothing that might suggest any deviation from the straight way of Most High Poverty, she includes not just prudent counselors or concerned relatives, but any attitude or ideal, whether worldly or spiritual, that did not conform with "that perfection to which the Spirit of the Lord" has called her.

Clare was learning through personal experience that to live the pure gospel life which Francis had shown her meant a struggle daily renewed. Sometimes opposition would come from persons outside the monastery, even from the Pope himself. But more insidious still were the objections which would arise within one's own fallen nature. Many of the standards which women of noble rank commonly accepted and were expected to conform to ran directly counter to the poverty, humility, and servanthood of a Poor Lady.

No one doffed these ingrained mores simply by donning a gray lazzo habit and kicking off her shoes. Lady Poverty was an exacting mistress and in her school, students were forced to face continually any failures, large or small, against her high standards. Thus, trust nothing, agree with nothing which deviates from her narrow but very straight way.

In all of this, follow the counsel of our venerable Father, our Brother Elias, the Minister General, so that you may walk more securely in the way of the commands of the Lord. Prize it beyond the advice of the others and cherish it as dearer to you than any gift. If anyone would tell you something else or suggest something which would hinder your perfection or seem contrary to your divine vocation, even though you must respect him, do not follow his counsel.[19]

Here Clare reveals the secret of how she dealt with persons, even prelates, who wished to dissuade her from following what she knew was her call from the Lord. Respect them, she says, but do not follow their advice. It required both humility and great confidence in one's calling to do this.

In view of later events, the esteem which Clare evinces for Brother Elias' counsel appears surprising. Yet she must have found him very appreciative of the true call of the Poor Ladies and strongly supportive of her desire to live it in all its purity. Clare's own sister, Agnes, looked forward to Elias' visits and counted on his encouragement. Obviously, Francis, Clare, and Agnes saw more in the enigmatic character of Brother Elias than many historians of the Order have preserved for us.

... but as a poor virgin, embrace the poor Christ. Look upon him who became contemptible for you, and follow him, making yourself contemptible in the world for him. Your Spouse, though more beautiful than the children of men became, for your salvation, the lowest of men, despised, struck, scourged untold times throughout his whole body, and then died amid the sufferings of the Cross. O most noble Queen, gaze upon [him], consider [him], contemplate [him], as you desire to imitate [him].[20]

Here the flames shoot forth and the intense glow of Clare's passionate love for Jesus leaps high. Her pen seems tipped with fire as she speaks of him who is the whole love of her life and urges Agnes to share with her his beauty, his humiliation, his terrible suffering. From such contemplation, she must pass on to compassion, literally suffering-with.

> If you suffer with him, you shall reign with him,
> [if you] weep [with him], you shall rejoice with him;
> [if you] die [with him] on the cross of tribulation,
>   you shall possess heavenly mansions in the
> splendor of the saints
>   and in the Book of Life, your name shall be
> called glorious among men.
> Because of this you shall share always and forever
> the glory of the kingdom of heaven in place of
> earthly and passing things, and everlasting
> treasures instead of those that perish, and you
> shall live forever.[21]

Earlier in this letter, Clare had dwelt on the possession of heavenly treasures even in this world. But now she leads Agnes on to the hope of still greater joys promised in the life to come. This world is a place where both suffering and rejoicing are but passing moments. Our lasting and perfect joy is yet to be revealed.

> Farewell, most dear sister, yes, and Lady, because of the Lord, your Spouse. Commend me and my sisters to the Lord in your fervent prayers, for we rejoice in the good things of the Lord that he works in you through his grace. Commend us truly to your sisters as well.[22]

This tender farewell reveals Clare's appreciation of how the communion of saints is lived out in its reality. She experienced a surge of joy in beholding "the good things of the Lord" which were being wrought in the distant monastery of Prague. What enriched that community enriched hers as well. She also knew that the reverse was true likewise. Any community which began to fall away from its pristine fervor diminished all the other communities. Clare would express her conviction to all her sisters in her Testament by writing: "Not only has the Lord himself set an example and mirror for others [outside the monastery], but also has He set the same example and mirror for our sisters whom the Lord has called to our way of life."[23]

One of the dearest of those whom God had called to share Clare's way of life was Ortolana. The great courage which had led her across the seas to find and kiss the places where her Savior had lived had finally brought her to this sanctuary of poverty where she, like her daughter, "fixed the anchor of her soul on solid ground, to be tossed no longer from one place to another; not wavering or hesitating because of the straitness of the place or shrinking back because of its loneliness."[24]

We do not know just when God called Ortolana forth on her final pilgrimage to the heavenly Jerusalem, but a list, compiled in 1238, of the sisters then living at San Damiano, does not include Ortolana's name.[25] Ortolana by that time would have reached her early sixties, a ripe old age in those times of war, famine, and plague.

So for Clare another irreplaceable loss had to be sustained. The two persons who had most influenced the direction of her life, Francis and the dauntless Ortolana, were no longer at her side with their inspiration and wise counsel. To add to Clare's sense of desolation, Elias, whose advice Clare had urged Agnes to prize above all others, was now following a course which would eventually lead to his deposition as Minister General, his dismissal from the Order, and finally, excommunication.

In 1239, Elias, who had been sent by Gregory IX as his personal envoy to the Emperor Frederick II, defied Gregory's edict that anyone who remained in Frederick's entourage would be excommunicated. The heady wine of power and prestige, which he had always enjoyed, had gradually destroyed the Elias whom Francis had admired and Clare trusted. Many of the Provincials of the Order had been insistently asking Gregory to depose Elias because of his abuse of his position as Minister General.

Clare, finding herself almost totally without human advisors and support, is led to anchor her trust ever more completely in the one for whom she had willingly left all security. Now she is being called upon, not to leave others but to be left by them, a searching trial which is often the ultimate purification of a woman who loves much.

A vision reported by Sister Agnes of Messer Oportulo graphically symbolized the state to which this purification is bringing Clare. "I saw the Lady Clare in the midst of the greatest splendor. . . all rosy as though it were sending out sparks of fire. It surrounded the Lady Clare and covered all her head. And wondering what this could be I heard, not by a voice but in my own mind, the words: 'Spiritus Sanctus superveniet in te—(the Holy Spirit will come upon you or, literally, the Holy Spirit will over come in you)."[26]

Chapter XIX Endnotes

1. Cause of Canonization, Wit. 4, #11.
2. Legend of Celano, #33.
3. Cause of Canonization, Wit. 9, # 6.
4. Ibid., Wit. 3, #15.
5. Ibid., Wit. 9, #6.
6. Ibid., Wit. 3, #16.
7. Ibid., Wit. 11, #1.
8. Legend of Celano #20.
9. Second Letter to Agnes of Prague, #1, 2.
10. Ibid., #3, #4.
11. Ibid., #5, #6.
12. Legend of Celano, #5.
13. Ibid., #6.

14. 2 Cel., #205.
15. Ibid., #114.
16. Second Letter to Agnes, #8–13.
17. Gen 30:1.
18. Second Letter to Agnes, #14.
19. Ibid., #15–17.
20. Ibid., #18–20.
21. Ibid., #21–23.
22. Ibid., #24–26.
23. Testament of Clare, #6.
24. Legend of Celano, #10.
25. Quoted in Wadding, *Annales Minorem,* Rome, 1731.
26. Cause of Canonization, Wit. 10, #8.

XX   With Shining Trust

"Hunger and the hour for eating stands at the door," related Friar Thomas.[1] So do all the sisters as they assemble to enter the refectory for their noonday meal, the only full repast of the day. Sister Cecilia is in a turmoil. There is but a single loaf of bread in the house, and Clare has just told her to give half of it to the questing brothers who are staying in the chaplain's hut.

Dismayed but obedient, Sister Cecilia divides the loaf and gives it to them. When she returns the sisters are quietly waiting for the meal to be served. Unable to face them, Cecilia takes the half loaf to Clare who is too ill at this time to come to the refectory. Clare "orders her to divide the half loaf into portions and to set them before the sisters seated at table."[2]

Cecilia retorts that "if I am to divide the loaf into these portions, the Lord's miracle of the five loaves and two fishes will have to be repeated!" Mildly, but firmly, Clare repeats, "Go and do what I have told you!"[3]

Mentally throwing up her hands, Sister Cecilia takes the loaf back to the refectory and hacks off a generous portion which she passes to the nearest sister. She then chops off another large piece and gives it to the next in line. By the time she has cut several similarly large pieces and notices that the loaf under her hand seems as large as when she began, her reckless attitude vanishes. More carefully now she cuts another generous piece and sees her own wonder mirrored in the eyes of the sister who takes it.

The loaf does not diminish until every sister has received a satisfying portion. Sister Cecilia takes the last portion to Clare, trembling and conscience-stricken that, despite her doubts, the Lord has worked through her own hands, the very miracle whose possibility she had mocked.

Clare has no word of reproof, knowing that Sister Cecilia's obedience, when put to the test, had proven true. As Celano summarized it, "while the daughter hastened to fulfill the Mother's command, the Mother hastened to direct to Christ pious pleas for her daughters. By the divine favor, the little bread multiplied in the hands of her who broke it."[4]

The date when this wonder occurred has not been preserved. However, the fact that there was but one loaf in the monastery points to a period when Umbria was suffering from famine. Under ordinary conditions, the fertile Spoleto valley produced more than sufficient crops for the needs of the inhabitants. But all too frequently the yearly cycle of sowing and reaping was disrupted by the endless strife which racked the region, caused by the rivalries of the city-states or by invasion of imperial troops.

Emperor Frederick was resorting to terrorist tactics in his drive to unite the entire Italian peninsula under his rule. Between the years 1215–50, the Papal dominions, especially the Guelph cities of Umbria, were repeatedly sacked and devastated. Although Assisi was Ghibelline (on the Emperor's side), Frederick did not count too heavily on its loyalty, suspecting rightly that Assisi's main loyalty was for Assisi! The "Saracens" whom Frederick recruited for this business of intimidation were descendents of the Moors who had once dominated Sicily and Calabria. Non-Christian and semibarbarian, they were so feared that the merest suspicion of their presence was sufficient to freeze the blood in the veins of the most stout-hearted.

Thomas of Celano depicts the situation of Umbria in vivid terms: "By reason of the tempest and tumult which the Church suffered in various parts of the world under the Emperor Frederick, the valley of Spoleto had often to drink of the chalice of wrath. At the command of the Emperor, troops of soldiers and Saracen bowmen swarmed like bees into the valley to destroy its fortresses and besiege its cities. At one time the enemy hurled themselves in fury against Assisi. . . ."[5]

Defenseless and exposed, San Damiano stands outside the city's protecting walls, surrounded only by its hedge of trees. ". . . The Saracens, a wicked race that thirsts for the blood of Christians and shamelessly attempts any outrage" are creeping silently up the hillside in the predawn darkness of a September day in 1240.[6] They cannot fail to notice the unprotected little monastery. These are men who wantonly burn cities, sack villages, and seem to take delight in torturing women and children. Little respect would be shown to any nuns who fell into their hands.

According to Sister Philippa, "the sisters greatly dreaded the incursion of the Saracens. . . but the blessed Mother comforted them saying: 'My sisters and daughters, do not fear because God will be with us and the enemies will not be able to harm us. Trust in our Lord Jesus Christ, and he will preserve us. I will be your hostage so that no hurt shall touch you. Should the enemies come so far put me in front of them."[7]

Though the sisters try to calm their fear, their sense of uneasiness remains. Early one Friday morning, they suddenly see to their horror that Saracen soldiers are silently scaling the courtyard wall and dropping stealthily into the cloister. In stark terror they run to Clare's pallet in the upstairs dormitory. According to Sister Benvenuta "Clare was then very ill, but she raised herself in bed and called the sisters, comforting and reassuring them."[8]

With the aid of Sisters Francesca and Illuminata, she has herself taken downstairs to the refectory. The friar-chaplain, aroused by the sisters' cries of alarm, runs to the chapel in order to remove the Blessed Sacrament and save it, if possible, from profanation. He, like the sisters, then seeks refuge in the refectory. Clare requests this unnamed but heroic friar to carry the Blessed Sacrament before her.[9] Slowly the heavy refectory door, their last defense against the invading soldiers, is swung back. The sisters, huddled fearfully behind Clare, find themselves staring into the gleaming eyes of the invaders. Between them stands only the frail form of their Mother leaning upon the arms of two sisters.

Suddenly Clare sinks to the ground and with tears prays: "Lord, look upon us, your poor servants for I cannot guard them. Then Sisters Francesca and Illuminata hear a voice of wonderful sweetness saying, 'I will always defend you.' Whereupon Clare prays also for the city saying, 'Lord, be pleased also to defend this city.' and again that same sweet voice answers, 'The city will suffer many dangers but will be defended.' "[10]

Behind Clare, the sisters are praying desperately but expecting the worst. To their amazement, Clare suddenly rises up from the ground, turns her back on the soldiers and calmly assures the sisters: "Do not be afraid; I am your safeguard, and no harm will come to you, now, or in the future, nor at any other time as long as you obey God's commandments."[11]

Even as Clare is speaking, the Saracen bowmen suddenly turn and leap back over the wall more quickly than they had entered, leaving the courtyard to the morning sunlight and the cooing of the doves. Gradually, the sisters recover from their shock and realize that they have been miraculously preserved from a fate worse than death. Only Sisters Illuminata and Francesca had heard the sweet voice which they knew had come from the Host. That evening Clare gathers all the sisters together and commands them not to speak of all this to anyone during her lifetime.

According to Clare's youngest sister, Beatrice, who had lived through these harrowing hours "the following day the whole army departed which had been encamped about the city of Assisi."[12]

Despite the turmoil and dangers of these years, the work of the Spirit goes forward in its quiet forcefulness. In 1239 Clare sends some sisters to establish a house in Milan. Two houses in Perugia have also been founded, that of St. Luke and that of Our Lady of the Angels. The good seed has found fertile soil in Spain where, after the successful expulsion of the Moors, a period of comparative peace reigns. New houses multiply there, including those at Salamanca, Burgos, Mantua-Migliarino, and Calahorra. These have been founded, not directly from Assisi but from the earlier foundations made on the Iberian peninsula.

In Poland, Salome, the widow of King Colman, brother of St. Elizabeth, has established a community of Poor Ladies at Zawichost which she herself will enter in 1240. Later, she moved to a new community established near Cracow where she died in 1268. She is venerated as Blessed Salome of Cracow. Before her death, she heard of the horrifying massacre of the fifty-nine sisters at Zawichost by the Tartars around 1260.

Early in the year of 1238, Clare pens a letter which rejoices her heart. Her love for the courageous princess in far-off Prague has grown from admiration to an affection so intimate that she now addresses Agnes as "more loved than all other human beings."[13]

Agnes, it would seem, had written to Clare for fuller details about the life of poverty and penance being lived at San Damiano. Clare responds with a letter rich in contemplative insight, a letter which clearly demonstrates that in Clare's mind penance and poverty are not ends in themselves but only a means toward the "one thing necessary," ever-growing union with Jesus and, through him, with the Father in the love that is the Holy Spirit.

> To the Lady [who is] most respected in Christ and the sister loved more than all other human beings, Agnes, sister of the illustrious king of Bohemia, but now the

> sister and spouse of the Most High King of heaven:
> Clare, the most lowly and unworthy handmaid of
> Christ and servant of the Poor Ladies: the joys of
> redemption in the Author of salvation and every
> good thing that can be desired.[14]

Agnes is greeted as the sister of the King of Bohemia, a title
which is contrasted now with her dignity as sister and spouse of
the King of heaven. Her brother, Wenceslaus III, had tried without success to compel Agnes to follow through on their father's
plan for her to marry Frederick II. If he had succeeded, it would
not have been the first time that a daughter of a royal family was
arbitrarily summoned from her convent, dispensed from her
vows, and forced into a political marriage.

Frederick's mother, Constance of Sicily, had been taken
against her will from a monastery when she was nearly forty.
Henry IV, son of Frederick Barbarossa, wished to gain control of
southern Italy. To further this plan, he decided to marry Constance who stood in line to inherit the crown of Sicily if her
nephew, then king, should die without issue, which he did in
1189. Henry, therefore, through Constance, became the ruler of
Sicily, a claim bloodily contested by other members of Constance's family. It was while trying to subdue these rebellious
factions that Henry was killed, leaving Constance with his three-
year-old son and heir, Frederick.

From similar turbulence and intrigue, Agnes had begged to
be spared. Clare now rejoices with her over the peace and fulfillment she is finding in the austere life of a Poor Lady.

> I am filled with such joys at your well-being, happi-
> ness, and marvelous progress through which, I un-
> derstand, you have advanced in the course you have
> undertaken to win the prize of heaven. And I sigh
> with such happiness in the Lord because I know you
> see that you make up most wonderfully what is lack-

ing both in me and in the other sisters in following the
footprints of the poor and humble Jesus Christ.[15]

Clare here praises and encourages Agnes in her choice of life
and the exemplary manner in which she is living. Again the
theme arises that the fervor and holiness of the community in
Prague is making up for whatever is lacking in the San Damiano
community.

How is Agnes doing this? By "following in the footprints of
the poor and humble Jesus." This brief phrase succinctly summarized the Franciscan calling and was chosen by both Francis
and Clare to describe their way of life.

> I can rejoice truly—and no one can rob me of such
> joy—because I now possess what under heaven I have
> desired. For I see that, helped by a special gift of
> wisdom from the mouth of God Himself and in an
> awe-inspiring and unexpected way, you have brought
> to ruin the subtleties of our crafty enemy and the
> pride that destroys human nature and the vanity that
> infatuates human hearts.[16]

How well Clare knew what distress and havoc could be
wrought by that "pride which destroys human nature!" For she
has seen it devastate whole cities and has lived her entire life
under the scourge of war engendered by vanity and ambition.
Agnes, she knew, had also been exposed to these same destructive influences. So it is to a "special gift of wisdom" that she
attributes Agnes' courageous counteraction to these passions by
choosing to live in the only manner which makes peace possible
on this earth, i.e., without desire for possessions, prestige, or
power.

Clare's joy over this is an echo of the Second Letter of John
where the elder exclaims: "Nothing delights me more than to
hear that my children are walking in this path (of truth)." Clare

goes on to set out precisely what Agnes is doing to deserve such praise.

> I see too that by humility, the virtue of faith and the strong arms of poverty, you have taken hold of that incomparable treasure hidden in the field of the world and in the hearts of men with which you have purchased that field of Him by Whom all things have been made from nothing. And to use the words of the Apostle himself in their proper sense, I consider you a co-worker of God Himself and a support of the weak members of his ineffable Body.[17]

It it noteworthy that Clare considers the great treasure, which Agnes has made her own through humility, faith, and poverty, is hidden, not only in the "field of the world" but also in the "hearts of men [and women]." Clare perceives and has built her life on the reality of this treasure and is not merely employing poetic rhetoric. This treasure is love, a love at once human and divine. The spark of love found in human hearts she sees as being caught up and divinized by the Spirit of Love himself, while the torrent of divine love is channeled, humanized, as it were, by passing through the hearts of men and women.

This is the dynamism which enables one to be in all literalness "a co-worker of God" on behalf of all the members of his mystical Body. Clare's grasp of this spiritual reality forms the basis of her appreciation of the apostolic power of the contemplative way of life to which she and her sisters are pledged. The Poor Ladies are meant to be a complement to the brothers. While the friars tramp the roads of the world, the sisters immerse themselves in the boundless energy of divine love, seeking to channel it through the brothers into the hearts of those who hear them.

With such a challenge to inspire her, is it any wonder that Clare can urge Agnes to abounding joy?

Who is there, then who would not encourage me to rejoice over such marvelous joys? Therefore, dearly beloved, may you too always rejoice in the Lord. And may neither bitterness nor a cloud [of sadness] overwhelm you, O dearly beloved Lady in Christ, joy of the angels and crown of your sisters!

Place your mind before the mirror of eternity!
place your soul in the brilliance of glory!
Place your heart in the figure of the divine
substance!
And transform your whole being into the image
of the
    Godhead Itself through contemplation!
    So that you too may feel what his friends feel
    as they taste the hidden sweetness
    which God himself has reserved
    from the beginning for those who love him.[18]

Here Clare is describing heights of contemplative experience with the calm assumption that they are the normal term of prayer for every son and daughter of God. Subtle scriptural allusions abound as Clare attempts to express the inexpressible. She writes with the sure instinct of one who is in tune with the workings of the Spirit. She could assert, in the words of St. Paul, that "Our hope being such, [I can] speak with full confidence."

Clare employs the theme of the mirror which was popular in the spiritual literature of her period. If we think of a mirror only as a shiny surface in which we see our own reflection, we shall fail to penetrate the profound meaning in Clare's use of this image. The medieval concept was that one gazed into a mirror to see there what one should *become*. The image which Clare urges Agnes to behold in the "mirror of eternity" is the Eternal One, the Beloved One. When gazing upon this Image, one is gazing upon one's truest self, for it is in this very Image that we have been created. By means of such loving contemplation, one will be transformed into a living reflection of the Image beheld. One shall become the "mirror of eternity" for others.

The underlying motif of this conception of mystical experience is found in 2 Cor 3:18: "All of us, gazing on the Lord's glory with unveiled faces, are being transformed from glory to glory into his very image by the Lord who is the Spirit." The context of this quotation is the revealing work of the Spirit. For it is the Holy Spirit who enables us to gaze upon Jesus who became "see-able" by the Spirit's overshadowing of the virgin flesh of Mary. He now works ceaselessly in us to accomplish this same marvel, i.e., to fashion the Word of God into a "see-able" Image in our bodies.

This theme is paramount in Clare's view of the spiritual life for had she not seen it lived out with dramatic realism in Francis? Bonaventure highlighted this in his account of the Stigmata when he wrote: Francis "opened the Gospel three times, and each time it opened at the passion; so Francis understood that he must become like Christ in the distress and agony of his passion. . . just as he had been like him in all that he did during his life. . . . The fervor of his seraphic longing raised Francis up to God and, in an ecstasy of compassion, made him like Christ. God let him see that, as Christ's lover, he would resemble Christ crucified perfectly not by physical martyrdom but by the fervor of his spirit. . . . True love of Christ now transformed his lover into his Image."[19]

Clare fully understood what such a transformation would require."

> Since you have cast aside all [those] things which, in this deceitful and turbulent world, ensnare their blind lovers, love him totally who gave himself totally for your love. His beauty the sun and moon admire; and of his gifts there is no limit in abundance, pre-

ciousness, and magnitude. I am speaking of him who is the Son of the Most High, whom the Virgin brought to birth and remained a virgin after his birth. Cling to his most sweet mother who carried a son whom the heavens could not contain; and yet she carried him in the little enclosure of her holy womb and held him on her virginal lap.[20]

Clare evidently loved the liturgical portrayal of the mystery of the Incarnation as it is found in the Office of the Blessed Virgin. She shares the wonder that One so great, whose presence causes the sun and moon to pale in their splendor, contracts his devastating magificence to enter Mary's womb so gently that her fragile humanity is not annihilated or her virginity violated.

Clare proceeds to draw from this soaring vision some concrete conclusions and practical applications:

Who would not dread the treacheries of the enemy of mankind, who, through the splendor of momentary and deceptive glories, attempts to reduce to nothing that which is greater than heaven itself? Indeed, is it not clear that the soul of the faithful person, the most worthy of all creatures because of the grace of God, is greater than heaven itself? For the heavens with the rest of creation cannot contain their Creator. Only the faithful soul is his dwelling place and [his] throne, and this [is possible] only through the charity which the wicked do not have. [He who is] the Truth has said: Whoever loves me will be loved by my Father, and I too shall love him, and we shall come to him and make our dwelling place with him.[21]

In this passage Clare expresses her wondering joy that our great God not only conserves life in all his creatures but actually comes and shares in it by the most intimate of presences. Our model for this is Mary. She carried the Lord physically. We are called to carry him spiritually, though not less really. Clare highlights the insight that it was through Mary that God was made able to embrace poverty. If we also seek to embrace poverty, which is, in truth, our fundamental condition, we shall discover that we are embracing the very God who is holding us and all the cosmos in existence.

Clare delights in the amazing paradox of greatness found in humility, of munificence found in poverty. She echoes Francis' oft repeated theme that we can be not only a sister/brother and spouse of Christ but also his mother by carrying him enthroned within us and fostering his life in others.

Only now, after having established the raison d'être of the life of a Poor Lady, does Clare respond to Agnes' questions about the penitential observances at San Damiano.

> Now concerning those matters which you have asked me to clarify for you: which are the specific feasts our most glorious father St. Francis urged us to celebrate in a special way by a change of food, feasts of which, I believe, you already have some knowledge—I propose to respond to your love.
>
> Your prudence should know then that, except for the weak and the sick, for whom [St. Francis] advised and admonished us to show every possible care in the matters of food, none of us who are healthy and strong should eat anything other than Lenten fare, either on ferial days or on feast days. Thus, we must fast every day except Sundays and the Nativity of the Lord, on which days we may have two meals. And on ordinary Thursdays everyone may do as she wishes, so that she who does not wish to fast is not obliged. However, we who are well should fast every day except on Sundays and on Christmas.
>
> During the entire Easter week, as the writing of St. Francis tells us, and on the feasts of the Blessed Mary

and of the holy Apostles, we are not obliged to fast, unless these feasts occur on a Friday. And, as I have already said, we who are well and strong always eat lenten fare.[22]

Here Clare sets down for Agnes a rule of fasting which though severe is tempered with admirable prudence. It is noteworthy that before she describes the fast required for all, she mentions that Francis prescribed special consideration for the needs of the weak and the sick. In the Rule which Clare would compose, she specifically mentions that the young, the weak, and those who serve outside the monastery may be "mercifully dispensed as it shall seem good to the abbess." Also Clare repeats Francis' dictum that "in time of manifest necessity" no one is obliged to corporal fasting.[23]

The general rule for fasting is very simple, all the sisters who are able eat only one full meal each day except on Sundays and Christmas, during Easter Week, and on feasts of Mary or the Apostles. On these days the sisters may partake of two meals but even then the food is "lenten fare" which excludes flesh meat. The practice at San Damiano of giving each sister the option to fast or not on ordinary Thursdays (the day traditionally assigned to honor the Blessed Sacrament) is quite intriguing. It appears to be one more example of the reverence Clare had for the freedom and individuality of each of her sisters and of her desire to enhance it. Love, she deeply believed, could never be compelled. It could exist and grow only where there was liberty of spirit. She would not deprive her sisters of their right to freely choose what they wished to give to the Lord. Perhaps it is unfortunate that this custom was not incorporated into the Rule written some years later.

One must smile at the phrase, repeated three times that "*we* who are well and strong . . ." fast every day. For by this time, 1238, Clare was anything but well and strong. Yet she cannot be accused of deception when writing thus to Agnes for, in all ways but one, Clare *was* well and strong. The vigor of her spirit, the overflowing vitality of her inner life, supported the frailty of her physical constitution to a remarkable degree. She was willing to concede, however, that:

> Our flesh is not bronze nor is our strength that of stone. No, we are frail and inclined to every bodily weakness. I beg you, therefore, most dear one, to refrain wisely and prudently from an indiscreet and impossible austerity in the fasting that I know you have undertaken. And I beg you in the Lord to praise the Lord by your very life, to offer to the Lord your reasonable service and your sacrifice always seasoned with salt.
>   May you do well in the Lord, as I hope I myself do. And remember me and my sisters in your prayers.[24]

Clare had had to learn the hard way that the sacrifice most pleasing to the Lord was that which was seasoned with discretion. Perhaps she had heard through others that Agnes was tending toward extremes in the matter of corporal fasting. Her humility does not let her command Agnes to desist but instead she earnestly begs Agnes to use the wisdom and prudence which Clare knows she possesses.

It is possible that this detailed description of the penitential practices observed by the San Damiano community completed the information which Agnes needed to draw up a similar rule of life for the monastery in Prague. In the early spring of 1238, Agnes submitted a petition that Gregory permit her community to follow the form of life and poverty observed by Clare rather than the Rule which he had drawn up for all the other houses of Poor Ladies. It has been conjectured that Clare may have hoped that Gregory would grant to a royal princess what he had denied to her.

If so, both Agnes and Clare were disappointed, for on May 11, 1238, Gregory sent a firm refusal to the Prague community. He simply could not see how a community of enclosed nuns could subsist by relying entirely on Divine Providence and the work of their own hands. He deemed ownership of property and assured revenues essential to the well-being of any religious community. Very few would disagree with this attitude even today. Despite the clear fact that Clare and her sisters could do it, he obviously felt this form of poverty could not be universally observed by all the Poor Ladies. Still Clare could not and would not relinquish her struggle to correspond to the call to total poverty which Francis had shown to her. To her dying day, Clare would pursue her right to follow "as a poor virgin the poor Christ."

One of the main reasons that Gregory advanced for refusing Agnes' petition was the unsettled state of political affairs. Emperor Frederick had, by this time, abandoned any pretence of being a faithful son of the Church. He blatantly initiated his plan to conquer and annex the Papal territories he had once so solemnly vowed to defend. The aging but indomitable Gregory was the only figure in Europe whom Frederick recognized as influential enough to thwart his plans.

As part of his design to crush Gregory, Frederick fielded a formidable army in the Umbrian valley. The commander was Vitale d'Aversa, a professional soldier famed for his ruthlessness, a captain who never gave up a fight until the "enemy" was totally vanquished, preferably annihilated. Celano provides us with a graphic picture of the situation: "Vitale d'Versa, a man thirsting for glory and mighty in battle, led the imperial army of which he was captain, against Assisi. He stripped the land of its trees, laid waste the whole countryside, and then undertook to besiege the city. With threatening words he swore he would not withdraw until the city was his. Things soon came to such a pass that men feared the worst for the city."[25]

Although Assisi has stout walls and is well placed for defense on the flank of Monte Subasio, the citizens know they cannot survive a long siege. It is early summer and the winter stores of provisions are depleted while the new crops have been burnt by D'Aversa's troops. In addition to the normal complement of city-dwellers, Assisi also harbors throngs of the dispossessed and burned-out families from the hamlets and castelli dotting Assisi's environs.

The officials of the city face a double-edged dilemma. They can try to hold out against D'Aversa, knowing that even if the walls and gates are successfully defended, starvation could wipe out the citizens as surely as the sword. Or they can surrender the city and throw themselves on the mercy of D'Aversa, knowing that he has none. They would only be opening themselves to pillage, rape, and destruction, for no ethical restraints check the kind of men whom Frederick generally employed.

Bonifazio, a contemporary poet of the period, has celebrated in verse what any conquering army normally inflicts upon its victim.

> Here the [conqueror] shows no pity,
>   He demolishes the walls, destroys the palaces,
> burns the houses, murders and sacks.
> Nothing is respected,
> neither the innocence of babes
> nor the tender age of children,
> nor the youth of adolescents.
> And not even the feebleness of the old
> saves them from the arrow.
> Here it is the will of the [conqueror]
> to repudiate every charity,
> forget every compassion,
> trample down every justice.
> War alone is his intention.[26]

Given this description of how a Christian army waged war, it is scarcely surprising that terror paralyzed many on whom the imperial troops marched. Sister Francesca relates that "when the Lady Clare was told that the city of Assisi was about to be given up into the hands of the enemy, she called the sisters together saying: 'We have received great good from this city, therefore we must pray God to save it.' She then commanded the sisters that early on the morrow they should gather round her, which they did."[27]

As the sisters assemble, pale in the gray light of dawn, Clare removes her veil and strews ashes on her head. She bids the sisters to do likewise and then sends them to lie prostrate in prayer before their Eucharistic Lord. All that day they pray, many with tears, as they think of loved ones huddling within the doomed city. Some of the sisters eat nothing at all that day while others fast on bread and water.

Like the "little ones" who, clothed in sackcloth were made to lie down in the temple courts at times of national crisis in Israel, the sisters' very bodies express the supplication of their hearts. Indelibly etched in Sister Agnes' memory is the sight of Clare "praying for this intention most humbly with many tears, her hands joined and her eyes turned upward to heaven."[28]

Early on the morning of June 22, 1241, the sentries on the walls of Assisi peer through the arrow slits to see what the rising light will reveal. To their utter amazement, they behold the entire army decamping in disordered haste with bands of soldiers dispersing in all directions. With no army to lead, D'Aversa, Celano tells us, "has to depart without accomplishing his plans." He adds triumphantly "and he never harasses that land further for he soon after perishes by the sword."[29]

The sentries cautiously stand up to look over the rim of the ramparts. Suddenly they are shouting in joy, proclaiming that the dreaded D'Aversa and his entire army are disappearing into the morning mist! The doom which all expected has passed like a dream in the night.

From behind the green shoulder of Monte Subasio, sunlight shafts upward into a tranquil June sky. The fresh dawn is sweet with dew and the song of larks spiraling above a quiet countryside.

According to Sister Francesca "the city of Assisi remained free from any foreign domination" until after the death of Clare.[30] The citizens recognize through whom their incredible deliverance has come. They form a jubilant procession through the unbarred gates and pour down the hillside to San Damiano. There they proclaim their gratitude to the Poor Ladies whose intercession has brought them swift salvation from their King.

This setback does not deter Frederick from pursuing his campaign to wipe out the implacable Gregory. He determines to march on Rome and take the aging Pontiff captive. But once again Gregory frustrates the Emperor's designs. On August 22, 1241, Gregory hands back to his Lord the talents which have been entrusted to him, talents which he has faithfully administered during the fourteen stormy years through which he has guided the Church and the destiny of most of Europe with a strong and steady hand.

Again the church bells toll through the length and breadth of Christendom as the news rapidly spreads. Nowhere is Gregory more deeply and sincerely mourned than at San Damiano. Although Clare rejoices that the aging Pope has received the reward so richly deserved, she mourns the loss of one more link with those first idyllic days when she and Francis had set out to keep their tryst with Lady Poverty. For Hugolino had been with them almost from the beginning, protecting the young Order from misunderstanding by church authorities, guiding them with wisdom and deep respect for Francis' unique gift for the Church.

All through the years, twenty-three of them Clare notes with a slight shock, Hugolino has been the one to whom she could always turn in all her perplexities and needs. Even his adamant stand regarding the Rule for the Poor Ladies had sprung, Clare knows, from his desire to provide the best possible support for her spreading Order. His personal esteem and care for her had evoked her devotion and trust. She now does what she can in terms of ceaseless prayer and intercession for him. The loss of such a friend and protector is no small grief for Clare. Who will take his place?

In Rome, this same question is being raised but with even greater urgency. The ten cardinals then in the city are quickly shut up within the walls of a run-down Palace called the Septizonium. Frederick II and his forces are in control of the city and he has made it clear that only a prelate favorable to him must be elected.

Despite this pressuring by the imperial arm and the fetid heat of the Roman summer, two months go by with no candidate among the cardinals receiving the needed two-third majority for a valid election. One cardinal dies during these exhausting months and others, most of whom are aged, become ill. In desperation the electors finally settle upon Gofreddo Castiglioni, a known partisan of Frederick.

On October 25, 1241, this aged and infirm prelate becomes the 181st Pontiff of the Catholic Church, assuming the name of Celestine IV. Most of the cardinals flee to Agnani as soon as they are released from the conclave. However, Frederick's men manage to capture and imprison two of them.

The new Pope Celestine is so ill that he dies seventeen days after his election, even before he can be solemnly consecrated. Eighteen confusing months will elapse before the scattered and imprisoned cardinals can reassemble for another conclave.

While the bark of Peter seems to be left floating aimlessly on the waves, hidden reserves of strength keep it intact and united. For Clare, as for all the faithful, this period of waiting deepens their trust in the power of the Holy Spirit and in Christ's promise that he will be with his Church until the end of time.

Now while darkness seems determined to prevail, Clare must struggle to keep her own light of faith burning brightly. Like the sanctuary lamp which silently consumes its store of oil before the Lord, Clare allows her vital energies to be absorbed before the

Crucified Lord who had charged her great friend and father: "Francis, rebuild my Church which you see is falling into ruin."

Chapter XX Endnotes

1. Legend of Celano, #15.
2. Cause of Canonization, Wit. 6, #16.
3. Ibid.
4. Legend by Celano, #15.
5. Ibid., #21.
6. Ibid.,
7. Cause of Canonization, Wit. 3, #18.
8. Ibid., Wit. 2. #20.
9. Ibid., Wit. 9, #2.
10. Ibid.
11. Ibid.
12. Ibid., Wit. 12, #8.
13. Third Letter to Agnes of Prague, #1.
14. Ibid., #1, #2.
15. Ibid., #3, #4.
16. Ibid., #5, #6.
17. Ibid., #7, #8.
18. Ibid., #9–14.
19. Legenda Major, Ch. 13, #2, #3, #5.
20. Third Letter, #15–19.
21. Ibid., #20–28.
22. Ibid., #29–37.
23. Later Rule Ch. III, #9.
24. Third Letter, #38–42.
25. Legend of Celano. #23.
26. Arnaldo Fortini, *Francis of Assisi*, trans. Helen Moak, (New York: Crossroad, 1981), p. 58.
27. Cause of Canonization, Wit. 9, #3.
28. Ibid., Wit. 10, #9.
29. Legend of Celano, #23.
30. Cause of Canonization, Wit. 9, #3.

XXI Lamp for Many Feet

Vibrant June sunshine pours through the top of the open half-door opposite Clare's pallet. Propped up against a support, she can see the olive leaves shimmering in the breeze. It is so quiet that Clare imagines one can hear the plants leaping up toward Brother Sun, unfolding their leaves and growing taller almost as one watched. She lays the corporal she has finished hemming in her lap, glad to rest and enjoy the gentle peace of the fresh morning.

She is alone in her corner of the dormitory for the other sisters are all busy about the myriad tasks which warmer weather makes possible. Many are working in the garden for not all the new plants springing up are of desirable varieties. Tubs are set out in the courtyard near the well. Doing the laundry on a day like this is pure pleasure.

As Clare carefully folds the finished corporal, she frowns slightly. The piece of linen she had intended to work on next lies beyond her reach. She is too weak just now to even rise from her cot without aid. This frustration, so familiar to all who must depend on others for even their smallest needs, is no stranger to Clare. She sighs and asks no one in particular to please bring her the cloth.

Suddenly, the little cat which has been dozing in the sunshine raises her head, a seeming question in her eyes. Intrigued, Clare repeats her request, indicating the linen piece on a low table. According to Sister Francesca, this little cat took hold of the material and "started to drag it along the floor as best she could to bring it to Clare. Seeing this, Clare said to the little cat, 'O you

319

bad one, you don't know how to carry it; why do you drag it along the ground in that way? Then the little cat, seeming to have understood those words, began to roll up the cloth so that it no longer touched the floor."[1]

Later when a sister looks in to ask if Clare needs anything, Clare smiles at the kitten, now purring contentedly on her blanket, and responds that all her needs are well taken care of.

As she works, Clare's thoughts and prayers may have strayed to concerns far more pressing than a piece of linen. Emperor Frederick has finally been pressured by King Louis IX into releasing the cardinals he has been holding prisoner. At last a papal conclave can convene. It opens in June of 1243, almost eighteen months since the death of Gregory IX. The cardinal-electors waste little time and on June 25, Cardinal Sinibaldo Fieschi is proclaimed Sovereign Pontiff with the name Innocent IV. The joy of Christendom that the bark of Peter once more has a pilot at its helm is immense. Cardinal Fieshi had been named to the sacred college when he was only twenty-seven. Considered as one of the greatest canonists of that period, he had worked closely with Gregory IX. He may have met Clare and the sisters at San Damiano through Gregory, although there is no record of this. What is certain is that he knew of them and interested himself personally in their affairs from the beginning of his pontificate.

Innocent's most immediate problem following his election was the political chaos wrought by Frederick II's ambitious bid to unite all Europe under his scepter. It is highly unlikely that Innocent's election was agreeable to Frederick since he had been a close associate of Gregory, Frederick's most doughty opponent. Still, when Innocent offered to negotiate with the Emperor about their conflicting interests, Frederick decided to respond. Inevitably, the intractable stand of the Pope and Frederick's insatiable appetite for power doomed the success of any negotiations.

Then Frederick invited Innocent to meet with him for a personal conference. The Pontiff knew that to respond would be tantamount to walking through prison doors. So, while Frederick and his army were on their way to Rome, Innocent resolved on a radically new tactic. Aware that the Emperor had many partisans in Rome who would be glad to betray the Pope to him, Innocent disguised himself and escaped by night to the port of Civitavecchia where a fleet was waiting to carry him to safety in his native Genoa. From there Innocent went over the Alps to reside in Lyon where he could count on the powerful protection of King Louis of France.

From this position of comparative safety, Innocent began to exercise a vigorous and decisive leadership of the Church. He summoned a General Council to meet in Lyon in 1245. Although there were a number of major issues to be discussed, everyone knew that the essential purpose of the Council was to deal with Frederick.

> At the third session of the Council, Innocent proceeded to the expected act of deposition. The prelates assembled in the nave of the cathdral bearing lighted tapers. The Pope, seated on a raised throne in the choir, read a long recital of Frederick's offenses—heresy, sacrilege, and perjury prominent among them, and then came to his appointed conclusion. "After careful consultation with our brothers and the Holy Council we declare that the aforesaid Prince . . . is rejected and deprived of all honor and dignity by God, to which we add our sentence of deprivation also." As the words of the condemnation rolled forth the prelates extinguished their tapers, Thadeus of Suessa [Frederick's advocate] swept out of the cathedral crying that a day of wrath had come upon the world, and, as he left, the fathers of the Council began to intone a solemn Te Deum.[2]

This act by Pope Innocent infuriated Frederick, who until this time, had generally tried to present himself as a persecuted and misunderstood son of the Church. In actual fact, the Pope's pronouncement did little to change the political situation. No prince in Europe was willing to accept the imperial dignity in Frederick's place for none wished to antagonize this powerful and magnetic leader of men. The only immediate effect was clarification of the issue so that no one could now pledge allegiance to Frederick and expect to be considered a faithful member of the Church.

Pope Innocent sent a personal message to Brother Elias who was still at the court of Frederick, summoning him to Lyon to justify his conduct. When he refused to come, the Pope had no choice but to publicly excommunicate him again. This was not a pleasant duty for Innocent since his ties with the Franciscan Order were deep and strong. In fact he had some Franciscans in his personal household and one, Brother Niccolo di Carbio, acted as his chaplain and confessor.

Conditions in the Second Order also disturbed him. He was aware that among the Poor Ladies, there was a dismaying degree of diversity in observance of the Rule formulated by Hugolino. Although they all nominally professed it, various dispensations and interpretations had created a variety of life-styles which, to the canonist Innocent, was painful to behold. Just before the death of Pope Gregory in 1241, a wandering group of women calling themselves Minoresses, had claimed affiliation with the Second Order. These Gregory had to denounce.

In 1245, Innocent decided that it was imperative to establish uniform observance among the Poor Ladies and to resolve the ever thorny question of their relationship with the friars. The brothers had, through many letters, made known their desire to be freed of the care of the Poor Ladies. On the other hand, the sisters were writing petitions that the ties between the two branches

be retained and strengthened. Innocent decided in favor of
the Poor Ladies by solemnly reconfirming Hugolino's Rule
on November 13, 1245. He made it binding on all the Houses
in Italy, France, and Germany. But if he thought that now
there would be peace, he was quickly informed of his mistake.

Although Hugolino's Rule did allow for the dependence of
the Poor Ladies upon the friars, other prescriptions in it had
always been unacceptable to Clare. She had professed this Rule
in all things except those sections which were counter to the
original Form of Life and the Privilege of Poverty which had
been approved before Hugolino composed his Rule in 1219.

Many of the other monasteries shared Clare's feelings. Agnes
of Prague had been trying, albeit unsuccessfully, to be allowed to
follow the usages and customs which had been granted to San
Damiano as a special privilege. Some houses of Poor Ladies felt
that Hugolino's Rule bound them too closely to Benedictine observances. However, those communities which had formerly
been Benedictine did not always see it that way. The heart of the
struggle lay in the matter of poverty. Although poverty was not,
and could not be, an end in itself, its radical observance distinguished the Franciscan charism and safeguarded it. Its faithful practice helped to guarantee that direct dependence on the
providence of God which undergirds all true Franciscan
spirituality.

Clare most likely wrote to Innocent expressing her convictions, as did many other communities of Poor Ladies. Innocent
had explicitly stated that he had reconfirmed Hugolino's Rule at
the request of the sisters themselves but evidently that request
had not been unanimous for he found himself besieged with
letters asking him to revoke this decision. He decided to give the
matter further thought. However, desperate crises arising in
Europe at this time also claimed his attention so that he could
not act immediately upon the petitions of the Poor Ladies.

Eastern Europe was being devastated by the Tartars, who taking advantage of the disunity among the princes of western Europe, were relentlessly driving westward. Soon they were battering on the very gates of Vienna. A new crusade to recapture Jerusalem from the Turks was also urgently needed. In addition, Innocent was anxious to repair the schism which had torn the Greek and Latin rites apart again. He set operations in motion to cope with these problems, but it would be years before he would see the fruit of his labors. And the greatest of his troubles, Frederick, continued to do all he could to harass, discredit, and vanquish the power and influence of the Church.

With all of these major worries pressing upon him, it is a testimony to Innocent's sincere concern for the family of St. Francis, that he devoted his energy to formulating a more acceptable Rule for the Poor Ladies. He brought to this task all his considerable skill as a canonist, as well as his finesse in reconciling different factions. The only thing he lacked was an understanding of the vision which had inspired Francis and Clare when initiating the life of the Poor Sisters. In 1247, Innocent revoked his decree which bound all the monasteries to the observance of Hugolino's Rule and on August 6 of that year, presented them with a new Rule which he had himself composed. His purpose in doing so, he announced, was his wish to resolve the need for dispensations which Hugolino's Rule had made necessary and which were "marring the unity of the Order."[3]

This new version retained clauses entrusting to the First Order the care of the Poor Ladies and recommended that the sisters follow the usages of the friars in the form of the Office they prayed. However, the spirit of the Rule was anything but Franciscan. He mitigated the penitential aspect of the life of the Poor Ladies and permitted, though did not demand, common ownership of movable and immovable goods and property. Clare searched in vain for that soaring and life-giving breath of the Spirit which was the heart of the joy, the freedom, and the poverty of Francis' great dream.

Once again she was faced with the dilemma of telling a high-ranking prelate, this time the Pope himself, that a Rule he had composed on behalf of her community was not acceptable to them. It was not acceptable for the friars either, who at this time of expansion, did not want to have the added "burden" of caring for the sisters. Once more letters flew to Lyon from all over Europe which convinced Innocent that his attempt at compromise had pleased no one, as is so often true of compromises. On July 6, 1250, Innocent declared that no community of Poor Ladies would be forced to accept his Rule, which thereby lost its binding force.

While Innocent sighed over the impossibility of pleasing either friars or sisters, Clare concluded that the only way a Rule which was true to the original inspiration of her Order could be drafted, would be if it were composed by someone who knew, loved, and lived that shining vision. It should be, she strongly felt, based on the Rule approved for the friars and incorporate those precious "writings" which Francis himself had given her.

The only person she knew who could do this was herself. But she was a woman . . . and women do not write their own Rules. Canonists do this for them, and all canonists are men. However, Clare was not one to allow convention to bar her from undertaking a work to which she felt called by the Holy Spirit. So sometime after 1247 and the promulgation of one more unsatisfactory Rule for the Poor Ladies, Clare gathered together all the texts of these Rules, including those of 1221 and 1223 for the friars. She assembled also the writings of Francis which she so cherished, took up her quill in the name of God and began a work which would not be completed until she lay on her deathbed.

An incident which occurred in 1246 may have contributed to Clare's sense of urgency about having a Rule which truly reflected the will of Francis for her and her sisters. Her health was continuing to deteriorate and more than once she had lain at death's door. Clare felt that to die before ensuring that Francis' original vision was properly protected by an appropriately written Rule, would be to fail in the trust which he had laid upon her.

In early July of 1246, Clare had experienced some resurgence of strength which enabled her to be up and around. As always she sought out little ways in which to serve her sisters. Some of the lay sisters had gone into Assisi to beg for alms of food after the heat of the afternoon had diminished. Clare may have seen them off with the injunction she frequently gave them to "praise God for every beautiful green and flowering plant they saw; and for every human being they saw, as well as for every creature, [they should] always and for all these things praise the Lord."[4]

Since the sisters would be late in returning home, Clare offered to remain up and wait for them. The other sisters had worked hard during the day and she wished them to be able to retire early for the repose she knew they needed. They would all be wakened soon enough to pray Matins at midnight. Perhaps Clare felt the desire to pray in solitude during this tranquil period when twilight slowly faded and the noises of the day were hushed. She had relished these peaceful hours from her earliest days at San Damiano when it was her delight to remain in chapel, absorbed in prayer, until the Night Office.

As the day's heat gave way to refreshing coolness, Clare relaxed her tired body and absorbed the beauty of her earthly homeland. Umbria has been described by many as possessing an unusual and subtle loveliness. The softness of the air seems to temper the harshness of the sun and imparts a special luminosity to the colors of the landscape. The lush valley, cradled between gentle mountain heights, retains an aura of peace despite the many bitter battles which have been fought there throughout its long history of human habitation. For some, this area possesses a certain mystic quality that makes it seem inevitable that a man of Francis' stature and holiness could be produced there and nowhere else.

Both Clare and Francis were molded by their homeland as

fully as they were by the culture of their times. Its very physical qualities played a formative part in the development of their spiritual lives. The caves deep in the side of Monte Subasio were like a womb to which Francis returned again and again to experience the rebirth of his spirit. The high, immovable mass of Monte Subasio brooded over Clare's life like the strong, protective shoulder of her heavenly Father. "I lift up my eyes toward the mountains; whence shall help come to me" was a prayer Clare had learned at her mother's side. And through the years she had learned ever more deeply that

> The Lord is your guardian; the Lord is your shade;
> he is beside you at your right hand.
> The sun shall not harm you by day
> nor the moon by night.
> . . . .
> The Lord will guard your life. . .
> both now and forever.[5]

As far as we know, Clare never ventured any further from Assisi and its environs than Perugia, a city built likewise on a rising height and overlooking the undulating contours of the Spoleto valley. It is unlikely that Clare consciously reflected on the role that the very color and shape of her native land played in her personal development. But we do know that she loved it. She had seen it endure the yearly round of seasonal changes and yet remain essentially unchanged whether the valley was golden with wheat or swept barren by winds storming down from frozen heights in winter.

She had listened to its myriad voices, the silken tongue of new spring leaves and the rasping complaint of dried oak groves in late fall. Perhaps, as twilight now draws on, she smiles as the song of nightingales reaches her from the woods further down the slope. Marveling gratitude floods Clare's heart for the sheer grace which had led her to the altar at the Portiuncula thirty-four years before. She may have thought then that she was renouncing her father's house and her rightful patrimony. But she had soon discovered, with an exaltation akin to that which she had beheld on the face of Peter Bernardone's disowned son, that to live in total dependence on the bounty of her heavenly Father ensured her an immortal inheritance, both here and in the world to come.

Despite the passing years and the gradual weakening of her body, Clare felt she was growing younger day by day, for each new day revealed deeper and richer wonders. In all the descriptions which the sisters gave of Clare after her death we glimpse, not a wornout, bedridden invalid but a vibrant woman, still caught up in the enthrallment of her first love.

Clare ceaselessly found new delight in the simplest bits of material creation which surrounded her. Sister Angeluccia mentions that once during an Easter season, the antiphon: "I saw water coming from the temple on the right side" threw Clare into such an ecstasy of delight that "she ever after bore it in mind."[6] Holy water was a most precious sacramental to her. After every meal and each evening after Compline Clare had it "brought for herself and her sisters. Often she would say to them, 'Sisters and daughters, you must always remember and keep in mind that holy water which came from the side of our Lord Jesus Christ when he hung on the cross.'"[7]

As with her Father Francis, nothing was too humble or common to remind Clare of her Lord. But she did not appreciate creation only for its symbolic significance. Each created thing was cherished in its own right so that Sister Water was precious, not just because it reminded her of the redeeming love of Christ but because it was so utterly beautiful in its lowliness and service. Its essential purity and preciousness derived simply from its being what it was created to be.

Perhaps on this summer evening Clare surrenders again to the enchantment of seeing the radiance of Sisters Moon and Stars gradually emerge as the fiery ardor of Brother Sun disappears behind the western mountains. These lamps of the night had also been named "precious" by Francis in the song he had composed when he had lain sleepless in her garden.

On that night when Francis had experienced his whole being achieving unity with all that existed, he had spontaneously given these sisters of the night the name of the light which had ever shone through the darkness for him— *clarite*. It was more than just a coincidence. By so naming the lights in the heavens, he had paid an exquisite courtesy to Clare and acknowledged that profound truth that "in every sense of the word, [Clare] was for him Sister Light, not only by the advice she gave him but, at a deeper level, by the spiritual influence of her being, on the innermost forces in his soul."[8]

Clare, like Sister Moon, had always turned toward her Brother Sun, reflecting back to him his own shining vision when it seemed to have grown too dark for Francis himself to see it. No matter how many events, personages, or years came between Clare and that moment of enlightenment when she first perceived her future way beaming from Francis' eyes, she never lost its radiance or allowed it to be clouded over.

Now, through the contented song of the crickets and sleepy chirps of the retiring birds, Clare hears the soft footfalls of the begging sisters coming down the path from Assisi's Porta Nuova gate. She rises to unlock the heavy door. Perhaps due to her weakness, she has to jerk it sharply to swing it inward on its old leathern hinges. Sister Angeluccia, who is coming toward the door, starts in horror as she sees the huge door tear loose from its moorings and fall inward on Clare, pinning her helplessly beneath its massive weight. "Thinking that she must surely be killed, Angeluccia sets up a great cry . . . that brought other sisters running to the scene. They find the door still lying on Clare, since Sister Angeluccia is powerless to move it by herself."[9]

To their immense relief, they hear Clare quietly assure them that she feels no weight at all. The cries of the sisters had aroused the brothers who were sleeping in the chaplain's hut that night. They come quickly and, according to Sister Angeluccia, it takes three of them to raise and replace the door.

The shock of this brush with Sister Death, from which she seems to have been preserved only by a miracle, may have strengthened Clare's determination to commit to paper the Rule which was written in her heart. She could see only too clearly what might ensue if she did not, for daily she observed the upheavals in the brotherhood caused by differing interpretations of Francis' Rule, the Rule which he had striven to write "simply and plainly" and desired to have understood "plainly and simply."

In addition Clare could not forget what Gregory IX had written to Agnes of Prague when she had asked to be allowed to follow the form of life observed at San Damiano in those points where it differed from the Rule he had given the Poor Ladies in 1219. His refusal read: "Being established that this Rule must be everywhere uniformly observed by all those who profess it, if one attempted to act otherwise it could give birth to some serious and intolerable scandals; especially because all the other sisters, seeing the integrity of the Rule thus violated, could—because of the confusion which would be born from it—be shaken in the observance of it; may such a thing never happen!"[10]

Clare certainly shared Gregory's heartfelt concern for the unity of the Poor Ladies. Although his Rule had not been wholly satisfactory, it was sufficiently so that Clare had felt she could profess it so long as she would be allowed to follow the earlier formulations of her way of life given to her by Francis himself and which had been guaranteed by Innocent III in the Privilege of Poverty. Gregory had himself reconfirmed this Privilege for the San Damiano community but had adamantly refused to extend it to any other monasteries except possibly a few which had been established prior to the composition of his Rule in 1219 or which had received a special permission in the matter.

Prominent among these would have been the monastery at Monticelli where Agnes had been sent. If so, this would clarify the ambiguous statement in Agnes' letter to Clare that "the Lord Pope has agreed with me, as I said, and with you, in all things in accordance with your desire and mine, concerning the question of property."

The multiplication of new monasteries of Poor Ladies gave an added impetus to Clare's decision. These new communities, many of which did not have the benefit of spiritual guidance by the friars, had only the basically Benedictine Rule of 1219 on which to base their conception of the way of life of Clare and her sisters.

Clare decided to use the Later Rule of 1223, approved for the friars, as the basic outline for her own Rule. Yet she did not try to merely adapt its precepts for women. She sought to interpret and express the spirit which gave life to the written precepts. She searched through all the other writings of Francis which were available to her. Among them were the Earlier Rule, so redolent of Francis' burning ardor, his Testament, and the few but, oh so precious "words," which Francis had written expressly for Clare in her first years at San Damiano.

Clare recognized that the way of life which she had freely chosen and lived for over thirty-five years had benefited by the support which the specifications of Hugolino's Rule had given it. She therefore drew from it most of the structural and governmental details about life within a monastery. But into even such legalistic norms she tried to infuse the flame of Francis' joy and spirit. The direct borrowings from the Benedictine Rule which she retained were those which were in full accord with the spirit of sisterhood and minority which she considered the essence of the life of the Poor Ladies.

The norms governing enclosure which Hugolino had imposed in 1219 were stricter than those being observed by any other order of nuns of that period with the exception of the reformed Cistercian nuns. These had caused Clare no apparent distress, since from the first she had chosen to live a very secluded form of life. This Hugolino must have observed, but his norms, drawn from the usages newly established for the Cistercian nuns, were more rigid and detailed than what Clare and her sisters were living.

The title given to Clare's Rule—"The Rule and Life of the Poor Sisters of the Strict Enclosure"—echoed what Clare had always lived. The first chapter of this Rule is taken almost word for word from the first chapter of Francis' Later Rule. The additions she made were only those which specified that her vocation had come to her from God *through Francis.* Thus, where Francis prescribed obedience and reverence to the Lord Pope, Clare amplifies this:

> Clare, the unworthy handmaid of Christ and the little plant of the most blessed Father Francis, promises obedience and reverence to the Lord Pope Innocent . . . and just as at the beginning of her conversion, together with her sisters she promised obedience to the Blessed Francis, so now she promises his successors to observe the same [obedience] inviolably.[11]

In addition Clare binds all the sisters to obey not only "the canonically elected abbesses: but also the "successors of the blessed Francis."[12]

Chapter II of Clare's Rule reveals how creatively she worked with the texts she had at hand. The first article, which deals with the acceptance of candidates, is remarkable in that Clare skillfully combined points from four different sources to express her mature thought on this important matter. It opens with the same words as the corresponding article in the Later Rule but Clare inserts a phrase of cardinal importance which was in the draft of the Earlier Rule but mysteriously omitted in the approved Rule. In the Earlier Rule, Francis had written: "If anyone, desiring by *divine inspiration* to accept this life, should come to our brothers, let him be received by them with kindness . . . ."[13] Clare echoes Francis' conviction about the source of a vocation and retains the phrase "by divine inspiration."[14]

For Clare, as for Francis, the Originator of the call to live the gospel life in poverty and littleness, is the Holy Spirit. The intimate experience of this Spirit's intervention in their own lives had convinced them of this. Francis had begun his Testament with the significant words: "The Lord granted me, Brother Francis, to begin to do penance in this way: . . . no one showed me what I should do, but the Most High Himself revealed to me that I should live according to the form of the Holy Gospel."[15]

The uniqueness of this inspiration arose, not so much from the idea that he, Francis, was to live the gospel life – all Christians are called to do this – but that he was to build a form of religious life *only* on that. He specified no particular apostolate as the means by which the brothers were to spread the Good News. No. Just let the brothers *become* the Good News themselves and it will direct them in what they should do. This is the special insight which Francis insisted had been made clear to him through no human mediation but directly by the Holy Spirit.

Clare, in her turn, cherished the fact that it was in the "enlightenment of the Holy Spirit" that Francis first prophesied about the Ladies who would come to dwell at San Damiano and who would "glorify our heavenly Father throughout his holy Church by their celebrated and holy manner of life."[16] It was not the "holy works" of these Ladies but their lives which would give glory to God and build up the Church. Clare added this significant conclusion: and our blessed Father prophesied this not only for us, but also for those who were to come to this [same] holy vocation to which the Lord has called us."[17]

Clare's own vocation had come to her when "the Most High Celestial Father saw fit to enlighten her heart by his grace." But to this Clare invariably added that the instrument for this inspiration had been "the example and teaching of our most blessed Father Saint Francis."[18]

Francis seemed to be more than simply a mouthpiece of the Holy Spirit for Clare. By his example he appeared as almost an incarnate expression of the Holy Spirit in her regard. True, the "Son of God had become for [Clare] the Way but Clare had come to know this Way through Francis who filled the role of Friend of the Bridegroom."[19]

It was as if the young Clare had carried within herself a light which she could not perceive until Francis came and held a mirror before her eyes. In that mirror (which was Francis' life) Clare recognized the call she had. Thomas of Celano gives the strong impression that Francis had also recognized the grace given to Clare for he was "impressed by the fair fame of so gracious a maiden [and] desired to see and speak with her." His intention is described as a "desire to *restore* her to his Lord."[20]

Francis, as we know from abundant testimonies, would have been the last person to decide on his own to take women into his young community. Yet we find him acting with no apparent hesitation, encouraging the lovely daughter of a noble family to come and follow the path marked out for him by Lady Poverty. And Clare came, simply and trustfully.

Clare later wrote that when Francis saw her joyously embracing "poverty, hard work, suffering, shame, and the contempt of the world," he was "moved by compassion" to confirm her vocation of having "the Holy Spirit as her Spouse and . . . of choosing to live according to the perfection of the holy Gospel."[21]

This experience of having the enlightenment and solicitude of the Holy Spirit come to her through another human being, Francis, impressed Clare profoundly. From then on, this kind of mediation became for Clare a fundamental concept of her apostolate and the radical explanation of the choice she made for an enclosed, contemplative way of life. She came to define her own role and that of her sisters as being mirrors and transmitters of the Holy Spirit to others.

She warned her daughters that, having been called to "such great things" they must live in such a way that in them the other sisters may behold their own true selves.[22]

Just as Francis had enabled young Clare de Favarone to see her own spiritual beauty and calling, she and her sisters were to fulfill this "service" for others. Such a vocation requires full awareness on the part of each sister of her own glory and grace, as well as a self-effacement so total that each can simply hold her life up before another as a mirror in which that other may come to see her own spiritual beauty, as well as the heights to which she is called.

Again we come across the concept of the mirror in Clare's spirituality. She believed that one looked into a mirror to discern, not only what one was but what one was to become. Clare, when writing to Agnes of Prague, spoke of Jesus as a mirror (who) as he was suspended upon the wood of the Cross, urges passersby to behold all this (i.e., his manner of loving).[23]

Clare realized that a call to embrace the life of a Poor Lady is a sheer grace from the "Father of mercies." It implies that one has been in-Spirited in such a manner that one can behold in the pattern of living of the sisters, an image of what one is and is called to become ever more clearly. To each sister, Clare says that she must "look upon that mirror each day . . . and continually study *her* face within it, so that she may adorn herself within and without . . . with all the virtues [she beholds]."[24]

In her Rule Clare does not entrust the discernment of a vocation to the abbess alone; with the friars it belongs to the "ministers provincial and to no other."[25] The abbess is required to consult all the sisters and obtain their consent.[26] Why should every sister actively approve and welcome new members? Because the goal of the gospel life that Clare holds up for all the Poor Ladies to strive for is holy unity where through "freely accepting (this form of life) the sisters live together in unity of mind and heart and in the profession of highest poverty."[27]

Chapter XXI Endnotes

1. Cause of Canonization, Wit. 9, #8.
2. Christopher Hollis, *The Papacy* (New York: Macmillan, 1964), p. 83.
3. Ignatius Brady, *The Legend and Writings of Saint Clare of Assisi* (St. Bonaventure: The Franciscan Institue, 1953), p. 5.
4. Cause of Canonization, Wit. 14, #9.
5. Ps 121:1, #5–7.
6. Cause of Canonization, Wit., 14, #8.
7. Ibid.
8. Eloi Leclerc O.F.M. *The Canticle of Creatures, Symbols of Union* (Chicago: Franciscan Herald Press, 1977), p. 82.
9. Cause of Canonization, cf. Wit. 14, #6.
10. *Bullarium Franciscanum* (1-Romae, 1759), p. 243.
11. Rule of Clare Ch. I, #3, #4.
12. Ibid., Ch. I, #5.
13. Earlier Rule, Ch. 2, #1.
14. Rule of Clare, Ch. II, #1.
15. Testament of Francis, #1, 14.
16. Testament of Clare, #4.
17. Ibid., #5.
18. Rule of Clare, Ch. VI, #1.
19. Testament of Clare, #2.
20. Legend of Celano, #5.
21. Rule of Clare Ch. VI, #2.
22. Testament of Clare, #6.

23. Fourth Letter to Agnes of Prague, #24.
24. Ibid., #15–17.
25. Later Rule, Ch. 2, #1.
26. Rule of Clare, Ch. II, #1.
27. Bull approving Rule of Clare, 1253.

XXII With Love Undimmed

While Clare labors to define the basic elements of the way of life which she, inspired by Francis and led by the Spirit, had embraced, monasteries of Poor Ladies continue to multiply. The ideal of evangelical poverty and simplicity had already stirred the religious aspirations of many before Francis and Clare launched their modest endeavor to enflesh this ideal in their own lives. The wildfire enthusiasm which greeted Francis' "poverty movement" had its roots in the facts of the age in which he was born.

But where other groups which had espoused gospel poverty often did so as a form of protest against abuses engendered by power and wealth in the Church, Francis' conceived his call as one to rebuild the Church. He was against nothing. He simply sought the liberty to delight always in the gifts of his Lord and to live in harmony with his ever-recreating will. No man saw more clearly than he that the "Lord loves all things that are and loathes nothing that he has made, for he fashioned all things that they might have being and the creatures of the world are wholesome."[1] It was to restore this wholesomeness that Jesus had come to live among his own creatures. He lived and died as the most human of men and rose from the dead as the most divine.

Clare shared Francis' intuitive perception of the deep and hidden glory of all that is. She knew that only the pure of heart could see God in all created things and only the poor in spirit could possess the kingdom of heaven which was already burgeoning to life within them. The pure of heart and poor in spirit were those who desired the fullness of life so passionately that they cast off all encumberances which might limit their embrace of it. Clare knew that the surest guide to this goal was the most divine and yet most human institution on earth, the Church.

Clare carried also in her heart the mandate to "rebuild My Church" which had been Francis' first positive direction from his Lord. Her Rule begins and ends with the statement that the Form of Life of the Poor Sisters is to observe the holy gospel. Intimately linked with this statement is the declaration that the sisters shall be "always submissive and subject at the feet of . . . holy Church and steadfast in the Catholic Faith." Clearly she believed that it was only possible for her sisters to "forever observe the poverty and humility of our Lord Jesus Christ and of his most holy Mother and the holy Gospel," if they enjoyed the guidance and protection of the Church.[2]

Her joy was genuine when she was informed in 1248 that Cardinal Rainaldo dei Conti di Segni had been appointed as Cardinal Protector of the Poor Ladies. He had been a Cistercian, called out of his monastery in 1227 by Pope Gregory IX and named a Cardinal-advisor to the Holy See. He became Bishop of Ostia, Gregory's former See, in 1231. By nature a devout and peaceful man, he was eminently qualified to appreciate Clare's determined struggle to obtain approval of a Rule for the Poor Ladies which would ensure the purest transmission of the original charism which she had received from Francis and had guarded so tenaciously.

According to Celano, Cardinal Rainaldo was to Clare "a father by reason of his office, a protector by his solicitude, and ever a devoted friend in purest affection."[3] It is very likely that he encouraged Clare to formulate an acceptable Rule for her sisters and promised that he would do all in his power to secure the approval she considered crucial.

It is probable that Clare recognized that time was running out for her. The long years of patience and waiting were past, and the time for action was at hand. Everything, however, seemed against the success of her plans. Pope Innocent IV was virtually out of reach in Lyon, political turbulence racked Europe from what was later called the Bering Sea to the Mediterreanean, and armed conflicts flared everywhere. Moreover the First Order had not only withdrawn almost all its support but was actively pursuing a course which seemed a betrayal of Francis' ideals. Like Esther of old, Clare could have prayed: "My Lord, our King, you alone are God. Help me, who am alone and have no help but you."

The sense of desperation which may have gripped Clare comes through in lines from her Testament:

> Later on Francis wrote a form of life for us, [indicating] especially that we should persevere always in holy poverty. And while he was living, he was not content to encourage us by many words and examples to love and observe holy poverty; [in addition] he also gave us many writings so that, after his death, we should in no way turn away from it. [In a similar way] the Son of God never wished to abandon this holy poverty while he lived in the world, and our most blessed Father Francis, following his footprints, never departed, either in example or teaching, from this holy poverty which he had chosen for himself and for his brothers.
>
> Therefore, I, Clare, the handmaid of Christ and of the Poor Sisters of the Monastery of San Damiano — although unworthy—and the little plant of the holy Father, consider together with my sisters our most high profession and the command of so great a father. [We also take note] in some [sisters] of the frailty which we feared in ourselves after the death of our holy Father Francis, [he] who was our pillar of strength, and, after God, our one consolation and support. [Thus] time and again, we bound ourselves

to our Lady, most holy Poverty, so that, after my
death, the sisters present and to come would never
abandon her.

And . . . I have always been most zealous and solicitous to observe and to have the other sisters observe
the holy poverty which we have promised the Lord
and our holy Father Francis.[4]

One of Clare's most faithful and truest friends among the
friars, Brother Philip of Atri, had given up his duties as Visitor
in 1246, presumably from old age and failing strength. He had
been the witness of Clare's earliest conversations with Francis,
his height (he was nicknamed "The Tall") in amusing contrast to
Francis' slight but vibrant figure. According to Beatrice, Clare's
youngest sister, it was he who had accompanied Francis when
Clare and Agnes were first taken to San Damiano to begin living
their tryst with Lady Poverty.

The extraordinary radiance which had thenceforth flowed
from San Damiano and aroused enthusiasm throughout Christendom, was described by Pope Alexander IV as "like the brilliance of lightning."[5] He expanded this metaphor in a beautifully balanced poem which has the cadence of a dance, the
dance which Clare had become through her sensitivity to the
rhythm of the Spirit.

On earth this light . . . was kept within cloistral
   walls,
yet shed abroad its shining rays;

it was confined within a convent cell,
yet it streamed forth without.

For though Clare was hidden,
her life was known to all;

though Clare was silent,
her fame cried out;

though Clare was enclosed in her cell,
she was preached to men in all the cities.[6]

In recent years, more houses of Poor Ladies had been established in France, that land for which Francis had such predilection. A new monastery had opened in Beziers around 1240 and another in Bordeaux in 1246. In 1250 Sister Maria of Assisi established a new foundation at Avignon. Around 1251, more houses came into being in Switzerland, Germany, and Hungary.[7]

Clare realized she must compose a Rule for all these monasteries which would not only be acceptable to the canonists in high places but which also glowed with the fire and freedom of Francis' vast dream. It seemed that such a "marriage" would be impossible to achieve but Clare was never daunted by mere impossibilities. She knew, precisely and clearly, what she wanted. Her working with the previous forms of her Rule, was creative and original. Even in the driest and most mundane of sections, glints and gleams of the fire of her spirit shine through. These insertions and addendas are of critical importance in appreciating Clare's full vision and wisdom.

In article eight of the second chapter, Clare echoes Francis' description of profession as a being "received to obedience." This was the customary phrase in use at that period; for the formula "Living in obedience, without property and in chastity" had been spelled out only at the Fourth Lateran Council in 1215. But where Francis speaks of promising "to observe our life and Rule,"[8] Clare says "promising to observe always our life and *form of poverty*."[9] This variation may be of some significance for Clare would not ordinarily change the words of her revered guide without reason.

It would seem that Clare's concept of poverty was so rich and multifaceted she considered "form of poverty" equivalent with "Rule of Life." Perhaps the key to understanding this equivalence lies in Clare's petition, made during her earliest years at San Damiano, for the Privilege of Poverty. As can be seen, she had felt content that this, joined with Francis' directives, was sufficient to define the life of the Poor Sisters. If the Poor Ladies truly vowed to "renounce *all desire* for temporal things," "proposed to have no possessions whatever" (i.e., have nothing they could call their own) and did this so that they could "cleave to the footprints of Him" who became poor for us, what more was needed?[10] "Poor virgins embracing the poor Christ" had no impediment to following him who is "the Way, the Truth, and the Life."

If the sisters were not seeking to entrust their lives totally to him "who feeds the birds of the air and the lilies of the field," the most exacting legislation would be of no use.[11] Whatever form the Rule took for the sisters, Clare saw it as only a clarification of how to live this "form of poverty" which they were to embrace totally and forever.

Clare, wise and appreciative of the ways of women, prescribed the garb by which the sisters were to express their dedication to poverty. It was a feminine copy of the friars' habit, made of the same poor material and girded with a cord. She included the little mantle or "caperon" which the brothers also wore when working. A veil took the place of the hood which the brothers received when professed. Like Francis, Clare was far from rigid in this matter and counsels the Mother to "provide them [the sisters] with clothing prudently, according to the needs of each person and place, and seasons and cold climates, as it shall seem expedient to her by necessity."[12]

Clare's special genius shines out in the final article about clothing. She recognized how responsive is the feminine psyche to clothing. A woman is subtly but surely influenced by the way she dresses and conversely, the clothing a woman chooses to wear is generally expressive of her own self-image and values. Therefore, Clare did not merely say: "the sisters shall wear always the poorest of garments" but provides an appealing motive based on love. "For the love of the most holy and beloved Child who was wrapped in the poorest of swaddling clothes and laid in a manger, and of his most holy Mother, I admonish, entreat, and exhort my sisters that they always wear the poorest of garments."[13]

The Rule goes on to prescribe that the sisters "shall celebrate the Divine Office according to the custom of the Friars Minor."[14] According to the research into the usages of that period, the brothers used the Gallican psalter joined with the Breviary of the Roman Curia. This formed a simpler and shorter arrangement of the Liturgy of the Hours, better adapted to the friars whose apostolic ministry kept them on the move. Moreover, the recitation of the full monastic Office would probably have required a larger group of men living together than was customary among the friars.

Clare's reason for prescribing that the sisters pray the same form of the Office as the brothers sprang primarily from her constant endeavor to have her sisters united as closely as possible to the First Order. She may also have seen the utility of praying this form of the Office because the houses of the Poor Ladies were usually small and had a limited number of sisters. It is probable that there were no more than about twelve choir sisters at San Damiano at any given time. The size of the choir itself would scarcely have permitted more than that. Even twelve would have had to stand elbow to elbow!

So Clare prescribes a form of choral prayer which a small group of women could pray together with relative ease. She adds the monition that it is to be "read without singing."[15] Most likely, Clare's intention was to avoid the magnificence and splendor which attended choir exercises in most monasteries of women at this period.

For the sisters who cannot read and also for those who "for some reasonable cause, sometimes are not able to read and pray the Hours," Clare prescribes the praying of the Pater Nosters, modeled on the practice of the lay brothers of the First Order.[16]

Following the articles about community prayer are those which treat of fasting. The two were always intimately linked in Clare's mind. In the Rule, she describes the same practice which she had outlined in her letter to Agnes of Prague in 1238. But here she does not specify that the sisters do not fast on Sundays because Church practice automatically forbade fasting on the Lord's Day and any reader of her Rule at that time would have known this. Nor does Clare mention the option permitting each sister to decide whether or not she will fast on ordinary Thursdays. The reason for this omission is not known.

Clare shared Francis' profound devotion to Our Lord in the Sacrament of the Altar. Yet, compared to his fervent outpourings and admonitions to his brothers, she wrote almost nothing on the centrality and importance of the Eucharistic Presence in the life of the Poor Ladies. However, her example spoke with such eloquence that eight hundred years later, Clare is invariably linked with devotion to Jesus' Sacramental Presence. The long hours she habitually spent praying in the chapel, the implicit confidence she manifested in the Sacrament's protective and saving influence; the innumerable altar linens and vestments to which she tirelessly applied her skilled needle, all testify to her vibrant devotion which pervaded every moment of her days and nights.

Clare, bound by the practice of her times, could not urge her sisters to frequent Communion, although she did mandate an unusual number of days each year on which the sisters could receive Communion. All the sisters saw how devoutly she re-

ceived the Sacrament of her Lord's Body and Blood. Sister Benvenuta of Peroscia, who had joined Clare at San Damiano about
four months after Clare had fled her parents' home, testified
that Clare "went often to confession and with great devotion and
awe often received the Body of our Lord Jesus Christ, and when
she received it, she trembled all over."[17] Other sisters noted the
tears which reception of this Sacrament often evoked in Clare.[18]

In early November of 1250, Clare's health took such an alarm-
ing turn that the sisters thought she was near to death. After
Mass on the feast of St. Martin, November 11, the priest brought
Communion to her where she lay ill. Sister Francesca saw "a
wonderful light over the head of the Lady Clare, and the Host
appeared to her transformed into a most beautiful Child.
After . . . Clare had received it with her habitual great devotion
and many tears she said these words: "All the heavens and earth
could not worthily praise our Lord God for what he has granted
me this day.'"[19]

Sister Francesca was asked whether any of the other sisters
had seen this. She responded that she did not know, she only
knew what she had seen herself.

In her Rule, Clare recommended monthly Confession and
specified seven days on which the sisters could receive Holy
Communion. In addition to the major feasts of the Church year,
Clare included the feast of St. Francis, another indication of her
appreciation of his holiness. She prescribed that at a time when
Christians so rarely approached the Communion Table that the
Fourth Lateran Council had found it necessary to bind the faith-
ful to receive Holy Communion at least once a year.

In Chapter IV of her Rule, Clare describes the role of the
abbess in the communities of the Poor Ladies. One commentator
has observed that if "we wish to understand the community
spirit of an Order, we should above all examine the position of
the superior."[20] Outside of the Rule, Clare uses the title Abbess
only once to describe the superior of the Poor Sisters. She never

applies it to herself, preferring to use such terms as handmaid, servant, and, occasionally, Mother.

Clare adopts several points from the Benedictine Rule which specify how the abbess should regard her position and conduct.

> Let the one who is elected reflect upon the kind of burden she has undertaken, and to whom she is to render an account for the flock committed to her. She should strive as well to preside over the others more by her virtues and holy behavior than by her office, so that, moved by her example, the sisters might obey her more out of love than out of fear. She should avoid particular friendships, lest by loving some more than others she cause scandal among all. She should consult with all her sisters on whatever concerns the welfare and good of the monastery; for the Lord often reveals what is best to the lesser [among us].[21]

To this portrait of a Mother who cares earnestly for the welfare of her community, Clare adds some important additions which she has drawn, directly or indirectly, from the writings of Francis, as well as from her own experience and wealth of compassion: "She should console those who are afflicted and be, likewise, the last refuge for those who are disturbed; for if they fail to find in her the means of health, the sickness of despair might overcome the weak."[22]

To this Clare wisely adds: "She should preserve the common life in everything, especially in the church, dormitory, refectory, infirmary, and in clothing. Her vicar is bound to do likewise."[23]

Clare is here prescribing the relationship of sisterhood and servanthood which should characterize the superior of any house of Poor Ladies. She intends that these attitudes be given clear and literal expression. Clare was writing in an age when abbesses of most religious communities were given the veneration and honor equal to that of a bishop. This sprang from the intermingling in the medieval mind of spiritual dignity with temporal prestige. Clare had no quarrel with the mentality of her age as regards veneration accorded to royalty or ranking prelates. Her letters to Agnes are proof of this. But she did not see how this mentality could have any place within a community of Poor Sisters.

She believed, as did Francis, that "the Abbess is to be so familiar with them [the sisters] that they can speak and act toward her as ladies do with their servant. For that is the way it should be, that the Abbess be the servant of all the sisters."[24]

No superior, however humble and saintly, can function effectively without the support of her sisters so Clare reminds them "that for God's sake they have renounced their own wills."[25] Taught by her own experience, Clare develops this theme in her Testament by adding: "Seeing the charity, humility, and unity' they have toward one another, their mother might bear all the burdens of her office more lightly. Thus what is painful and bitter might be turned into sweetness for her because of their holy way of life."[26]

She copies what Francis had written in his Rule that "the sisters be on their guard against all pride, vainglory, envy, greed, worldly care and anxiety, detraction and murmuring, dissension and division."[27] It is significant that the final two vices which Clare warns against are additions of her own. Clare recognizes the extreme importance of fostering a spirit of holy unity within each monastery of the Poor Ladies. Her addition of "dissension and division" to the list Francis had composed reflects her awareness of how destructive these particular failings can be within an enclosed community.

Not only had Clare observed at close hand the painful divisions which were plaguing the First Order but had traced them to their root cause which was a failure to appreciate Lady Poverty in her true role. Francis loved Lady Poverty but not as an end in herself. Outward poverty helps to ensure and safeguard poverty of spirit. Without it, humility and purity of heart are replaced by ambition and possessiveness. True charity turns into a possessive owning or using of others. Factions and divisions inevitably follow. When such develop within the confines of an enclosed community, the possibility of deep contemplative prayer is dangerously threatened.

Clare exhibits her concern for holy unity in all her writings, adopting St. Paul's words: "Let them be ever zealous to preserve among themselves the unity of mutual love, which is the bond of perfection."[28]

Continuing to follow the order of the Later Rule, Clare here inserts a practical directive toward maintaining this mutual love. In the thirteenth century, a point from which pride, vanity, and division often took its origin was learning. There were three ways in which a person could gain status and a sense of superiority over others. One was through distinctions of social class. Another was to seek renown through courageous action on the battlefield, while the third was to gain esteem through the acquisition of higher learning. Clare recognized how the first and third of these could, and often did, wreak havoc within enclosed communities.

Therefore, she dwelt strongly on the relationships of servanthood and sisterhood among her sisters. At this point in the Rule, she singles out learning. "And those who do not know how to read should not be eager to learn."[29] Clare's intention here is not to hold up cultivated ignorance as a value but rather to point up the truth that a sister's personal worth does not lie in what she can or cannot do but rather in what she is and what she is striving to become. In this, all the sisters are on a basis of equality. The article which immediately follows bears this out:

> Rather, let them devote themselves to what they must desire to have above all else: the Spirit of the Lord and his holy manner of working, to pray always to

him with a pure heart, and to have humility, patience in difficulty and weakness, and to love those who persecute, blame, and accuse us; for the Lord says: Blessed are they who suffer persecution for justice's sake, for theirs is the kingdom of heaven. But he who shall have persevered to the end will be saved."[30]

This paragraph is taken word for word from the Later Rule except for one scriptural text which Clare omits. It would be unlikely that this was merely an oversight on her part since she had spent years praying over and formulating the Rule she wished to have approved for the sisters. The omitted text reads: "Love your enemies; pray for your persecutors." Possibly Clare, with her acute insight and understanding of a woman's way of loving, preferred that her sisters not view anyone among them as her "enemy" or "persecutor."

Rather, their prayer should be directed toward acheiving fuller acceptance of all that befalls them, not with grim stoicism but with that special quality of feminine maturity which has learned that "all things work together for the good of those who love God." This is a type of grace-filled surrender which knows how to trust in the One who loves them. Everything which occurs within the monastery has its ultimate source in God. Are not all her sisters brides of Christ? Clare would have them focus their vision on the kingdom which is already growing among them and persevere in unwavering hope.

At the exact center of Clare's Rule, we find four chapters which express the essence of the spirituality which should animate and give life to all the other prescriptions.[31] Chapter VI appears to be entirely Clare's personal composition in which she imbeds two short quotations from the "Writings" which Francis had given to her. It may seem strange that a section dealing with the founding of the Order and the profession of perfect poverty should be found in the middle, rather than at the beginning of the Rule. However, Clare generally had good reason behind whatever she wrote.

She had modeled her Rule as closely as she could on the order of Francis' Rule of 1223. That Rule opened and closed with the statement of the brothers' first purpose and final goal: to live according to the holy gospel and in submission to the Roman Church. Clare recognized this primacy and chose that her Rule also be enclosed between these same twin statements of purpose.

Yet she did not wish that her account of the founding and Vision of the life of the Poor Ladies be relegated to the status of a mere prologue or become a document separate from the Rule. She had seen how Francis' Testament had become a source of contention among the friars who disputed its binding power. A vision, an ideal, can never be an obligation of conscience in itself. Thus, when the brothers had asked Pope Gregory whether the Testament which Francis had written bound them under pain of sin, he correctly responded that it did not. Francis himself had said that "the brothers [should] not say: This is another Rule; because this is a remembrance, an admonition, an exhortation, and my testament, which I, little Brother Francis, prepare for all of you, my blessed brothers."[32]

However, a Last Will and Testament is not something which members of a family can lightly ignore. The degree to which a brother takes the last words of his spiritual father to heart and strives to live by them is an outward expression of his esteem for the writer of these directives. Francis was never one who wished to compel others through threats or coercion. He longed for the spontaneous response which springs from love. Those who love the Vision have no need of any further rule!

Clare tried to avoid similar problems among the sisters by a unique ploy. She enshrined the Vision which was to animate all the Poor Ladies at the very center of her Rule. This entire section is repeated in her Testament, a document which was probably written in stages during the final years of Clare's life. It is the most personal of her writings, a unique revelation of all she held most dear.

Clare wished to make it clear that the Vision which she had received from Francis and is holding up to her sisters cannot be disregarded; and, on the other hand, it should not be separated from the structural elements of their life. She, like Francis, desired that all her sisters "present and to come . . . strive to follow the way . . . we have been taught by our blessed Father Francis."[33] They were to do so because they were "bonded" or covenanted to one another and to the Vision through a testament (covenant) which they had freely accepted.

Clare's mind, as well as that of her contemporaries, was formed on scriptural thought patterns. Their way of seeing the world and of understanding humans and their place in it were still quite close to the Semitic world-view. Thus Francis and Clare could count on the deference which would be spontaneously accorded to a person's last wishes.

Another consideration, also based on scriptural patterns, which may have influenced Clare's placement of this supremely important section at the center of her Rule, is the order of the Bible itself. At the precise center of the Bible is found the Book of Psalms. This collection of poetic prayers and remembrances contains the distilled essence of the entire Scriptures. In medieval times, the various psalms were frequently interpreted as descriptive prophecies of the life, suffering, and triumph of Jesus, as well as containing a summary of the entire Old Testament. In fact this single book was often referred to as the Bible in miniature.

The medieval mind would not have failed to note the significance that this book was placed at the literary heart of the Bible. Clare surely shared this mindset. By placing the section which expressed the raison d'être of her entire Rule at the physical center of her document, she automatically gave it a place of unique importance which would not go unnoticed by her contemporaries.

Another fact which supports the possibility that this placement was not a matter of chance is that it and the four following chapters which form a close unit with it, interrupt the logical flow of thought about the norms of the enclosure which begin in Chapter V, and are picked up and completed only in Chapter XI. Between these rather dry and legalistic prescriptions, we find the Vision of Clare for the Poor Ladies, together with the will of Francis regarding poverty and communal relationships. Here is enshrined the ideals of sisterhood and holy unity which Clare felt were essential if her sisters were to serve the Lord in freedom of soul.

Can we also see in this arrangement the purpose of material separation from the world as Clare conceived it? In the Rule, the chapters on the subject of enclosure stand on either side of the Vision like protecting ramparts. Unhindered by contrary winds and fueled to white heat by the banked coals of profound contemplative living, the Flame of the Spirit can leap high.

Material separation from the world appears as an integral element in Clare's conception of the vocation of the Poor Ladies. Yet she introduced into this accepted norm for feminine religious life a startling innovation, something so contrary to worldly prudence that she had to fight for it until she entered her death agony. This new factor was a form of poverty so radical that it drove the sisters to live day by day in total dependence on the bounty of their heavenly Father. They were to literally "seek first the kingdom of God" and then to trust that whatever was necessary to sustain them in this quest would come in its own time.

Clare had petitioned for the privilege of living without any security for the morrow. She and her sisters were to live in small, obscure convents where they would make do with whatever the Lord pleased to send them and with what they could produce by their own labor, i.e., their garden plot and skills of their own hands. Although Clare does not include in her Rule Francis' prohibition about receiving money as alms, her own practice would indicate that San Damiano depended mainly on alms received in kind rather than in coin.

Clare's resolve to live an enclosed life in radical poverty, both individual and communal, purified the practice of material separation from the world of some of its less admirable companions which had, in the name of prudence, become associated with monastic life. In the legitimate concern for a reasonable security, monasteries had become holders of vast tracts of land which brought with it wealth, prestige, and power. Clare wished to live as a "little poor one" of God, the title which Francis had given her and her sisters in the Canticle which he had composed for them.

She inserted Francis' Last Will, sent to her in loving concern as he was approaching his final hours at the Portiuncula: "I, brother Francis, the little one, wish to follow the life and poverty of our most high Lord Jesus Christ . . . and I ask and counsel you, my ladies, to live always in this most holy life and poverty. And keep most careful watch that you never depart from this by reason of the teaching or advice of anyone." Clare loyally and fearlessly defended her right to observe this injunction of Francis and bound all "the Abbesses who shall succeed me in office and all the sisters . . . to observe it inviolably to the end."[34]

Clare then defined precisely what this meant in regard to material goods: "They are not to receive or hold onto any possessions or property [acquired] through an intermediary, or even anything that might reasonably be called property, except as much land as necessity requires for the integrity and the proper seclusion of the monastery; and this land is not to be cultivated except as a garden for the needs of the sisters."[35]

But this clarification, strict as it sounds, was only the bottom line of her conception of radical poverty. In Chapter VIII, Clare copies Francis' directives to his brothers as given in Chapter VI of the Later Rule:

> The sisters shall not acquire anything as their own, neither a house nor a place nor anything at all; instead, as pilgrims and strangers in this world who

serve the Lord in poverty and humility let them send
confidently for alms.[36]

Clare, like Francis, shared the medieval concept that the poor
have a place within the normal social structure. Their presence
not only gave the more affluent an opportunity for winning
pardon for their offenses through works of mercy but they also
served as living reminders of the Lord Jesus who "was a poor
man and a transient and lived on alms, he and the Blessed Virgin and his disciples." In addition, Francis believed that "alms
are a legacy and a just right due to the poor, which our Lord
Jesus Christ acquired for us."[37]

Building on this, Clare quotes Francis further by saying that
the sisters should not "feel ashamed since the Lord made himself poor for us in this world. This is that summit of highest
poverty which has established you, my dearest sisters, as heirs
and queens of the kingdom of heaven; it has made you poor in
the things [of this world] but has exalted you in virtue. Let this
be your portion, which leads into the land of the living. Dedicat-
ing yourselves totally to this, my most beloved sisters, do not
wish to have anything else forever under heaven for the name of
our Lord Jesus Christ and his most holy Mother."[38]

At first glance these paragraphs may seem in opposition to
Clare's earlier statement that the sisters may have a place to live
with sufficient grounds to allow for privacy and a vegetable garden. But if we discern the full wisdom of Clare's concept of
poverty, we may recognize this is a description of what the previous statute makes possible.

The key phrase is that "the sisters shall not acquire anything *as
their own.*" Clare's concern here is to highlight how deeply poverty is meant to invade each sister's inmost being. The form of
profession which the sisters made contains the phrase "sine proprio"—without property. This is a technical term usually taken
to be simply a variant expression of the vow of religious poverty.

However, it appears to carry, in Francis' thought, and therefore also in Clare's, a much profounder meaning.

The practice of making profession of the three vows of poverty, chastity and obedience had only been canonically formulated in 1215 and did not have the glibness of an all-too-familiar fomula. The practice, which applied to each individual religious, as well as to the community as a whole, of living "sine proprio" meant, not just a lack of material goods but rather a free choice to live without ever calling anything their own, i.e., without appropriating anything to themselves.

Within the very circumscribed area of their small enclosure, Clare also exhorts her sisters to live as strangers and pilgrims! We may not simply conclude that Clare inserted this line from Francis' Rule merely because he had used it. We have already seen that she made additions and deletions of her own wherever she judged it necessary. In fact, in this same section, Clare has changed the phrase that the friars were to *go* confidently for alms to read that the sisters were to *send* confidently for alms. We may not conclude, therefore, that Clare expected her sisters to become strangers and pilgrims by literally wandering the roads of the world but neither may we say that Clare included this only as a piece of charming imagery.

Clare had learned through intimate experience that although her body remained within the limits of San Damiano, her soul traveled the wild way of the world of the Spirit, where one is indeed a "stranger" and where one is ever a pilgrim, seeking with Abraham "the city . . . whose designer and maker is God."

The sisters' temporal abode was, paradoxically, both transitory and the place where they already experienced being in their homeland. Like Abraham, they were already "sojourning in the promised land (but) as in a foreign country." This "now and not yet" tension was expressed by their "serving the Lord in poverty and humility." This attitude made it possible for them to live without taking the cares of this world very seriously, and least of all, themselves! Such radical poverty bore the fruit of liberty and laughter, of a playfulness born of a single-mindedness which permitted them to take the "*one* thing necessary" very seriously indeed.

The sisters did not seek to live without love and concern but without desire and attachment. "Do not wish to have anything else [except poverty] forever under heaven for the name of our Lord Jesus Christ and his most holy Mother."[39] It is characteristic of Clare that she added Mary to every mention of following the Lord. Her reason is evident. She is a woman and is speaking to women first of all. The most beautiful of models for any woman is Mary, the humble handmaid of the Lord, the "little poor one" par excellence.

Perhaps Celano captured the quality of Clare's own imitation of Mary when he speaks of Clare as "the footprint of the Mother of God" and "a most shining light for womankind."[40]

Before Clare developed the section on nonappropriation, she dealt with the subject of work. Deftly she wove together points taken from the Later Rule of Francis, from his Testament, and from the monastic usages found in Hugolino's Rule.

> The sisters to whom the Lord has given the grace of working are to work faithfully and devotedly ... at work which pertains to a virtuous life and to the common good. They must do this in such a way that, while they banish idleness, the enemy of the soul, they do not extinguish the Spirit of holy prayer and devotion to which all other things of our earthly existence must contribute.[41]

Clare, like Francis, considered work as a grace by which the human person is allowed to "help" his Creator bring all things to their finest development. This grace was given to Adam in the Garden before his fall. Part of the punishment for original sin was that work which was intended to be a joyful co-creation with

God, became fraught with hardship and frustration. It would seem that part of Francis' dream to restore Lady Poverty to her place of honor included the recognition that work needed to be purified of selfish goals and given back the original dignity it once had in God's plan for the human race.

Francis did not see that the primary goal of work was to amass the goods of this earth. Nor did he view work as a penalty imposed by God after orignal sin with the implication that humankind was originally created to live in effortless ease. For Francis, the only appropriate purpose of work was to glorify the Creator by enhancing, in one's own small way, the goodness of all created things. He allowed the brothers to accept recompense for whatever work they might do for others but they were to receive it as a gift of alms, not as something due to them. In fact, Francis seems to assume that frequently such recompense would be less than what the work done deserved.

The brothers were not working simply to earn a living but to express their ideal of minority and servanthood. The single stipulation which Francis and Clare made regarding the type of work done was simply that it be appropriate, that is, it should be of the kind which would foster the spirit of prayer.

Clare omits any mention of the sisters receiving payment of any sort for work. The sewing to which she devoted herself, the making of altar linens, was not sold but rather seems to have been given freely to "poor churches" around the area.

By working with a deep poverty of spirit, the sisters could labor with profound reverence for the created things they handled, seeking to bring them, not only to their natural perfection, but to also give them a "voice" through which they could offer conscious praise to their Creator. Francis had reverenced all the gifts of creation; those which grew from "our sister, Mother Earth" as well as the works of human industry. Everything could be seen in reference to God; paper on which his name could be written; beautiful materials and precious metals which could adorn the earthly sanctuaries of the Lord; bread, which was the fruit of human toil and nature's rhythms. As Francis' great dream the night before he composed the Canticle of Brother Sun indicated, everything on the earth had been transformed for him into the preciousness of glowing jewels once he had passed through the crucible of renunciation and loneliness.

Clare wished her sisters to find joy in the work of their hands. She directed that the various chores within the monastery be arranged "for the common good."[42] This would mean for the good of the sister assigned to the task as well as for the group as a whole.

Alms which a sister received, either on behalf of the monastery or as a personal gift were to be distributed according to need. Clare allowed a personal gift to be used by a sister if she had need of it, "otherwise, let her in all charity give it to a sister who needs it."[43] This directive demonstrates once more Clare's deep respect for the freedom of her sisters as well as her implicit confidence in their good will and discretion. She expected her sisters to be both simple enough to receive and sensitive enough to the needs of those around them to share whatever they had received.

Clare copied out Francis' directives that the sick were to be treated with special care and compassion. This responsibility did not rest soley on the Abbess or the appointed infirmarian. "*All* are obliged to serve and provide for their sisters who are ill just as they would wish to be served themselves if they were suffering from any infirmity."[44]

Francis' Rule assumes that his brothers are on the road most of the time, but that does not mean they have no community life. "Wherever the brothers may be together or meet [other] brothers, let them give witness that they are members of one family."[45] The love and concern which they had for each other was to form the "home" where they lived together in common love.

Clare realized that no matter how secure the enclosure or

stout the walls, her sisters would only have community when they lived so that "each can make known her needs to the other with confidence. For if a mother loves and nourishes her daughter according to the flesh, how much more lovingly must a sister love and nourish her sister according to the Spirit!"[46]

The sick in heart and soul were to be treated as compassionately as those with physical ailments. Although the Mother should have to "admonish two or three times" any sister who might have sinned against "the form of our profession," yet all must . . . "beware not to become angry or disturbed on account of anyone's sin; for anger and disturbance prevent charity in oneself and in others."[47]

Francis had considered it so crucial to avoid anger toward a brother that he prescribed it in the Earlier Rule, maintained it in the Later Rule, and enlarged upon it in what is now Admonition XI. He felt that if a brother retained the right to judge another and to display even righteous anger toward him, he failed against both justice and poverty. "That servant of God who does not become angry or upset at anything lives justly and without anything of his own."[48]

Clare urged that all the sisters have such love for each other that they "pray that the Lord enlighten her [the erring sister's] heart to do penance" and if they themselves have been the cause of trouble for another, each should "not only prostrate herself humbly at the feet of the other and ask pardon, but also beg her earnestly to intercede for her to the Lord that he might forgive her."[49]

The responsibility of knowing, living, and growing in the special charism of their Order rested, in Clare's thought, not just on the superiors but on all the sisters. This is implied by her directive to the abbess who shall "humbly and charitably correct them [the sisters], not commanding them anything which would be against their soul and the form of our profession."[50] The sisters themselves must know well what the "form of our profession" truly required of them. They must must be intent on always advancing "in serving God more perfectly and above all to observe most holy poverty in a more perfect manner."[51]

What this means in practical daily living is summed up by Clare in these lines from her Testament:

> In the Lord Jesus Christ, I admonish and exhort all my sisters, both those present and those to come, to strive always to imitate the way of holy simplicity, humility, and poverty and [to preserve] the integrity of [our] holy manner of life, as we were taught by our blessed Father Francis. . . . Thus may they always remain in the fragrance of a good name, both among those who are afar off and those who are near.[52]

Clare does not explicitly treat of what a sister should do if she feels she cannot conscientiously follow a command from her Abbess. Francis had counseled his brothers to continue in obedience to their local superior in all other matters and to take their difficulty to their minister. The sisters' only higher superior was generally their Cardinal Protector, but recourse to him would seldom be convenient because of the troubles and wars rampant at that time. Clare counsels something more difficult but also more productive of peace and unity.

"The Abbess is to be so familiar with them that they can speak and act toward her as ladies do with their servant. For that is the way it should be, that the Abbess be the servant of all the sisters.[53] Let her also be so kind and so available that all [of them] may reveal their needs with trust and have recourse to her at any hour with confidence as they see fit, both for her sake and that of her sisters."[54]

In other words, Clare wished that the lines of communication be open at all times between the Abbess and her sisters, something which can become particularly difficult at times within enclosed communities. But where this injunction is followed, Clare's practical wisdom is immediately apparent. To be able to do this is part of the goal of poverty, the attitude of inner emptiness and humility which only the Holy Spirit, the living bond of unity, can produce in a person and in a community.

This central and most important section of Clare's Rule closes with the scriptural exhortation, "He who perseveres to the end will be saved." Clare reveals her deep concern for perseverance in her Testament where she writes with wisdom born of sad experience:

> Because the way and path is straight and the gate through which one passes and enters into life is narrow, there are few who walk on it and enter through it. And if there are some who walk that way for a time, there are very few who persevere in it. How blessed are those to whom it has been given to walk that way and persevere to the end!
>
> Therefore, as we have set out on the path of the Lord, let us take care that we do not turn away from it by our own fault or negligence or ignorance nor that we offend so great a Lord and his Virgin Mother, and our Father, the blessed Francis, and the Church Triumphant and, indeed, the Church Militant.[55]

It is characteristic of Clare that she considers the failure of any one sister to follow the way to which she has been called as doing injury to the entire Church, both on earth and in heaven, as well as to their own sisters and their own souls. The WAY is everything to Clare who said it most simply when she wrote: "Christ Himself became our WAY."

The sisters' duty toward the Church is reiterated in the conclusion of the Rule thus: "may we observe forever the poverty and humility of our Lord Jesus Christ and of his most holy Mother and the holy gospel which we have firmly promised."[56]

Chapter XXII Endnotes

1. Wis. 11:24; 1:14.
2. Rule of Clare, Ch. XII, #11.
3. Legend of Celano, Ch. XXVI, #40.
4. Testament of Clare, #10–12.
5. Bull of Canonization, #3.
6. Ibid., #4.
7. It is not possible to assign absolutely certain dates to many of these foundations or to state the precise number of communities established during Clare's lifetime because of the loss of records.
8. Later Rule, Ch. 2, #11.
9. Rule of Clare, Ch. II, #8.
10. Privilege of Poverty, #1.
11. Ibid., #3.
12. Rule of Clare, Ch. II, #11; Later Rule, Ch. 4.
13. Rule of Clare, Ch. II, #18.
14. Ibid. Ch. III, #1.
15. Ibid.
16. Ibid., Ch. III, #2: Later Rule, Ch. 3.
17. Cause of Canonization, Wit. 2, #11.
18. Ibid., Wit. 3, #7 Wit. 9, #10.
19. Ibid., Wit. 9, #10.
20. Ignatius Brady, *Legend and Writings of St. Clare of Assisi* (St. Bonaventure: Franciscan Institute, 1953), p. 145.
21. Rule of Clare, Ch. IV, #6, #7, #8, #13.
22. Ibid., Ch. IV, #9.
23. Ibid., Ch. IV, #10.
24. Rule of Clare, Ch. X, #3; Later Rule, Ch. 10.
25. Rule of Clare, Ch. X, #2.
26. Testament of Clare, #20.
27. Rule of Clare, Ch. X, #4.
28. Ibid., Ch. X, #5.
29. Ibid., Ch. X, #6.
30. Ibid., Ch. X, #7.
31. The original text was written without division into chapters

and articles but the order of the text is the same. For the sake of clarity, I will continue to use the accepted numerology for chapters and articles.

32. Testament of Francis, #34.
33. Testament of Clare, #17 (Brady trans.).
34. Rule of Clare, Ch. VI, #3, #4.
35. Ibid., Ch. VI, #5.
36. Ibid., Ch. VIII, #1.
37. Earlier Rule, Ch. 9, #5, 8.
38. Rule of Clare, Ch. VIII, #2.
39. Ibid., Ch. VIII, #2.
40. Prologue to Legend by Celano.
41. Rule of Clare, Ch. VII, #1, #2.
42. Ibid., Ch. VII, #5.
43. Ibid., Ch. VIII, #5.
44. Ibid., Ch. VIII, #8.
45. Later Rule, Ch. 6.
46. Rule of Clare, Ch. VIII, #9.
47. Ibid., Ch. IX, #1, #3.
48. Admonition XI, #3.
49. Rule of Clare, Ch. IX, #2, #4.
50. Ibid., Ch. X, #1.
51. Testament of Clare, #14.
52. Ibid., #17.
53. Rule of Clare, Ch. X, #3.
54. Testament of Clare, #19.
55. Ibid., #21, #22.
56. Rule of Clare, Ch. XII, #11.

XXIII While Daylight Lasts

The gales sweeping over the shoulder of Monte Subasio have given way to gentler breezes. A pale green haze hovers within shrubs and trees as spring warmth teases open swelling buds. Meadows are carpeted with wild flowers. Behind the ox-drawn plows, birds swoop down to snatch up edibles from freshly turned furrows.

Within San Damiano, a silence deeper than usual reigns. It is Holy Thursday in the year 1250, and the sisters have set aside all but the most necessary chores. They have just had the rare privilege of receiving Holy Communion during the services commemorating the Lord's Supper. Now as they leave the choir, their bare feet soundless on the stone flaggings, each sister seeks out her preferred place of prayer.

Clare climbs slowly to the dormitory above the chapel wherein the altar is now stripped and the sanctuary lamp extinguished. Although she is weak and probably in pain, Clare's thoughts are turned toward the Mystery which has ever held her in awe. "Her memory often recalled to her him whom love had impressed so deeply on her heart," wrote Celano, adding that when she taught the novices to "bewail Christ Crucified" she was often caught up into tears herself, "exemplifying in her actions what she taught by word."[1]

Wearily Clare lies down on her pallet as evening darkens the sky. A full moon is rising. Perhaps Clare reflects that this same moon had once shone through the olive trees in a garden named Gethsemani when a Man knelt there in the shadows, terribly alone and overcome with agonizing dread.

In prayer she follows the Lord in his prayer, and in soul sorrowful even unto death feels and shares the sorrow of Christ, and is caught up by the remembrance of his arrest, his imprisonment and mockery. Thus lying on her bed all that night and the next day, she remains so wholly absorbed and rapt out of herself that while her eyes stare steadily at one object she seems crucified with Christ and completely insensible. A certain trusted daughter (probably Philippa Gislerio) comes several times to her to see if she might need anything and always finds her in the same position. But when Friday night comes, . . . (she) lights a candle and by signs, without words, recalls to the Mother the precept of St. Francis.

For the Saint had commanded that no day should pass without her taking something to eat. As the sister stands by, Clare returns as it were from elsewhere and asks her: "What need is there of a candle? Is it not day?" "Mother," replied the other, "the night has gone and the day has passed and another night is at hand!" Clare makes answer: "Blessed be this sleep, dearest daughter, for I have long desired it, and now it has been given to me. Beware lest you tell anyone of this sleep as long as I shall live."[2]

Sister Philippa promises, recognizing the true nature of this refreshing "sleep." Francis, she might have recalled, had also tried to conceal the nature of his experience on La Verna. Ever since Clare had seen the wounds of Christ in the hands of Francis, her own devotion had been fired to white heat. She had a particular affection for a prayer to the Five Wounds, praying it frequently and having it said while she was in her final moments.

Celano informs us that "she girded her flesh with a little cord with thirteen knots as a secret reminder of the Savior's wounds." He adds that Christ's "holy wounds were for her at times a source of sorrowful affection, at others a reason to flee sweeter joys."[3] The wounds which Francis had borne visibly were invisibly imprinted in Clare's pain-racked and shattered body.

The effectiveness of Clare's union with the Crucified One was dramatically illustrated when a woman from Pisa came to the monastery toward the end of Clare's life. Sister Balvina remembered that she had come loudly praising God who had heard her anguished pleas through the prayers of Clare. The woman related that she had been liberated from the oppression of five evil spirits, adding that "the evil spirits had said 'The prayers of this [one] consume us like fire.'"[4]

Clare's last years were ones of increasing weakness as "the strength of her body succumbed to the rigor of penance in her earlier years. For 'strength is made perfect in weakness.' Though she was burdened with the weight of her infirmities and seemed to be hastening to her end, it pleased God to delay her death. A sword of overwhelming sorrow pierced the hearts of her daughters as Clare began to grow worse than usual" toward the end of 1250.[5]

"At this time a certain handmaid of Christ, a virgin consecrated to God in the Monastery of San Paolo (which had once sheltered the young Clare) had the following vision: it seemed to her that with her sisters she was present at the illness of the Lady Clare at San Damiano and that Clare lay on a precious bed. Then as the sisters were weeping and awaiting amid tears the passage of the Blessed Clare, a beautiful woman appeared at the head of the bed and said to the sorrowing sisters: 'Do not weep, daughters, for her who is to win the victory; she shall not die until the Lord come with his disciples.'"[6]

The sisters, when told of this, surmised that the enigmatic words meant the Pope and his Cardinals would visit Clare before her death. Such a visit seemed an impossibility in November of 1250. Pope Innocent dared not leave his refuge in Lyon for fear of betrayal into the hands of Frederick. This most merciless of the Church's foes controlled all of southern Italy and many cities in the north. For a time, he had suffered a series of reverses but during 1250 he had recouped his losses and seemed stronger than ever.

His relentless war on the Church was gaining momentum when suddenly Europe rocked with the news that while riding to yet another battle, this invincible leader had died of dysentery in Apulia. Although Frederick's son, Manfred, tried to carry on his father's campaign, he seemed but an eaglet in comparison with his imperial father.

Thus in the spring of 1251, Innocent felt free to begin his return trip to Rome. He made the journey in cautious stages, testing the loyalty of various city states. He resided first in Genoa, his native city; then moved on through Milan and Bologna, arriving in Perugia in November. This city became his residence until April of 1253.

Cardinal Rainaldo, learning that Clare was again mortally ill, hastened from Perugia to visit her. Deeply grieved by the sight of Clare's suffering, he did all he could to hearten her. "He nourished the invalid with the Sacrament of the Lord's Body and encouraged the other sisters. . . . Then Clare earnestly and tearfully begged the Father for this one thing, that for the name of Christ, he would ever be mindful of her and the other Ladies. Above all, she begged that he would ask the Pope and the Cardinals to confirm to her the Privilege of Poverty (i.e., her own Rule which would guarantee this Privilege for all the Poor Ladies)."[7]

Rainaldo took a copy of the Rule Clare had composed, promising to do all he could to fulfill her request. Clare slowly recovered from this latest brush with death, but she would never again be able to perform these little services of love for her sisters which had been her delight. Celano wrote: "Illness so took possession of her later years that she who in good health had been enriched with merits of good works was in sickness enriched with the merit of suffering."[8]

Clare now longed for only two things: to see the seal of Papal approval affixed to her Rule, and then to fly to the embrace of her Lord. On September 16, 1252, Cardinal Rainaldo sent the following document to Clare.

> Rainaldo, by the mercy of God, Bishop of Ostia and Velletri, to his most beloved mother and daughter in Christ, the Lady Clare, Abbess of San Damiano at Assisi, and to her sisters present and to come: health and fatherly blessing.
>
> Because you, beloved daughters in Christ, have contemned the pomps and delights of the world and, following the footprints of Christ himself and of his most holy Mother, have chosen to live in monastic seclusion and to give yourselves to the highest poverty that you may thereby serve the Lord in freedom of soul: we commend your holy proposal in the Lord and desire indeed to bestow a benevolent regard on your petitions and holy desires.
>
> Wherefore moved by your pious prayers we, by the authority of the Lord Pope and our own, confirm to you forever and to all who come after you in your monastery and by these letters sanction with our protection the form of life and manner of common living and highest poverty which the Blessed Father Francis in word and in writing gave you to be observed, and which is here set forth."[9]

This Bull brought Clare a measure of reassurance but did not fully satisfy her for it seems to restrict the observance of her Rule to San Damiano, in the same manner as the Privilege of Poverty was granted only to the Poor Ladies living in the Assisi community. Clare knew that this was not enough. She could not die until she had fulfilled completely the trust she had received from Francis.

The year 1252 had brought with it much suffering for Clare, but it had also had its measure of small joys. Sister Christiana of

Parisse remembered a happy day in early summer when Clare's compassion had wrought a small miracle for her. "I had long been deaf in one ear," she later declared, "and had tried many medicines which were all unavailing. At length our Mother made the sign of the cross over my head and touched my ear which was immediately opened so that I now hear perfectly."[10]

What Clare could no longer accomplish through her own service, she strove to perform through the power of her Lord. Celano has indicated that, although Clare called herself a "useless plant in the garden of the Lord," she was actually effecting works of immense benefit for the Church during this time of her more intense suffering.

Clare felt that no suffering could compare with the immense grace of having been called by God through Francis to walk the way of highest poverty. "This is made evident," Celano noted, "by the fact that during twenty-eight years of continual illness she uttered neither murmur nor complaint; holy words and acts of thanksgiving alone came from her lips.."[11]

Clare suffered so peacefully and joyously that the sisters vied with each other for the privilege of sitting with her during the long days and nights of pain and helplessness. One night, however, late that same year, Clare did utter a small complaint to her Lord.

When Christmas eve arrived, Clare was so seriously weakened that it was impossible for her to join her sisters in choir, even on that holiest of nights. She would miss not only the exultant Night Office celebrating the Birth of the Lord but also the Midnight Mass during which the sisters were privileged to receive Holy Communion. A number of sisters had offered to remain with Clare in her solitary nook but she had not wished to deprive anyone of participating fully in the joys of this night.

Left alone in the dim attic dormitory, Clare strains her ears to hear the sisters' singing below in the chapel but the stone floor proves an effective barrier. She sighs and murmurs, "O my Lord

God, here I am alone with you in this place."[12] The bells ringing out from the basilica of San Francesco, a mile away, catch her attention.

Suddenly, the peal of a great organ surges through the darkened room. Deep, strong chanting as of hundreds of friars reaches her ears. Breathlessly, she listens to the magnificent music of the Christmas eve liturgy being celebrated across the valley at San Francesco. Her heart soars and the dusky rafters looming above her seem to dissolve into the splendor and lights of that magnificent basilica which she has never seen. "It was as though she had been actually present," Sister Balvina later said.[13]

Clare volunteered only a few details about this consoling experience so it is not certain whether it was only an auditory participation, as the earliest sources indicate, or whether it was also visual. After the services at San Damiano, the sisters hurry upstairs to share their joy with Clare and to try to comfort her for not having been able to join them. A radiant Clare greets them with the words: "You all left me alone when you went to the chapel for Matins, but since I could not rise from bed the Lord himself looked after me."[14]

As 1253 opens, the sisters realize that their Mother will most certainly not be with them when it closes. Perhaps they are responsible for a great and unexpected joy which came to Clare toward the end of January. Her sister Agnes comes home! Thirty-three years have passed since the parting of these two sisters who were so closely bonded in heart and spirit.

Time after time, in recent years, Agnes has received a message from San Damiano that Clare was dying. Weeks, and sometimes months, passed while she waited with anxious heart for further news. Now nothing can keep her from flying to Clare's bedside.

The sight of her sister, so weak and emaciated, overwhelms Agnes. She bursts into tears and, according to Celano, begs Clare not to depart and leave her so soon after this long-awaited reunion. To comfort her, Clare responds gently: "It is God's good pleasure, dearest sister, that I go hence. But do you cease weeping, for you shall come to the Lord soon after me, and before you do the Lord shall grant you great consolation."[15] Agnes accepts Clare's words and, as far as we know, asks no further questions.

Agnes and Clare have both been pleading with the Lord for the welfare of someone whom they love and had trusted in the early days of the Order—Brother Elias Bombarone. After the dissolution of Frederick's court in 1250, Elias had retired to a hermitage near Cortona with a few devoted followers but had not been reconciled with the Church or the Order. He immersed himself in his favorite avocation, church building, and soon a new structure in honor of St. Francis began rising in Cortona.

As Holy Week of 1253 approaches, the sisters learn that Elias is mortally ill. Their prayers grow more earnest. On Holy Saturday, Brother Elias is received back into the fold of Peter along with other Lenten penitents. He receives the sacraments on Easter Sunday and dies peacefully two days later. Although he was not received back into the Order, Clare and Agnes are grateful that God, in his mercy, has brought home another errant son.

Agnes of Prague now comes to Clare's mind. She wishes to send one last letter to her who had become a soul-sister. Too weak to write herself, Clare must dictate the letter and possibly it is her own sister, Agnes, who acts as scribe. There is a freedom of spirit in the letter which could only have been expressed in the presence of someone with whom Clare had always shared her deepest loves.

The fragrance of the Paschal season permeates the letter. Quotations from the Book of Revelation, which is read during the period following Easter, abound. Clare writes as a daughter of the Resurrection, liberated to love without restriction from without or hindrance from within.

> To her who is the half of her soul and the special shrine of her heart's deepest love, to the illustrious Queen and Bride of the Lamb, the eternal King: to the Lady Agnes, her most dear mother, and, of all the others, her favorite daughter: Clare, an unworthy servant of Christ and a useless handmaid of his handmaids in the monastery of San Damiano of Assisi: health and [a prayer] that she may sing a new song with the other most holy virgins before the throne of God and of the Lamb and follow the Lamb wherever he may go.[16]

The Latin in which the letter was originally composed allowed for a play on the recipient's name (Agnes) and the Lamb (Agnus). Clare's prayer for Agnes does not now refer to perseverance but rather that she may experience the Paschal joy of singing, even here on earth, the new song that the holy virgins are singing in heaven.

Saint Augustine wrote beautifully about the "new song" which all baptized Christians are called to sing. He said that this song is sung not only with one's lips but also with one's heart and one's life. This new song is in the singer so intimately that the singer *becomes* the song of praise his whole being utters.[17]

Clare pays graceful tribute to Agnes' fidelity and holiness by this comparison. But Clare has a deeper purpose in writing. Poised on the threshold of eternity, she longs to convey the tenderness of her feelings at this moment of farewell.

> O mother and daughter, spouse of the King of all ages, if I have not written to you as often as your soul and mine as well desire and long for, do not wonder or think that the fire of love for you glows less sweetly in the heart of your mother. No, this is the difficulty: the lack of messengers and the obvious dangers of the roads. Now, however, as I write to your love, I rejoice

and exult with you in the joy of the Spirit, O bride of
Christ, because, since you have totally abandoned the
vanities of this world, like another most holy virgin,
Saint Agnes, you have been marvelously espoused to
the spotless Lamb who takes away the sins of the
world.[18]

Ten to fifteen years may have elapsed between this farewell
letter to Agnes and Clare's previous one. The turbulence of the
1240s can easily account for the perils of the road and the dearth
of messengers able to reach far-off Bohemia. Agnes would have
been aware of this, but Clare feels the need to mention it so as to
reassure Agnes of her constant love.

Clare's greatest joy is still over Agnes' bridal relationship with
their Lord. The mention of St. Agnes of Rome brings to Clare's
mind poetic phrases from the liturgical office of her feast and
Clare cannot resist "singing" them.

Happy, indeed, is she to whom it is given to share
this sacred banquet, and to cling with all her
heart to him

whose beauty all the heavenly hosts admire
unceasingly,
whose love inflames our love,
whose contemplation is our refreshment,
whose graciousness is our joy,
whose gentleness fills us to overflowing,
whose remembrance brings a gentle light,
whose fragrance will revive the dead,
whose glorious vision will be the happiness
of all the citizens of the heavenly Jerusalem.[19]

These cadenced phrases evoke the melodies of the troubadours and we hear in them how a people sang their loves and

sorrows. Clare's people sang wherever they were. Men sang, not only in chapels and monasteries, but on the road, behind the plow, and wherever they found anything beautiful to celebrate. Women crooned over the cradles and keened over the many graves which broke their hearts. At the loom, the grinding stones, to and from the wells, they sang the many songs and lauds which brought a measure of harmony into lives which were often short and sad.

We know that Francis, troubadour of the Great King, composed and sang many lauds for his Lord. He even took the "hard sayings" of the Master and sang them so enticingly that men by the thousands were drawn to such joyous challenges as selling all they have, carrying the burdens of the Lord, and dying that others might know life.

The only hint we have of Clare's love for music is the lilting style of her letters. Like Francis, she cannot speak of the "most beautiful of the sons of men" in mere prose. Transmuted into poetry by the beauty of the King, Clare's words celebrate One who transforms all who gaze upon him.

> Inasmuch as this vision is the splendor of eternal glory, the brilliance of eternal light and the mirror without blemish, look upon that mirror each day, O queen and spouse of Jesus Christ and continually study your face within it, so that you may adorn yourself within and without with beautiful robes and cover yourself with the flowers and garments of all the virtues, as becomes the daughter and most chaste bride of the Most High King.[20]

Again Clare employs the image of the mirror which is so rich for her. Christ is the mirror of one's own deepest identity. So she urges Agnes to study her *own* face as she looks upon the Lord. Like the bride of Psalm 45, Agnes is to be clothed in raiment embroidered with the beauty of her Spouse. As did St. Paul, Clare expects that as Agnes "grows in knowledge, she will be formed anew in the image of her Creator until Christ is everything in her." The "flowers and garments" Agnes is to adorn herself with are those attitudes of Christ for which Clare had a special fascination.

> Indeed, blessed poverty, holy humility, and ineffable charity are reflected in that mirror, as, with the grace of God, you can contemplate them throughout the entire mirror.
>
> Look at the parameters of this mirror, that is, the poverty of Him who was placed in a manger and wrapped in swaddling clothes. O marvelous humility, O astonishing poverty! The King of the angels, the Lord of heaven and earth, is laid in a manger! Then, at the surface of the mirror, dwell on the holy humility, the blessed poverty, the untold labors and burdens which He endured for the redemption of all mankind. Then, in the depths of this same mirror, contemplate the ineffable charity which led him to suffer on the wood of the Cross and die thereon the most shameful kind of death. Therefore, that Mirror, suspended on the wood of the Cross, urged those who passed by to consider, saying: "All you who pass by the way, look and see if there is any suffering like my suffering! Let us answer him with one voice and spirit, as he said: Remembering this over and over, leaves my soul downcast within me. From this moment, then O queen of our heavenly King, let yourself be inflamed more strongly with the fervor of charity![21]

This rich passage is Clare's final Laud. From the threshold of eternity, she bequeathes to Agnes the song which has formed the theme of her life. William of St. Thierry spoke of this love of which Clare sings: "You, Lord, first loved us so that we might love you—not because you needed our love, but because we could not be what you created us to be except by loving you."

Clare would have been familiar with his works, as well as with the writings of William's close friend, Bernard of Clairvaux, who composed his commentary on the Song of Songs at his request. These love-inspired homilies are evidently in the background of Clare's thought whenever she quotes passages from the Song of Songs. But with an original twist, Clare links such mystical contemplation with meditation on the poverty and humility of the God-man.

> As you contemplate further his ineffable delights,
> eternal riches and honors, and sigh for them in the
> great desire and love of your heart, may you cry
>   out:
> Draw me after you!
> We will run in the fragrance of your perfumes,
>   O heavenly Spouse!
> I will run and not tire,
>   until you bring me into the wine-cellar,
>   until your left hand is under my head
>   and your right hand will embrace me happily
>   [and] you will kiss me with the happiest kiss of
>   your mouth.[22]

Clare herself is now running with swifter flight than ever toward that eternal embrace which Innocent III had pointed out to her when he had approved her petition for the privilege of poverty in the springtime of Clare's first love. Although this gift of supreme price is nearly within her grasp, Clare still values the precious spiritual friendship which binds her soul with that of Agnes. Poignantly, she begs Agnes not to forget her.

> In such contemplation, may you remember your poor
> little mother, knowing that I have inscribed the happy

> memory of you indelibly on the tablets of my heart,
> holding you dearer than all the others.
>   What more can I say? Let the tongue of the flesh be
> silent when I seek to express my love for you; and let
> the tongue of the Spirit speak, because the love that I
> have for you, O blessed daughter, can never be fully
> expressed by the tongue of the flesh, and even what I
> have written is an inadequate expression.[23]

Clare despairs of words to express her heart's love and invok-
es the very Spirit of Love himself to speak for her. Clare's genius
for friendship shines out here in limpid beauty. In her the art of
love reached fullest flowering for she had become the love she
ever contemplated. Her farewell is tender, echoing Jesus' emotions at the Last Supper. It seems she can hardly bear to close
this letter which she knows will be her last.

> I beg you to receive my words with kindness and
> devotion, seeing in them at least the motherly affec-
> tion which in the fire of charity I feel daily toward you
> and your daughters, to whom I warmly commend
> myself and my daughters in Christ. On their part,
> these very daughters of mine, especially the most pru-
> dent virgin Agnes, our sister, recommend themselves
> in the Lord to you and your daughters.
>   Farewell, my dearest daughter, to you and to your
> daughters until we meet at the throne of the glory of
> the great God, and desire [this] for us.
>   Inasmuch as I can, I recommend to your charity
> the bearers of this letter, our dearly beloved Brother
> Amatus, beloved of God and men, and Brother Bon-
> agura. Amen.[24]

Clare's love overflows to include the scribe and the bearers of
the letter who will carry this token of her affection to Agnes.
In 1253, we behold in Clare the full flowering of her natural

and supernatural gifts. Her womanhood has achieved an exquisite femininity, and her personality radiates a marvelous wholeness. Pope Alexander IV, her beloved Rainaldo will laud her as "the new woman of the Valley of Spoleto, who poured forth a new fountain of the water of life to refresh and benefit souls, a fountain which has since flowed in many streams through the whole of Christendom and watered many nurseries of religious life."[25]

Toward the end of April 1253, Pope Innocent IV and his entourage moved from Perugia to Assisi, taking up residence at San Francesco. The splendid basilica was approaching completion, and the consecration of the upper nave was set for May 25. According to Nicholas of Carbio, a friar who was then bishop of Assisi, Pope Innocent arranged to visit Clare at San Damiano.

This visit by the Holy Father and the Cardinals was interpreted by Celano as the fulfillment of the prophecy made three years earlier that Clare would not die until the "Lord and his disciples" would come. He supports his point by explaining that "the Supreme Pontiff, who is above man and below God, represents the person of the Lord, while the Lord Cardinals closely surround him, like the disciples, in the temple of the Church militant."[26]

Two temples of the Lord are approaching their moment of consecration. The soaring upper church of San Francesco, so full of light and adorned with frescoes of gleaming color, and the "alabaster vase" of Clare's body, alight with the glory of the Lord, which shall soon be broken to "fill the whole building of the Church with the fragrance of her sanctity."[27]

Chapter XXIII Endnotes

1. Legend of Celano, #30.
2. Ibid., #31.
3. Ibid., #30.

4. Cause of Canonization, Wit. 7, #14.
5. Legend of Celano, #39.
6. Ibid., #40.
7. Ibid.
8. Ibid., #39.
9. Bull of Approval for the Rule (Brady trans.).
10. Cause of Canonization, Wit. 5, #1.
11. Legend of Celano, #39.
12. Cause of Canonization, Wit. 3, #30.
13. Ibid., Wit. 7, #9.
14. Ibid.
15. Legend of Celano, #28.
16. Fourth Letter to Agnes of Prague #1–3.
17. Sermon 34, St. Augustine.
18. Fourth Letter to Agnes, #4–8.
19. Ibid., #9–13.
20. Ibid., #14—17.
21. Ibid., #18—27.
22. Ibid., #28–32.
23. Ibid., #33–36.
24. Ibid., #37–40.
25. Bull of Canonization, #11.
26. Legend of Celano, #40.
27. Bull of Canonization, #5.

XXIV Song in the Morning

August heat, radiating through the low ceiling, turns the dormitory above the chapel into an oven but the sisters seem unaware. Despite their heavy hearts and the oppressive air, peace permeates the long room like a gentle breeze. Clare is dying and they cannot tear themselves away from her bedside except for the most urgent of duties.

"Worn out by her long illness," Celano wrote, "a new weakness now takes hold of her which betokens her approaching call to the Lord and prepares the way for her everlasting good health."[1] Since July 26, Clare has been unable to take any nourishment and her emaciated body is being consumed in the throes of starvation and dehydration. Despite this, she remains so quietly joyful that "she strengthens in the service of Christ all who come to her."[2]

Among her more frequent visitors is Friar Rainaldo, her confessor and possibly the chaplain of the community at this time. Described as a kindly man, he is deeply moved by the terrible physical distress Clare is enduring and expresses his compassion. Clare smiles gently and responds, "Dearest brother, ever since I have known the grace of my Lord Jesus Christ through his servant Francis, no suffering has troubled me, no penance has been hard, no sickness too arduous."[3] The sisters nearby nod in agreement despite their tears.

"Unmindful of rest or food," relates Celano, "the sisters maintain their constant vigil."[4] Among them are Clare's two sisters, Agnes and Beatrice, the ever-faithful Pacifica and lifelong companions, Philippa Gislerio, Benvenuta of Peroscia, and Christiana di Suppo. Daughters of her cousins, among them Balvina and Amata di Martino, are also watching in sorrow as mortal life slowly ebbs from Clare's body.

Clare is still vitally aware of the needs of those around her and obtains miracles of healing for them, even when not directly asked. Sister Francesca has suffered for six years from such a severe pain in her head that, according to her own statement, her memory had been affected. She silently "makes a vow to Clare as she lay dying and is instantly cured, never experiencing that pain again."[5]

As it becomes known outside the monastery that Clare is approaching her final hour, the townspeople and country folk throng the chapel at San Damiano. Although they cannot see Clare within the cloister, they come away visibly affected by a peace and almost unearthly joy which seems to envelop the little convent.

"Daily she is honored as a very saint by the frequent visits of Cardinals and prelates," Celano records.[6] Among these are her beloved Cardinal Rainaldo, Friar Nicholas who has replaced old Guido as bishop of Assisi, and many of the brothers whose lives had been so intimately linked with Francis' and hers in the early days.

During the first week of August, Pope Innocent comes to visit Clare once more for, according to Celano, "he considered her to surpass all the women of the time."[7] He finds Clare alert but so weak that she cannot tender him the usual reverence of kissing his slippered foot despite her intense desire. He extends his hand with the Fisherman's ring "which she grasps most gratefully but begs that she might also kiss his foot. Unwilling to cause Clare any distress, Innocent mounts a low stool and extends his foot. Clare bends her head and kisses it above and below."[8]

In response to Innocent's solicitous inquiry, Clare makes two requests. Would he grant her an indulgence for the remission of all her sins? "Would to God," Innocent bursts out, "that I had no more need for forgiveness than you!"[9] Graciously he imparts the desired blessing, assuring her of full absolution for all past failures and the most plentiful benediction which it lies in his power as Vicar of Christ to bestow.

Finally, Clare whispers her request for the one thing for which she has spent her life—Papal approbation of her Rule which will ensure that all the monasteries of Poor Ladies everywhere will be permitted to live the same form of life and highest poverty as she has joyously lived for forty-two years at San Damiano. Innocent probably gives her his oral approval immediately. But even this does not entirely reassure Clare. She must see the seal of the Fisherman's ring impressed on the written Bull. Innocent leaves her, assuring her that it shall soon be in her hands.

Sister Philippa, who has been at Clare's side all day, was impressed when, after the Pope and his illustrious retinue had departed, Clare turned to her and the other sisters saying with a radiant face, "O my daughters, thank the Lord God for me, because all the heavens and earth cannot suffice to praise God for me since today I have received him in the Blessed Sacrament and have also seen his Vicar."[10]

It is typical of Clare that she placed the reception of her sacramental Lord ahead of even the exceptional honor of a Papal visit to her bedside.

After this day of joy, Clare's strength is wholly gone, though she remains aware of and responsive to what occurs about her. The sisters often hear her praying softly and as far as they can discern, it is only words of praise and gratitude which pass her parched lips. Once they distinctly hear her murmur: "Blessed are you, O my Lord, who have created me!"[11]

On Friday, Clare's young cousin, Sister Amata, is alone with her. Suddenly Clare whispers, "Do you see the King of Glory as I do?" She asks this several times, and Amata, though she sees nothing, knows that the King is very near.[12] The veil separating Clare from eternity is becoming translucent.

From time to time, Clare rouses herself to speak to all the sisters, urging them to "observe the Rule in its entirety and to always love poverty."[13] Sister Benvenuta with some of the other sisters is "sitting around the bed during the night of Friday to Saturday, weeping . . . . No one is speaking. Then in the silence they hear Clare saying in gentle tones: 'Go in peace for you will be well escorted for he who created you has provided for your sanctification, and after he had created you, he infused into you his Holy Spirit. He has ever guarded you as a mother does her little child.' Sister Anastasia asks wonderingly, 'To whom are you speaking? 'To my blessed soul,' is the quiet response."[14]

These trustful words sum up, as perhaps nothing else does, Clare's total relationship with her God: her Creator-Father who has held her in his hand since the moment of her conception; who has provided her, not only with natural life but also with life in grace through the death of his only Son; and who has, through his Spirit, brooded over her protectively all her life long. Now this same Spirit will unite her with her Lord as escort through the loneliest of human journeys. Perhaps Clare needs to remind herself of these truths at this moment because even she is not immune to the assaults on our human faith and hope which tests every person at this supreme hour.

Clare then continues to pray "speaking of the Blessed Trinity so subtly that the sisters cannot well understand her. Sister Philippa whispers to another sister standing by, 'You who have a good memory, remember what our mother is saying.'"[15] Clare's hearing, like that of many dying persons, is still keen and she catches these words. With a brief flash of humor she chides "the sisters who are present. 'You will remember what I am now saying as far as he allows it who is now causing me to speak!'"[16] Apparently Clare is not interested in a deathbed scribe.

Later Sister Angeluccia would say that Clare "had spoken of the Blessed Trinity . . . with such subtlety that even the very learned would hardly have been able to understand her."[17] Clare was speaking, not of what could be learned through books, but of what could be known only through the experience of a lifetime lived in intimate search for the Living God. She spoke as one who had gradually entered into a participation in the inner Life-Circle of Father, Son, and Spirit, as does a child who enters into ever fuller relationship with the members of its own family.

The night wears on. Sister Benvenuta, perhaps in an effort to keep awake, begins to consider what "great and marvelous holiness" is being revealed to her by this glimpse into the soul of one with whom she had literally knocked elbows in the crowded little monastery for nearly thirty years.

> And while she is thus meditating, it seems to her that the whole celestial court is preparing to honor this saint. Especially the most blessed Virgin Mary is preparing the garments for this new saint. While she is absorbed in this fancy, she sees all at once with her bodily eyes a great multitude of white robed virgins with crowns on their heads who come entering by the door into the room where Clare is lying. Among these virgins there is one unspeakably greater than the others, and beyond all words more beautiful. She has on her head a more wondrous crown than any; and above the crown there is a golden round vessel like a thurible from which comes such a splendor that it illumines the whole house. This virgin draws near to the bed of the holy Lady Clare, and she who is the greatest among them covers the bed with a veil which is so fine that although she is covered with it, yet the Lady Clare is still plainly visible. Then she, the greatest among the virgins, inclines her face over the face of the holy virgin blessed Clare, bending over her so that Sister Benvenuta cannot rightly distinguish one from the other; and this being done, they all vanish."[18]

Sister Benvenuta, almost afraid to breathe, glances about her in the now dim dormitory. Many sisters are about; some praying, others drowsing. She says nothing of her experience and later, when she recounts it for the bishop's commission, admits that she does not know if any of the others had also witnessed it. She is quite explicit, when closely questioned, that she had been wide awake and had seen the procession of virgins with her bodily eyes. This unexpected apparition was quite different from the inner musings she had been entertaining until she had been suddenly shocked out of her reveries.

Incredibly, Clare lingers on though it is clear to all, as Celano said, the "the Lord is near . . . standing already at the gate."[19] Clare asks if "the priests and her spiritual brothers can come to her and read the Passion of the Lord and other holy words" as they had done at Francis' death.[20]

> When there appeared among them Brother Juniper, that rare jester of the Lord, who often sang of the Lord in heartwarming words, Clare is filled with new delight and asks him if he has anything new at hand about the Lord. And opening his mouth, Juniper sends forth like sparks such flaming words from the furnace of his burning heart that the virgin of God finds great consolation in his parables.[21]

Out of her own peace, Clare seeks to comfort her daughters. "She recalls in words of praise the bounties of God and blesses all who are devoted to her, both friars and sisters."[22] Her words, probably preserved in what is now known as her Blessing, flow from a heart that loves tenderly and which recognizes that the greatest of all possible blessings is intimacy with the Lord, here on earth and ultimately in heaven. At the same time, Clare acknowledges her radical inability to impart such blessings. All is gift, a gift to be received with gratitude from the One Giver. She prays;

> Our Lord bless you and keep you. May he show his

face to you and be merciful to you. May he turn his countenance to you and give you peace . . . . On earth, may he increase [his] grace and virtues among [you] . . . . In heaven, may he exalt and glorify you . . . among all his saints.

I bless you in my life and after my death as much as I can and more than I can with all the blessings with which the Father of mercies has and will have blessed his sons and daughters in heaven and earth . . . . May the Lord be with you always and, wherever you are, may you be with him always.[23]

There remains yet one blessing which Clare feels she must obtain for her spiritual family before she can consent to die. She tells Sister Philippa that only "if the Rule of the Order is approved in a Papal Bull and I can kiss that seal, will I then be well content to die."[24]

Over at San Francesco, Innocent realizes that if he does not act with haste, Clare will die without seeing the written approval he has promised. Therefore he bypasses Curial formalities, and with his own hands adds a brief note to the page containing the approval which Cardinal Rainaldo had already composed. He makes a short notation on the parchment as to why the usual form has been waived and entrusts it to a friar to deliver with all speed.

Sunday, August 10, the document reaches San Damiano. "When the brother brings the sealed Papal Letter, although Clare is very near death, she takes it in her hands and places it on her mouth and kisses it."[25] An unknown hand later inscribed this touching note on the back of the parchment: "The blessed Clare touched and kissed this Bull out of great devotion many, many times."

With the Bull clasped upon her heart, Clare releases her hold on the last slender thread still binding her to earth. That afternoon she begins to sink rapidly. "Two of the holy companions of the blessed Francis stand near; one of them, Angelo, despite his own tears, comforts the others in their sorrow; the other, Leo, kisses the bed of the dying saint," wordless in his grief.[26]

Night falls and only the sisters remain to continue their watch at Clare's side. Clare is lucid but extremely weak. Once more she urges her sisters to fidelity to what they have promised "after which she makes so beautiful and holy a confession that Sister Philippa feels she has never heard the like."[27] Philippa later explained that Clare did this "because she feared to have in some way offended against the faith promised at her baptism."[28]

The sisters begin to pray and Sister Agnes of Messer Oportulo recites the Prayer to the Five Wounds which is one of Clare's favorites. Clare herself is praying with them but her voice is so weak that the sisters must strain to hear her. As far as they can make out, the "passion of Christ is continually on her lips together with the holy Name of Jesus."[29]

Toward dawn on Monday, August 11, Clare's breathing grows slower and lighter. The sisters are praying Psalm 116:

> How shall I make a return to the Lord
> for all the good he has done for me?
>
> The cup of salvation I will take up,
> and I will call upon the name of the Lord;
>
> My vows to the Lord I will pay
> in the presence of all his people.

Clare's lips are moving and as Sister Agnes bends close, she hears her murmuring the words of the next strophe:

> Precious in the eyes of the Lord
> is the death of his faithful ones.

Imperceptibly, as the eastern sky begins to brighten behind Monte Subasio, a last sigh escapes Clare's lips.

Thus Clare passed from this life to God,
shining indeed without a shadow,
without any stain of sin,
entering into the eternal light.[30]

Chapter XXIV Endnotes

1. Legend of Celano, #41.
2. Ibid., #44.
3. Ibid., #44.
4. Ibid., #43.
5. Cause of Canonization, cf. Wit. 9, #7.
6. Legend of Celano, #44.
7. Ibid., #41.
8. Ibid., #41.
9. Ibid., #42.
10. Cause of Canonization, cf. Wit. 3, #24.
11. Ibid., Wit. 3, #20.
12. Ibid., Wit. #4, #19.
13. Ibid., Wit. 13, #10.
14. Ibid., Wit. 3, #20, 22.
15. Ibid., Wit. 3, #21.
16. Ibid.
17. Ibid., Wit. 14, #7.
18. Ibid., Wit. 11, #4.
19. Legend of Celano, cf. #45.
20. Ibid., #45.
21. Ibid.
22. Ibid.
23. Blessing of St. Clare, #2, #8, #9, #10, #13.
24. Cause of Canonization, Wit. 3, #32.
25. Ibid.
26. Legend of Celano, #45.
27. Cause of Canonization, cf. Wit. 3, #23.
28. Ibid.
29. Ibid., Wit. 10, #10.
30. Ibid., Wit. 3, #32.

Epilogue: The Light and the Song

August 11 is the feast of Assisi's patron saint, Rufino, the first evangelizer and bishop of the Umbrian valley. In 1253, the joy of this annual festival is enhanced, rather than diminished by the news of Clare's death which "spreads like wildfire among all the people of her city." Once more crowds burst out of the city gates crying, "A saint! A saint has died!"[1] The Podestà and the civil guard come with great haste to set a watch about San Damiano where lies the city's most illustrious daughter. The bereaved sisters are permitted to keep Clare's body with them that day so that they may pray one more time with her still among them. Into her cold hands, they have placed the Bull, sign of Clare's triumph, so that it will be buried with her.

The following day, the whole Roman Curia moves to the little monastery, as well as every man, woman, and child in the vicinity who has two legs to carry them there. As the friars intone the solemn Office of the Dead, Pope Innocent suddenly halts them, declaring that they should be reciting the Office of Virgins instead. Cardinal Rainaldo tugs at his sleeve and quietly reminds him that this would be tantamount to canonizing Clare before her body is even in the tomb and that "one should proceed slowly in such things."[2] Reluctantly, Innocent permits the Office of the Dead to proceed.

During the funeral Mass, Rainaldo preaches, eulogizing Clare whom he knew so well, as one who had seen the emptiness and frustration of clinging to earthly things and had passed through them to embrace lasting realities. Then comes the moment of deepest bereavement for Clare's sisters. The city fathers "do not deem it safe or becoming that so precious a relic be left at such a distance from the citizens, so Clare's body is lifted up amid hymns and lauds, with the sound of trumpets and in solemn jubilation is borne in triumph to San Giorgio."[3]

Not long after Clare's death, her sister Agnes "is called to the nuptials of the Lamb and follows Clare into the delights of eternity. There both these daughters of the Church, sisters by nature, grace, and glory, together give God unending praise."[4]

Innocent wastes no time, and in October issues a Bull from the Lateran authorizing the opening of the process for Clare's canonization. Bishop Bartolomeo is charged with conducting the inquiries and comes to Assisi in November. All the sisters living at San Damiano are asked to give their testimony as well as persons living in Assisi who had known Clare or her family.

Innocent dies in December of 1254; so it devolves on his successor, Alexander IV, the faithful Cardinal-Protector Rainaldo, to conduct the canonization ceremonies for his revered spiritual friend and daughter, Clare. The Bull of Canonization, read aloud at the celebration of the Anagni Cathedral is a poetic masterpiece, a marvelous play on Clare's name.

> O wondrous blessed clarity of Clare!
> In life she shone to a few;
> after death she shines on the whole world!
> On earth she was a clear light;
> now in heaven she is a brilliant sun.
>
> O how great the vehemence of this light
> and how vehement the brilliance of this clarity!
> On earth this light indeed was kept within cloistral
>   walls,
> yet shed abroad its shining rays;
> It was confined within a convent cell,
> yet spread itself through the wide world.
> It was kept within,

yet it streamed forth without.
For though Clare was hidden,
her life was known to all;
though Clare was silent,
her fame cried out;
though Clare was enclosed in her cell,
she was preached to men in all the cities.

Little wonder indeed that a light
so burning and shining could not be hidden
but would break forth and illuminate the house of
  the Lord;
that a vessel of such fragrance could not be kept
  closed
but would diffuse itself
and fill the mansion of the Lord with its sweet
  odor.
Indeed, while Clare in the seclusion of her solitude
broke the alabaster vase of her body,
the whole building of the Church
was filled with the fragrance of her sanctity.[5]

When Clare died on August 11, 1253, there were at least forty monasteries of Poor Ladies in Italy and about sixty more strewn the length and breadth of Europe. Her light and her song has continued to spread through the centuries. In 1978 there were 974 communities of Poor Clares flourishing in every part of the world.[6] From New Guinea to California, from the African Cape to the Bering Straits, her song is being sung, her light still glowing.

Epilogue Endnotes

1. Legend of Celano, #47.
2. Ibid.

3. Ibid.
4. Ibid., #48.
5. Bull of Canonization, #2, #4, #5.
6. Ignacio Omaechevarria O.F.M., *Primeros Monasterios De Clarisas En Espana* (Burgosi Imprente de Aldecoa, Diego do Siloe, 18; 1978), p. 23.

Bibliography

Armstrong, OFM, Cap. Regis J. and Brady, OFM, Ignatius. *The Writings of Francis and Clare*. Ramsey, N.J.: Paulist Press, 1982

Bargellini, Piero. *The Little Flowers of Saint Clare*. Trans. Edmund O'Gorman, OFM, Conv. Padua: Messaggero Editions, 1972.

Brady, OFM, Ignatius. *The Legend and Writings of St. Clare of Assisi*. St. Bonaventure, N.Y.: The Franciscan Institute, 1953.

Dante Alighieri. *Divine Comedy, The Paradiso*. Trans. John Ciardi. New York: Mentor Book—New American Library, 1970.

Engelbert, Omer. *Saint Francis of Assisi: A Biography*. Trans. Eve Marie Cooper, 2nd Edition revised and augmented by Ignatius Brady, OFM and Raphael Brown. Chicago: Franciscan Herald Press, 1965.

Fortini, Arnaldo. *Francis of Assisi*. Trans. Helen Moak, New York: Crossroad, 1981.

Habig, Marion A., Editor. *St. Francis of Assisi—Omnibus of Sources*. Chicago: Franciscan Herald Press, 1972.

Hollis, Christopher. *The Papacy*. New York: Macmillan Company, 1964.

Leclerc, OFM, Eloi. *The Canticle of Creatures—Symbols of Union*. Chicago: Franciscan Herald Press, 1977.

Omaechevarria, OFM, Ignacio. *Primeros Monasterios de Clarisas En Espana*. Burgos: Imprente de Aldecoa, Diego de Siloe, 18; 1978.

Prescott, Orville. *Lords of Italy*. New York: Harper and Row, 1972.

de Robeck, Nesta. *St. Clare of Assisi*. Chicago: Franciscan Herald Press, 1980.

Roggen, OFM, Heribert. *The Spirit of St. Clare*. Trans. Paul Joseph Oligny. Chicago: Franciscan Herald Press, 1971.

Index

CPSIA information can be obtained
at www.ICGtesting.com
Printed in the USA
LVOW12s1425140817

544958LV00001B/4/P

9 781504 036894